'L.M.', Ida Constance Baker, was born in Stuston, Suffolk, in 1888. When she was only two months her family moved to Burma, where her father was an Army doctor, but they returned to London seven years later. Ida and her sister were sent to Queen's College School, then in 1901 moved to Queen's College. It was there, in 1903, that she met Katherine Mansfield (then Katherine Beauchamp) for the first time. Both were studying music - Ida the violin, Katherine the 'cello - and the friendship which developed between them was to survive almost unbroken until Katherine's early death in 1923.

Throughout those twenty years L.M.'s role - and desire - was to be for Katherine the friend and helpmate that no other person could be. She was excluded from Katherine's circle of literary acquaintances; she had no part in the creative and critical processes that absorbed Katherine so utterly. But apart from two major periods of separation, one in 1908-09 when Katherine returned to her native New Zealand, and another ten years later when L.M. visited her family in Rhodesia, their lives were intertwined. During Katherine's two early pregnancies, her disastrous first marriage, her long and vexed relationship with John Middleton Murry, L.M. was there for support. As Katherine's will to write grew at the same time as her health declined, L.M. remained steadfast in her care and practical concern. She tended to the menial tasks Katherine herself was unable to undertake; she travelled with her about Britain and to Italy and France in search of health and the peace to write; she kept house for Katherine and Murry in Hampstead; she provided money, food, comfort when required. When Katherine died at Fontainebleau at the age of thirty-four L.M. was not with her, but understood perfectly the significance of their final brief meeting just before: 'I felt as if I had come from the funeral of someone who has meant the world and life to me.'

L.M. continued to devote her life to helping others after Katherine's death, working particularly with children in the area of the New Forest that became her home. As numerous critical works about Katherine Mansfield were published, L.M. remained silent about her own special insight into Katherine's life, and it was not until the publication of *Katherine Mansfield: The Memories of LM* in 1971 that she attempted to set the record straight. She died seven years later at the age of ninety.

KATHERINE MANSFIELD

The Memories of LM

With a New Introduction by
A. L. BARKER

THE SECRET

In the profoundest Ocean
There is a rainbow shell,
It is always there, shining most stilly
Under the greatest storm waves
And under the happy little waves
That the old Greeks called 'ripples of laughter'.
And you listen, the rainbow shell
Sings – in the profoundest ocean.
It is always there, singing most silently!

Inscribed in a book on wisdom
from KM to LM 1912

For
Georgina
with love

Published by VIRAGO PRESS Limited 1985
41 William IV Street, London WC2N 4DB

First published in Great Britain by Michael Joseph Ltd 1971

British Library Cataloguing in Publication Data
Moore, Leslie
  Katherine Mansfield : the memories of L.M.
  1. Mansfield, Katherine—Biography
  2. Novelists, New Zealand—20th century—Biography
  Rn: Ida Constance Baker   I. Title
  823   PR6025.A57Z/

ISBN 0-86068-745-7

Printed in Great Britain by Anchor Brendon Ltd of Tiptree, Essex

The cover shows a detail from 'The Earl of Oxford and Asquith in a writing room at the Wharf, Sutton Courtney' by Sir John Lavery. Photo: Sotheby's.

Contents

Acknowledgements

I wish to acknowledge my grateful thanks to Mrs Mary Middleton Murry, widow of the late John Middleton Murry, for her kindness in allowing me to reproduce the letters and poems of Katherine, which are her copyright. My thanks are also due to the librarian, Queen's College, for permission to reproduce the photograph of the college library, appearing between pages 64–65.

Linking text by Georgina Joysmith

Illustrations

between pages 118-119

KM in New Zealand before 1903

The Library at Queen's College, Harley Street

KM with her 'cello at Queen's College

KM in Brussels, 1906

KM at Rottingdean, 1910

The black and silver Egyptian shawl, Rottingdean, 1910

LM (in black) in Rhodesia, 1914-1916

LM in Rhodesia

Chummie, Leslie Heron Beauchamp

Mrs Beauchamp

KM at Barons Court, 1913

KM, JMM and Richard Murry at 'The Elephant', Hampstead, 1918

The Villa Isola Bella, Menton

KM at the Villa Isola Bella, 1920

Introduction

These memories were not recalled in tranquillity, there is still a whiff of gunpowder about them. Katherine Mansfield's life-long friend, Ida Baker (L.M.), was unable to accept some of the interpretations put on the events and compulsions of that life and friendship. Nearly fifty years after Katherine's death she wrote this book as an attempt to set the record straighter.

Katherine Mansfield's own story may be traced throughout her work, her letters, and her *Journal*. It has been written up, chronicled birth to death, analysed, annotated, probed by her biographers and published between hard covers. She believed that truth was 'the only thing worth having'. The question is, can we have it? Can the splendours and miseries be crystallised into one pure grain? Apart from the impossibility of seeing into people's hearts and heads, time darkens some things and lightens others. The vision of Katherine as she appeared to people who knew her was different for each of them. And those who did not know her but have chosen to write about her may also choose *what* they write.

Katherine Mansfield was quite an actress, and as a writer she could embark on all sorts of lives and try some of them out for herself, almost as if she had a premonition that her own life would be short and not especially merry. She needed to love and be loved, and when she wrote to the people she wanted to bind to her she ran on, gushed, and gushed over. As she did to Ottoline Morrell: 'Who, among women, loves you as I love you? Who appreciates you and understands you more nearly than I? I want you – I want

you so immensely and so utterly for my friend ... ' To
Garnet Trowell: 'Dearest of all the world – you are never
out of my thoughts. I love you – I love you eternally ... Oh,
with you, I could conquer the world – Oh, with you I could
catch hold of the moon like a little silver sixpence ... ' To
William Orton: 'I think of you more often than you think
of me. You are always in my heart – even when my heart –
my beloved and my dear – has been most like the sand
castle and nearest the waves – you have been safe and secret
and treasured'. To S. S. Koteliansky: 'I am extremely fond
of you this afternoon. I wish you would walk into this café
now and sit opposite me ... But no, you will not; you are
dancing on the downs with the fair Barbara and Kissienka
is forgotten'. And, of course, to Middleton Murry: 'I love
you. I hug your blessed little head against my breast and
kiss you – I love you you bad wicked precious adorable and
enchanting boge'. 'How I love you – we are two little boys
walking with our arms (which won't quite reach) around
each others shoulders and telling each other secrets and
stopping to look at things ... We must not fail our love'.
'Do you feel in this letter my love for you today – It is as
warm as a bird's nest'.

Ida Baker's testament of their friendship is without
histrionics or vitriolics. She has no pretensions and does
not strive after effect. She employs such bridging phrases
as 'she did not tell me this in so many words'; 'He arrived
one day and there was much talk, but in the end he did
nothing'; 'she became depressed and miserable'. Of
Katherine's momentous admission as to the reason for a
dreadful black straw hat which she chose to wear for her
wedding to George Bowden Ida simply records that she
said the hat 'gave her courage'.

Yet there is in the book a charming vignette of Wingley,
the cat, on a French railway platform, and a vivid evocation
of early morning in Rhodesia. Because this unaffected style
is the direct expression of her unaffected self, the facts
come alive. The reader's sympathy is engaged as it is not –

always – by Katherine's own letters. Some of them provoke and even nauseate; some Katherine regretted having written. Many were never intended for general reading.

L.M.'s own name was Ida Constance Baker. Katherine called her 'Lesley' – borrowed from Katherine's brother – 'Moore', which was Ida's mother's maiden name. Names were important to Katherine: she had many for herself – Katerina, Kass, Wig, Jones, Sally, Tig, Kissienka – and wrote under *noms-de-plume*. Ida was variously called Godmother, Aida, Jones, The Faithful One, and, when she was out of favour, the Rhodesian Mountain and the Albatross.

For all her self-doubts and deprecation, and for all she wished otherwise, Ida Baker remained ineluctably herself. To her, Katherine wrote: 'I can't say "nice" things to you. In fact I behave like a fiend. But ignore all that. Remember that through it all I love you and *understand*.' She knew that Ida, without understanding *her*, could accept 'the whole with love'.

If Katherine Mansfield carried within her the converse of many of her qualities, was delicate, sensitive, a realist, a fantasist, a poseur, a passionate seeker after truth, tender-hearted, cruel, childish, cynical and 'more than half a man', these were the prerequisites of the writer. And each of us is androgynous to some extent.

Ida was born to be a helpmate, a woman who loved to serve. She would have made some man an ideal wife. She was the daughter of an Indian Army doctor. He is said to have been withdrawn and melancholic, and he could have had no love of life, for eventually he took his own. His chilling presence broods throughout Katherine Mansfield's story *The Daughters of the Late Colonel*. Constantia, the younger daughter, is thought to have been inspired by Ida herself, and she is drawn with a finely disciplined heavy hand. Ida considered the story to be a 'gentle caricature'. But it is about waste, blistering despite its delicately low key, and masterly in its evocation of futility. Katherine Mansfield was only eighteen when she wrote: 'I am so keen upon all women having a *definite* future', and she didn't mean just marriage, although it is about men and marriage that Constantia is wistfully wondering at the end of the story. The caricature is not so gentle, there are barbs.

When Ida first met Katherine at Queen's College in 1903 she already knew how to make herself scarce when she was not wanted – a faculty she would often be called upon to exercise. Katherine wrote magnanimously to a young man with whom she was in love: 'She is more than good to me, and we have both brought into her life all the happiness it contains. That's a strange fact, but I have to realise it. She never, by any chance, takes the initiative – must be shown everything – never thinks for herself, and is content, yes, radiantly content, to have a little spare room in our life, and, presumably, sew on buttons'. Presumably.

Some people's impressions were not magnanimous. Margaret Wishart, a friend from Katherine's young days, thought Ida only tolerated because of her loyalty: 'I couldn't help hearing . . . what an incubus she was.' Jinnie Fullerton, with whom Katherine stayed in Menton, said that Ida would 'never set the Thames on fire' – a judgement with which Ida agreed. Virginia Woolf disdainfully observed her as 'a munition worker called Leslie Moor . . . another of these females on the border land of propriety, & naturally inhabiting the underworld.'

These people did not realise that Ida Baker was a rarity. She never lost her essential strength and individuality, yet was willing to defer a life of her own and live joyfully, painfully, and to the full on the periphery of another. She was not a downtrodden pain, nor was she easily fooled. In her capacity to take people and love them as she found them, without first putting them through the hoops of her own demands and sensibilities, she was well-nigh impregnable.

With the dice loaded against her, Katherine needed all the help she could get. Certainly she made use of Ida, a whole range of uses, objective and subjective, for loving and hating, nursing her in her sickness, keeping her night-fears at bay, cooking the lunch, fetching the bathwater, settling the cat, any of the troublesome, trivial, life-supporting tasks which Katherine could not do for herself. Ida wished it so. While all else was shifting and crumbling and people were treacherous and egocentric (a word which haunted Katherine), Ida was steadfast and selfless. Katherine knew it. 'There is something quite absolute in Lesley . . . she's about the nearest thing to "eternal" that I could ever imagine.' One of Katherine's more predictable ideas (she who had so many conflicting selves) was that it was a second *permanent* self which made choice of a partner, for its own particular reasons. If the impermanent first self became unhappy with the arrangement, that was just too bad. There could be no divorce.

Katherine maintained that to her friendship was as sacred and binding as marriage, and she referred to Ida as her 'wife'. Casting Ida in that role was one more way of using her. Katherine affected to despise the conventional wifely functions and status, but she would have dearly loved to be able to fulfil them. The word 'wife' must have had a complex and bitter significance for her. On Ida as wife she revenged herself for the hurt, the talking-down, the forgetting, the torment and the 'killing' which she had to take – or thought she did – from Murry and from other people.

A sense of inadequacy plagued Ida all her life. It was due not to shortcoming in her but to the sheer impossibility of staying on Katherine's wavelength, within the range of such a unique and errant mind. When she put a would-be cheering message – 'Bear up' – in Katherine's luggage as she left to be married to George Bowden, there was no way she could know what she was asking Katherine to bear. The sight of Katherine dressed as for a funeral told her that it was going to be a question of endurance.

Inevitably Katherine tended to find Ida's care of her wearying and infuriating. She needed companionship – she also needed time to be alone. When she was by herself she could savour the 'detail of life, the *life* of life'. And she was so often in a heightened and feverish state occasioned by her illness and the tension it engendered. Then Ida fretted her with simple anxieties. If she couldn't help worrying when Katherine suddenly needed solitude and rushed out on a wintry night without waiting to put on her coat, not all Ida's best intentions could stop Katherine from feeling smothered. Katherine wrote in her *Journal*: 'I have even *torn* my heart out and told her how it hurts my last little defences to be questioned – how it makes me feel just for the moment an independent being, to be allowed to go and come unquestioned.'

But Ida recognised and respected Katherine's need to be free. She blamed herself, her lack of imagination, for not handling it right, and condemned innocent remarks of hers which offended. She had always been good at effacing herself: who but Ida would have passed the night on a staircase outside Katherine's and Murry's room rather than disturb them, or in a church crypt when she could not get home, and slept on the floor of Katherine's room so as to be at hand when needed? There was for a time a *ménage-à-trois* when Ida had only the curtained-off corner of a tiny kitchenette to sleep in and was obliged to stay hidden if visitors came. Keeping out of the way of Katherine's literary friends was one of the duties required of her.

She and Katherine were accused of lesbianism. George Bowden went so far as to blame the failure of his marriage on this 'perversion'. At the time, Ida did not know what was meant by a 'lesbian friend', and does not say what she thought when she found out. Katherine, like many another impressionable girl, fell passionately in love with certain of her schoolfriends. There were what have been darkly called 'relationships with women'.

Once, while attempting to console the unhappy Ida with kisses 'such as one delights to give a tired child', Katherine professed herself faintly revolted. It would seem pretty certain that any innocent frisson Ida experienced during these attentions was as much as she ever got from Katherine. If she was favoured with physical passion it was more likely to be the wrong side of Katherine's temper. A powerful moment described in Middleton Murry's journal, when Ida was supposed to have appeared naked and desiring Katherine to turn and look at her, and Katherine would not turn, would not look, and rejoiced at what she – or somebody – called Ida's 'humiliation and bitter disappointment', is by way of being third hand. It is recorded as possibly Murry's version of an incident related by Katherine who claimed to *know* that Ida was naked and willing Katherine to look on her nakedness. If Katherine did not turn and look, the implication is suppositious. And spiteful.

Ida has been accused of contriving, in this book, 'minute assassinations' of the men in Katherine Mansfield's life. Katherine had already assassinated most of them: witness the brilliant study of male egocentricity – as she saw it – in the character of Raoul Duquette, the 'little perfumed fox terrier of a Frenchman' of *Je ne parle pas Français*.

Periodically Katherine's ambivalent feelings erupted. From 1918 to 1920 was a terrible time for her. Her illness had been diagnosed as tuberculosis. There was no specific cure, thousands of people died of the disease every year. She was in great pain and acute anxiety, not only about her health but about her relationship with Middleton Murry. She was doing some of her most important work and the effort of creation excited her 'almost to madness'. So when Ida, anxious but uninvited, arrived to look after her at Bandol in February 1918, Katherine complained to Murry with a revulsion which was totally unbalanced: 'She's a revolting hysterical ghoul. She's never content except when she can eat me'. Ida quietly admits that she was not welcome, that she felt herself an intruder; Katherine did not want her 'daily routine and privacy broken into, even by me', and she adds, with a hint of her own unhappiness, 'perhaps at that moment, particularly by me'. To Katherine their enforced stop-off and stay in Paris in March 1918 was Hell. The city was under constant bombardment. Ida, as guardian against the horrors of the night, slept on the floor of Katherine's room. But Katherine found this unremitting care and self-sacrifice an intolerable burden. The disease was established in her and its ravages are terribly evident – as are her fear and despair – in a passport photograph taken at that time.

Writing of her problems in managing the house at Hampstead for Katherine and Middleton Murry, Ida condemns herself for her failures. While tidying the garden she happened to pull up a blazing great dandelion; it turned out to be the only thing of colour and glory in the neglected patch which Katherine had to look at. Ida never forgot, nor forgave herself, for Katherine's distress.

More serious, and more hurtful, was the 'idle afternoon' when she offered to Katherine the bundle of letters she had received from her over the years, and had cherished. One glance and Katherine ordered her to burn them. Burned they were, in that same neglected garden. Ida's treasures – Katherine's regrets?

In her philosophical old age Ida realised that time resolves everything, and 'desperation is not necessary'. But in those vulnerable days she saw her clumsiness and unawareness and, above all, her surpassing love, as the cause of their troubles.

Those troubles were transported to Italy in the autumn of 1919, and intensified. Alone with Ida in a tiny chalet in primitive living conditions, desperately ill, forlorn and unhappy, Katherine rounded again on her Faithful One, raged, cursed and physically abused her. To her distracted mind Ida appeared as a 'murderer', a 'deadly deadly enemy'. She expressed her pathological loathing in cruel, brilliant detail, such as only a writer of her calibre could command. She likened Ida to an albatross hung around her neck, dragging her down. Constancy was the quality which most offended her then. She longed to see it in Middleton Murry. But whereas Ida was at hand, eager to serve, to sacrifice, Murry wasn't. In her *Scrapbook* Katherine wrote: 'If he could only for a minute, serve me, help me, give *himself* up!' But Murry, too, was a writer, with a writer's faculty and necessity for self-absorption.

Ida, for her part, does not judge him. She thought that he too needed the devotion of a 'patient loving soul'. Her surmise that he felt his anxiety lifted when he could believe that Katherine, in Italy, was in the best possible place, and was reluctant to be involved again in the ever-recurring emotional storms and stresses is charitable – and almost certainly right. Katherine herself understood his dilemma. She acknowledged and perpetuated it in the story *The Man Without a Temperament*.

That frenzied hatred which caused Ida so much grief and bewilderment brings her to the sorrowful conclusion that she was fundamentally incapable of giving Katherine the mental support she needed while they were in Italy. There was no one who could come and take Ida's place. Katherine continued to keep Ida with her at night to ward off her fears – and the mosquitoes.

That terrible time, like other terrible times, passed. Katherine was able to revoke her hatred. Suddenly she felt something 'very like love' for Ida, and admitted that she might well have died without her. They found that they could talk about it, Katherine wondered why she had felt as she did. Perhaps she was 'under a curse' which she had to hide from everyone except Ida; Ida got the brunt of it. Ida of course believed the fault was hers, she had made herself a nothing, had suppressed her own desires to such an extent that now she had none, didn't think and didn't feel. That last desire must certainly have been left her. Katherine thought that Ida would recover if she could be loved and cherished and she would like to have done it. But she didn't.

Their final parting from each other came in the autumn of 1922. By then the wasting disease was so advanced in Katherine that she could scarcely creep about and knew herself a hopeless invalid. At this juncture she rebelled against medicine and science. She had no faith left in either. She longed for health, to be rooted in 'warm, eager, living life'. If she could live in and learn from the external world, 'the earth and the wonders thereof – the sea – the sun', she believed that she would lose the 'superficial and acquired' part of herself – and be a better writer.

She had come across a book with the high-sounding title *Cosmic Anatomy, or the Structure of the Ego*, a compound of occult doctrines, postulating the supremacy of the mind over the body. The Cosmic Anatomist suggested that it could even be an advantage to discard the body, that 'cumbersome machine', and free the surviving mind to develop certain spiritual mechanisms. Katherine was inspired and fascinated. Her flesh had become her prison and was engaged in the old torture of breaking her spirit. She rejected the orthodox treatments which had failed to cure her in favour of a discipline which promised to lift her above the degradation and hindrance of her sickness.

George Ivanovich Gurdjieff, a Caucasian Greek, had founded an institute at Fontainebleau to establish the harmonious development of man. He maintained that integration of the physical, emotional and mental centres could be achieved by conscious effort and voluntary suffering. When all artificial conceptions had been discarded and barriers broken down, self-knowledge would ensue. He himself was forceful and exotic, a dynamic personality. He was also shrewd, and must have been a considerable psychologist.

Katherine was eager, even desperate, to embrace his principles and follow them to the letter. 'Haven't I been saying, all along', she wrote in her *Journal*, 'that the fault lies in trying to cure the body and paying no heed whatever to the sick psyche?' This, her last great hope, was that when she had 'got the dying over' she would be inwardly purified and reborn. 'I am not in body and soul. I feel a bit of a sham . . . And so I am. One of the K.M.'s is so sorry . . . She has to die.' It seemed to her that then, and only then, could she put into words the whole truth which she glimpsed in her imagination. The last words she wrote in her *Journal* were 'All is well'.

She had said goodbye to Ida, and during the few weeks left to her they did not meet again, although Katherine's letters show her continuing need of her friend – and a concern for Ida's welfare. Ida's diary of the brief time she was allowed to spend at Fontainebleau with Katherine expresses in the simplest, fewest words her aching desolation.

The most saddening thing about this book is Ida's misprising of herself. She returns, is driven back, again and again, to the theme of insufficiency: 'I was not much help', 'I was not worth it', 'I had nothing to offer but a dumb sense of inadequacy', 'I never gave her the buoyant unfettered love that she needed', 'I had not enough imagination to do the right thing'.

Ida died in 1978, when she was ninety years old. Her passing was crisply noted in *The Times* of 25 July: 'Ida Constance Baker, friend and companion of the writer Katherine Mansfield, and the "L.M." of Katherine Mansfield's journal, died on July 4th.' But enough was said, Ida would not have wished for more.

After Katherine, she continued for the rest of her days to serve those who most needed her. As well as practical care and encouragement she gave an unquestioning regard which valued people for what they were, and not for what they ought to be.

'If only': these are desolate words from one whose life was as generous and loving as hers. 'If only I could have been myself', when it was precisely because she had been herself – Ida Constance Baker – that she could meet demands and fill omissions which other people were too self-centred to undertake.

If only Katherine had consulted other doctors, taken other advice and submitted to a proven medical regime as willingly as she did to the pseudo-mystical rigours at Fontainebleau, she might have been saved. She might have had that 'full adult, living, breathing life' in which to write many more books.

But conjecture, with hindsight, is fairly futile, and this one is wholly so. Katherine Mansfield wrote out of herself, and the extremities of her illness were an integral part of her. Joy inspired her, so did a profound sense of helplessness. She could not have uttered her 'cry against corruption' without intimate knowledge of spoliation and the imminence of death. Although she longed for '*real leisure*' to work in, she might have lived to discover that no such state is possible; for the writer it is always a race against time.

In her latter years Ida concluded that 'so much judging and by so many different standards' is a tragedy of life. She must have known that she was loved, respected, and still needed. We must hope that at the last she could stop judging herself by the impossible standards she had set in her youth. Desperation was never necessary.

A. L. Barker, 1985

Foreword

This detailed account by 'LM' of her long relationship with Katherine Mansfield is of very particular value. As a source of intimate knowledge pertaining to Miss Mansfield, LM commands a wholly unrivalled place. Through the twenty years of a close and intricate friendship LM stood irrevocably grounded in a loyalty that constituted the single, unwavering devotion in Katherine Mansfield's experience. LM's affection, in that fragmented, shifting, increasingly lonely life, persisted as an absolute.

The value of this record is twofold: (1) it presents with sharper focus a number of blurred elements in Katherine Mansfield's history; (2) it infuses that history with enriched vigour through its recital of the unspectacular minutiae of daily living which accrete to form the ground out of which the spectacular summits thrust. In general, our knowledge of the biographical facts is not significantly altered; but naked fact is often incomplete, and can be misleading. Here fact is at points clarified and the substance of the history takes on a heightened reverberance.

Destiny, though shrouded, presided over their first meeting, in 1903, when Katherine Mansfield, with her two older sisters, entered Queen's College, London, a willing exile from New Zealand. It was LM who was entrusted with the courtesy of showing the three young sisters to their room in the boarders' hostel of the school. Through the following three years an ardent schoolgirl bond developed. What is remarkable is that this bond survived the two years of separation after Katherine returned to Wellington in 1906. Then, and for long intervals thereafter, Katherine Mansfield sustained intense emotional experience, explored in depth and in nuance, through the medium of letters.

The twofold value of LM's recollections is especially important for the period from August, 1908, when Katherine Mansfield, not yet twenty, returned to London to embark upon a literary career, and the spring of 1912, when she and John Middleton Murry became allied, in a union which was to be confirmed by marriage

xxi

in 1918. This period was one of headlong self-assertion. Katherine moved in minor artistic circles in which she sought to impress, and did impress, by her assumption of the exotic and provocative. She knew that she was gifted. Life was hers to dominate. She had only to fulfill her gifts. To that purpose she was dedicated. But she was also wilful, emotionally voracious, and undisciplined in the sense that she had not yet been schooled to the knowledge that self-assertion bears results, results not always readily controlled. This was the period she later strove to eradicate by destroying all the personal testimony of her notebooks and journals.

Throughout these years LM stood staunchly by her side. She was the only person whom Katherine took into her confidence. She is able therefore to trace the course of Katherine's early love affair with Garnet Trowell – 'gentle, sweet-tempered, quiet Garnet' – whose child Katherine conceived, and to invest the factual record with the quality of lived experience. Equally, in her account of Katherine's hasty and disastrous marriage to George Bowden in March, 1909, at which LM was the only attendant, the civil ceremony in the Paddington Registry Office (with Katherine wearing a 'dreadful shiny black straw hat') springs into bleak immediacy: a barren ritual in a dirty, sparsely furnished, public room.

LM's presence on this occasion is significant. Twice she was out of England on visits to her family in Rhodesia, once for six months (1911), later for two years (1914–1916). Except for these periods of absence, through arrangement or through her own uncanny instinct she was with Katherine Mansfield at every subsequent crisis in her life, to their final departure together for Paris, when Katherine Mansfield left behind all her customary associations to enter the Gurdjieff Institute at Fontainebleau.

Katherine Mansfield's life was rarely tranquil, even when she was reduced to inactivity by ill health. Under repeated trials she grew chastened; but in these early years she could call upon a ferocious resilience. On her return in 1910 from a sojourn in Bavaria, where she suffered a miscarriage, her friendship with LM flowered into an even closer intimacy. Repeatedly, LM supplemented Katherine's funds from her own resources at moments of need. In this respect her generosity was total, even reckless one might say. She guarded Katherine through illness and convalescence. She participated in the final break with Mr. Bowden. She shared the progress of a second love affair (which again resulted in a doomed pregnancy). Apparently, Katherine surged on. What was courage, what stubborn bravado? It is clear that she was fortified by LM's selfless loyalty throughout these days. One is glad to hear of the 'small coats of lovely colours and soft velvet materials' Katherine fancied and the gay travel posters she displayed in the kitchen of her new flat at Gray's Inn Road, where she settled at the beginning of 1911. Here the two friends spent many hours in comfortable harmony, until LM's departure for her first visit to Rhodesia.

From the spring of 1912 onward, when Katherine Mansfield and Murry became allied, the personal records are now extensive: the augmented *Journal,* the unedited *Letters to John Middleton Murry,* the pertinent references in various other works (Lady Ottoline Morrell's memoirs, the biography of Lytton Strachey, for exanple), as well as the body of sources from antecedent years. Together the *Journal* and the *Letters to JMM* form an immensely rich and vibrant account. Yet the journal is never regularly kept – it erratically spurts forth and ebbs, and the long diary letters to Murry of course vanish when the two are not apart. LM, in her steady vigilance, is the single continuing witness to the last decade of Katherine Mansfield's life.

The relationship between the two was complex, and did not become less complex with time. Through her own developing career and through Murry's interests Katherine was no longer a youthful literary aspirant. Her sphere had enlarged to include a host of new acquaintances, a few new friends (among them the D. H. Lawrences, Lady Ottoline Morrell, and Dorothy Brett), homemaking in a succession of temporary flats and cottages, an active if essentially brittle social life, the tensions and emotional upheavals bred by her adjustment (and resistance) to Murry's character. Additionally, LM had been far out of reach in the months Katherine was devastated by her young brother's death during a military commission in France. On LM's return to England in 1916, after her two years' stay in Rhodesia, she found that she could no longer slip into her old place at Katherine's side. Ostensibly, their paths had diverged. Yet in the pattern she was to repeat through the remainder of her days, when Katherine turned away from Murry as she did the following spring to take a studio of her own, she turned at once to LM. She knew that here was bedrock, that no other inclination could prevail over the primary allegiance of LM's life.

For Katherine, in spite of oscillations and withdrawals, her primary allegiance was to Murry. To support two separate points of emotional focus, which did not fuse, often proved a complicated strain. The friendship with LM could not have endured if LM had not felt her destined role to be service to Katherine and the fostering of Katherine's gifts. Now and again, dimly, another pattern of existence hovered. Always Katherine's welfare intervened. When LM was needed, she came. When she was not needed, she was ready to retreat.

At points she was needed though she was not wanted. Early in 1918, under the threat of tuberculosis, Katherine left England, on her doctor's orders, for the milder climate of Bandol, in the South of France. Here she was soon overwhelmed by an anguish of loneliness, and despair at the worsening of her health. Immediately, on learning of her state, LM managed to break through all official wartime prohibitions in order to join her, unasked. She was stonily received. Yet she was *there,* and needed, when a week later Katherine suffered the frightening shock of her first hemorrhage.

Katherine had left England for Bandol on January 8, 1918. She was twenty-nine years old. She had exactly five more years of life ahead. Throughout this period she was subject to intense and agonizing pressures: physical torment, increasing physical weakness, the consuming need to incorporate her deepest powers in her work, a frantic hunger for order, stability, and peace. She strove to control her own existence, she was stubborn and determined still; but she was struggling against an adversary, impersonal, implacable, beyond the compass of human control.

Valiantly, she tried to unify the separate elements that claimed her concern. When she and Murry established their first real home in Hampstead, in the summer of 1918, she persuaded LM to join them as mistress-in-charge. 'For the sake of all that has been I ask that of you,' she wrote in a letter of candid good faith. The arrangement proved exacerbating, as one might have judged. The triple alliance revealed a triple edge. Often Katherine was confined to her room, extremely ill; often she and Murry were not in harmony. She could be captious, demanding, and severe. Not only was LM totally unfitted for the practical duties with which she was charged; she existed as a wraith within a private citadel. Yet the experiment has yielded a valuable residue in the intimate glimpses LM gives of the Hampstead life – the charming rooms, the bowls of flowers, the delicate fabrics the two women shaped, the Christmas party Katherine was well enough to enjoy 'wearing a rather frilly soft dress of plum-coloured silk'.

It was ominously clear, after the trial at Hampstead, that Katherine could not endure another London winter. Her doctor advised the Italian Riviera. She returned the following summer, to inhabit her own house for the last time. With that exception, she lived abroad, in Italy, France, Switzerland, until her final brief return to England in the summer of 1922.

In the autumn of 1919, with LM as companion, she settled in a pleasant furnished cottage, the Casetta Deerholm, at Ospedaletti, just over the French border. She worked steadily; daily she wrote her brilliant letters to Murry; but she was racked by violent inner struggle. Spiritually, she was utterly bereft; she was consumed by devastating loneliness and grief.

It was in these months that her hostility towards LM, first unleashed at Bandol in 1918, to subside later, flared to uncontrollable rage. What had she done, she asked Murry, that she must be imprisoned with her mortal enemy, chained to disease and blind destructive hate? Probably it is not safe to conjecture: but I believe this unnatural fury had other than the physical cause to which it has been ascribed. Illness merely exaggerated its degree.

LM went too far back in Katherine's life; she was the repository of too much. She was a channel to the past, with its record of failures, disappointments, disillusionments, and mistakes. But her cardinal sin was that she was not Murry. In each time of need it was she who was able to come, and who did come. Deep down, beyond all self-blame and self-accusation, Katherine felt betrayed. Murry had not given up his own pursuits to join her; he had chosen his work and his homeland. He had abandoned her to the embrace of death. In her bitterness and pain she turned the blade of her wild despair against LM.

The emotional situation must break; it could not continue to distend. It did break, in an acute attack of nervous illness through which LM nursed Katherine with patient care. Katherine acknowledged now her dependence on LM, the value of this constant, sorely tried devotion; she accepted what LM had to give, and with acceptance hatred dissipated. Thenceforward, through the various sojourns in exile, the two lived in closer amity, though Katherine's temper was always mercurial, and the old sparks flashed at times.

It is superficial to say, as has been said, that Katherine simply 'used' LM. She trusted her, and she was bound to her, fundamentally, by indestructible ties. Katherine was by nature hypersensitive, fastidious, and independent. She could not have drawn upon any person whom she did not freely trust. Further, as her letters to LM indicate, she could share with her some portions of her experience which she could not share even with Murry, indeed some of her private reservations concerning Murry.

After a quiescent summer at Hampstead, Katherine and LM travelled to Menton, to the charming villa, Isola Bella, Katherine had engaged. Under the radiant sun she grew stronger. Spiritually, she had ascended into a haven of peace. She was released into a burst of amazing creative energy. Within three months she had completed seven stories, among them the long and intricately constructed *Daughters of the Late Colonel*, which LM reports she finished at three o'clock in the morning and called for a celebration 'with tea!' The story also is a celebration, for in shaping Constantia, the younger of the 'daughters', she sensitively probed the stifled yearnings of LM's heart.

In February, 1921, Murry joined Katherine at Menton, to remain with her for the next eighteen months. After continued deteriorating health since the first of the year Katherine now resolved to seek the more bracing climate of Switzerland. Hereafter one follows LM's course with particular sympathy as she flutters about according to Katherine's needs. The journey to England, to dismantle the Hampstead house, a difficult and melancholy task. The journey to Switzerland during Murry's temporary absence in May: the formalities of tickets and visas to be carefully arranged, the supplies of food and 'little comforts' to be packed, the early setting forth to allow for the slow progress down the long platform unencumbered by jostling crowds. The search for suitable living quarters, at Baugy, Clarens, Sierre, finally the Châlet des Sapins at Montana set within a forest clearing rimmed by pines. A second journey to London to collect warm winter clothing for Katherine. Working at a French clinic, living apart, but near, in a rented room. All in all, for LM a dislocating time; but for Katherine, with the separate units of her life composed, a time of great peace and creativity. Again, within the span of a few months, she produced an amazing amount of work, including the long and beautiful *At the Bay*.

At this juncture, the pattern of Katherine's life becomes erratic. In spite of the clear benefits of Montana, at the end of January, 1922, with LM, she hurried off to Paris in search of a total cure at the hands of the Russian specialist Manoukhin, whom she knew only by repute. LM, after Murry had joined Katherine at her hotel, went back to deal with the châlet, of which the lease still had several months to run.

The frequent letters Katherine sent to LM from Paris reveal an irritable and agitated state of mind, intermixing impatience at the complicated details of practical matters, cajolery, genuine concern for LM's welfare, familiar gossip, nostalgic recollection, excitement at the success of *The Garden Party* (which had appeared in February), infinitely exact reports of her own health. They are letters which could be written only to a trusted intimate. And it was the trusted intimate Katherine summoned from England when the Paris treatments were over. The trip from Paris to Randogne-sur-Sierre under Murry's guidance had been violently disorganized: tickets lost, luggage mislaid, buffeting crowds, insufficient food. Katherine's need for LM's practised care was acute: she confessed that need.

This is not the place to rehearse Katherine's spiritual pilgrimage through its culmination in the closing months of her life. Gropingly, she had come to believe that only through a fundamental spiritual regeneration, accomplished through psychic discipline, could she effect a physical cure. Murry disagreed, in anxiety and gloom. To ease the strain between them, they found it best to separate, though they still often met. LM, unquestioning, accompanied Katherine to the Chateau Belle Vue, at Sierre. Here the paltry strength Katherine had gathered in Paris waned; she was restless, inwardly preoccupied. She made her will. Abruptly at the end of August she decided to visit England again. Together, the three left.

In London, Katherine moved swiftly, with a single stark purpose that gave her a new quality of ruthlessness. She sought out the Ouspensky circle, of which she had learned in Switzerland, whose philosophic thinking seemed to confirm her own. Through Ouspensky she was instructed in the mode of living at the Gurdjieff Institute, at Avon, near Fontainebleau. The occult mysticism of this group was highly repugnant to Murry; he escaped to the country with a friend. Katherine regretted his lack of sympathy; but she shoved his needs and interests aside to pursue her own. Suddenly, at the first of October, she crossed to Paris, with LM, ostensibly for a second series of Manoukhin's treatments, actually to investigate the Gurdjieff colony. She wavered; she pondered; she steeled herself to act. On October 17 she entered the Institute.

LM had gone with Katherine to Fontainebleau, her final journey of this kind. For a while she stayed on in Paris, assembling a suitable wardrobe for Katherine according to the very precise instructions she received. After a brief return to London, in Katherine's further interests, she took a farm job at Lisieux, disconsolate and bereft.

Katherine's last letters to LM of December, 1922, reveal a stirring to return, to renew the oldest affections of her heart. Her signal to Murry was undisguised. She invited him for a visit to the Institute. He arrived on the afternoon of January 9, to find her transfigured by radiant love. That evening as she was climbing the stairs to her room she suffered a violent hemorrhage. Within half an hour she was dead.

LM, summoned from Lisieux, sorted and packed her belongings. In the chapel she covered the bare wooden coffin with Katherine's brilliantly embroidered Spanish shawl, as she knew Katherine would wish. At the burial, she dropped a bunch of marigolds, a flower Katherine loved, into the open pit before the grave was sealed. No further service could she give.

Sylvia Berkman
Cambridge, Mass.

Preface

One day in the autumn of 1903, when we were just fifteen Katherine and I were walking in the gardens of Regent's Park near our school. Suddenly she turned to me with the question: 'Shall we be friends?' I hesitated both because I felt half committed to a Canadian girl at the school and because it seemed to me that friendship was something that *happened* spontaneously. But it was not long before I knew that I had found what I was to have and to be for the next twenty years. Friendship was to become the roadway of my life, and unconsciously my feet had been leading there.

Our relationship was remarkable in many ways. It existed before we met and after we had parted. Shortly before Katherine and I became friends I had had a strange experience following my mother's death. Grieving deeply for my loss, I had stood at the bottom of the garden; in the neighbouring paddock was a little pony which had resisted all our overtures of friendship. My attention had been caught and fixed on a brilliant star when suddenly the pony had come across the grass and had nuzzled his head against my breast and I had heard my mother speak to me. A year or two after this experience, KM told me she had just had a vivid dream, in which she saw my mother and me walking in a field in which was a pony.

Much later, when Katherine had just died, and our life together had ended, I was in great grief. Then one evening while I was working for Murry, she came into the room. I saw her face, radiant with light, as she smiled and passed through the room, telling me that all was well. Murry, looking up when she was gone, said quietly and simply: 'You have just seen Katherine'.

After this I shut the door on my life with Katherine and started again in the New Forest, from where I now write.

In 1947, Antony Alpers came from New Zealand to England to write a biography of Katherine (*Katherine Mansfield*, published 1954). Koteliansky, a friend of Katherine, told me he found him sincere and honest and thought I should help him as much as possible with his book. For four years I did all I could to interpret and explain Katherine's life for him, and to tell him of those parts of which I alone had knowledge.

I found later that he had not always accepted my interpretations, not trusting my knowledge and judgement and thinking among other things that I had been enslaved by Katherine and had suffered from that cruel sickness, jealousy. This was a pity because he was dedicated and absorbed in his work and wrote with love and some insight, and much of his book is valuable. But his appreciation came from a young New Zealand: a New Zealand from which Katherine had run away to find true understanding. It was not till much later that she realised her love, her deep love, for the country which did not then comprehend her.

Koteliansky had written to me in December 1926: 'To me you are Katherine's sole and only friend', and he and others have insisted that I should write all I knew of Katherine, saying it is my duty to correct the many false impressions of her. If I now lay bare the treasured secrets of my life, it is, therefore, with reluctance. These memories are not written to proclaim my friendship with Katherine, but to try and show her in a true and perhaps new light, guided by the silver line of our closeness and love.

Katherine herself wrote in the copy of *Bliss* which she gave me:

In spite of what I have said - and shall say.
You have been a 'perfect' friend to me.

Katherine Mansfield.

I shall do my best.

CHAPTER I

The Beginning: Queen's College
1903 – 1906

Katherine Mansfield and LM first met at Queen's College, Nos. 43 and 45 Harley Street.

LM was born in Stuston, Suffolk, on 19th January 1888, and at two months was taken to Burma. She had one sister, May, who was crippled by polio, and a younger brother, Waldo. When she was seven the family returned to England and settled in Welbeck Street. In 1897 the two sisters attended Queen's College School, the junior section of Queen's College, as day girls, moving to the college in 1901.

Katherine Mansfield and her two sisters came to the college in the autumn term of 1903. Their grandfather and great uncles had emigrated to New Zealand in the 1840s; and these grandchildren were the first generation to be sent back to England for their education. Queen's College was chosen as it was the school their three cousins, the Paynes – related through their mother – already attended and had recommended. Katherine's real name was Kathleen Mansfield Beauchamp, and her sisters were Vera (Vera Margaret), and Chaddie (Charlotte Mary). Katherine was fourteen when she came to the College, having been born on 14th October 1888; LM was then fifteen, nine months older.

They both studied music at the college and it was there that Katherine decided that she would not use the name Beauchamp when she became a famous musician. Keeping her first two names, she changed Kathleen into the more sophisticated Katherine. Two years later when LM was studying to be a professional violinist at an academy of music, she took her mother's maiden name, Katherine Moore. But, as it was inconvenient to have two Katherines, they decided that she should take the name of Katherine's young brother, Leslie, and thus evolved the initials LM and KM.

In the spring of 1903 my mother died and our family life was shattered. My father went to the country house in which they had hoped to live, and took my sister and brother with him. That autumn I became a boarder at Queen's College.

On returning early for the term, I was sent for by Miss Wood, the head of the boarding house, to meet the three Beauchamp girls who had come from New Zealand earlier that year and then to show them up to their room on the top floor of No. 41. Vera, I don't remember, but Chaddie and Katherine were much alike. I remember particularly how they both had their hair parted in the middle and drawn back neatly: Chaddie's fair, Katherine's nut brown and closely waving. Katherine looked at me steadily with calm, deeply dark eyes. We went up to their room which had a view high up out over the lead roofs and the mews behind the house where the horse carriages were kept and the coachmen lived, the sound of the horses' hooves on the paved ground mingling with the splashing of water and the voices and laughter of the cockney grooms.

The three beds in the girls' room were enclosed by curtains to make cubicles, but these they soon threw out. Katherine immediately chose her corner, the bed between the door and the bay window, and that became her home for the next three years.

Katherine adapted herself quickly to the new life; the delicately waving hair disappeared, turning into the then fashionable pads of back-combed rolls; the high stiff collars and leg-of-mutton sleeves successfully hid the shape of a young girl's shoulders; small waists and full skirts followed; and the Kass of New Zealand became Kathleen Mansfield Beauchamp written in large firm writing across her exercise book.

One day I noticed a book of poetry lying on Katherine's bed. I had myself read and written verses, but I knew of no one else who did. So, Katherine read poetry and even wrote it – and stories too! She also played the 'cello and was an avid correspondent. Amongst her letters were some to 'Caesar', young Arnold Trowell, her friend from New Zealand and great romantic idol; his photograph stood on her chest of drawers dressing table. I would sometimes watch Katherine lean out of the window, breathing, listening, absorbed and dreaming; I was beginning to *see* her.

One evening the three sisters were going out as I was coming up the stairs. At the top stood K, in a full, soft silk dress, her head tilted a little, her eyes glowing, her lips a little open as she sang to herself. Again I *saw* her, and the image is still vivid in my mind. A joyful young Katherine!

I spent many hours with her in their room while her sisters were elsewhere, listening to her playing the 'cello or talking, catching her flying thoughts in words. To find Truth, Katherine said, she would go down into herself, deep down, like sinking to the bottom of a dark well. Waiting at the bottom Truth would come to her. Katherine knew this when she was only fourteen years old, whereas it has taken me most of my life to find my way to the Peace which comes with this vision of Truth. And even now I cannot always find my way there. There was something of the other world about her.

Katherine had a real gift for the 'cello for she was intensely musical. Yet from earliest days she was practising the art of word painting, looking and *seeing* to make her true and perfect picture. Her writing had precedence over everything. It was her life. I remember so well, in later years, the frustration of the barren times: those empty, dry periods when she could not work, though so much was waiting to be written. By then her style had become fastidious; the manuscripts had few corrections, yet every word had to be exact and inevitable. Katherine rarely laboured over her stories. The whole was there, and her hand could not set it down fast enough.

Queen's College was founded by Frederick Denison Maurice in 1848 with the aid of the Governesses' Benevolent Institution, to give governesses an educational qualification. It quickly developed into a college of further education for women, girls being admitted from the age of fourteen. Also included amongst its students were married and older women who wished to study special subjects; these were known as non-compounders. Later, as the need grew, the school was added, which took girls from the age of seven to fourteen.

The school was run by a Committee of Education which was made up of the teaching professors, who were all men. A Lady Resident was the administrative head and had charge of the girls. Each new day started with her saying short prayers in the waiting room.

The idea of Queen's was to teach the students how to teach themselves and a certain amount of individual freedom was allowed. We had lectures rather than classes at the college, and each student was responsible for her own attendance; although, since we started at fourteen, there had to be a certain amount of supervision, and during the course of a lecture the assistant secretary came in and counted those present. We took notes and these were checked by the seniors: I believe Evelyn Payne was told to look after her young cousin, Katherine. We had our own internal exams; hardly anyone took external exams. Each girl was the assessor of her own progress, not a competitor. The object was to learn how to learn rather than to amass facts.

The main part of the college was in Nos. 43 and 45 Harley Street, and the house next door, No. 41, formed a hostel for the boarders; this was under the supervision of Miss Clara Wood. The upper part of '41' was connected with the upper floors of the college itself. From this height we could look down the well of the stairs in the college and watch our favourite professors striding to their different class-rooms. On the first floor there was an opening in the landing, carefully guarded by fine iron-work railings, which was known to us as the 'giraffe hole'. This gave us a view of the main corridor and on great occasions the younger members of the boarding house would look down through it and watch the older girls, wearing posies from their young admirers in the lower forms, walking along the corridor with their brothers and friends to the hall at the end where the dances were held.

There was also a library where silence was observed to allow for serious study, and a beautiful waiting room with a big bay window in which the time between lectures was spent. In this waiting-room there was a large painting of Queen Victoria in her carriage, visiting the college and being greeted by the staff and seven scholarship holders. We were, of course, under her patronage.

We had a college magazine, to which Katherine soon became a contributor and later sub-editor.* A curious thing happened to me while K was connected with the magazine. One night a short

* For one issue in December 1905 KM was co-editor. She wrote five stories for the magazine: *The Pine Tree, The Sparrows and You and I* (Dec. 1903); *Die Einsame (The Lonely One)* (March 1904); *Your Birthday* (Dec. 1904); *One Day* (July 1905); *About Pat* (Dec. 1905).

story came into my mind. I wrote it down, and took it to show Katherine. Before I gave it to her, she handed me something to read, which she had written for the magazine. I suppose I must have picked up her thought as she wrote, because the idea of my sketch was exactly the same as hers, though only vaguely expressed in my version. My dream-child was hastily smothered!

We also had a debating society, not a brilliant affair, though useful for the magazine, and an unusual group called the Swanwick Society, named after its founder. This group met once a month, each of us having learnt by heart one poem of our own choice. We did not always know it by heart! Miss Swanwick had, however, memorised many poems, and in her later life would claim that to repeat verse to herself was a comfort in any kind of trouble.

Life at the college was not all entertainment. For religious instruction we had as Professor of Theology the Rev. E. H. Pearce, sometimes supported by his sister, Miss Pearce. He had a parish in the city and his sister worked amongst the factory girls; he ran a club for them and tried to arrange 'evenings'. On one such evening the Beauchamp sisters and I were invited down: Katherine's 'cello, my fiddle, Chaddie's voice and Vera's piano. I don't know how much pleasure the girls derived from our activities, but I gathered two strange pieces of information there: that old women spent their time cutting wood into tiny bits to be used as raspberry seeds in the factory jam, and that the workers drank large quantities of vinegar.

By 1904 LM was no longer a boarder. Her father, finding the quiet of country life unbearable without his wife, had returned to London with her brother and sister, and had taken a flat in Montagu Mansions, just behind Baker Street. LM joined the family there and consequently did not see so much of the life of the boarders.

It was at this time that Katherine became fascinated by Oscar Wilde and his ideas. She was introduced both to Wilde's and to Walter Pater's work at Queen's College by Walter Rippmann the German Professor and Evelyn Bartrick Baker a fellow student; the influence on her opinions, her clothes and her writing was great. Her Notebook in 1906 is full of Wilde's aphorisms: 'Push everything as far as it will go'; 'The only way to get rid of temptation is to yield to it'; 'Conscience and cowardice are the same thing. Conscience is the trade-mark of the firm. That is all'; 'To realize one's nature perfectly – that is what each of us is here for'.

During her college days Katherine was often preoccupied with the question of different degrees of friendship. One day she suddenly asked me what I would do if I found she had done something really awful, like killing somebody with a hat-pin. I replied that I imagined that my first reaction would be to do something positive, not to criticise. I think she expected me to say that I would run away and leave her in horror at such an act. I had to explain to her what friendship was and always would be for me. Many years later she was to write me a letter in which she said that to her friendship was as sacred and binding a relationship as marriage. In the important things of life our values were always the same.

Katherine made several friendships at Queen's College. One such was EBB (Evelyn Bartrick Baker) whom Katherine called Eve. She was small, dark and slender, with an aloof air as though she was much older and more experienced than the rest of us. She has left me with the impression of a bunch of choice flowers – roses and carnations. She and Katherine spent much time together between and after lectures, walking and talking in the remoter corridors of the college. Years later Katherine wrote a sketch called *Carnation*, about a young girl languidly attending a French class in one of the large period classrooms of the college, carrying a single, dark-red, burning carnation.

Another friend was a rather wild young New Zealander, Ruth Herrick. She was younger than Katherine but shared her comings and goings in No. 41. They went to concerts together in large, floppy, black ties, and wide, soft felt hats and assumed a rather slouching walk, imagining themselves to be young bohemian musicians. Ruth became devoted to Katherine, perhaps too devoted. When college days were over the friendship faded: something must have happened, some unavoidable break and I don't think Katherine met her again. Ruth went back to New Zealand and I was sent a newspaper cutting years later showing her as Chief Girl Scout of New Zealand.

Gwen Rouse was another friend of these days: a tall, languid girl from the Isle of Man, much quieter and older than Ruth. She had a mouth that might have belonged to one of Dante Gabriel Rossetti's damsels. She and Katherine kept lightly in touch with each other for years.

Yet another friend I must speak of, since she meant so much to Katherine, was a very beautiful young Maori princess, Maata, whom Katherine had known in New Zealand. She was not at the college but had been sent to London and Paris to finish her education. Petite, with a pale touch of gold in her skin and sparks flashing from her eyes, she was a fascinating little being. She and Katherine enjoyed each other's company immensely and she must have made a refreshing change from the more unsophisticated, simple, English girl-students. To Katherine she brought a reminder of, and even a yearning for, the wild, unknown plains of her beautiful homeland. This feeling was to become stronger and stronger throughout Katherine's life.

Our German Professor, Walter Rippmann, also became a friend to Katherine during college days. He opened many doors for her exploration. During midday break, between the official classes, he was always available in his class-room for any questioning pupil, and I am sure he helped many girls to find themselves. I think that young creatures reaching out into maturity were all the better for some masculine attention in that large hive of women. Rippmann was interested only in girls of original or remarkable intelligence; they were sure of his sympathy and indeed he first met his own wife in this way.

To us plodders it was always rather intriguing to wonder what 'went on' during that quarter of an hour's extra coaching for which only the favoured few dared ask. On one occasion I did stay behind, on the pretext of clarifying a point. It was carefully explained and I came away none the wiser. To people like myself he was always immaculately correct, polite, suave and impersonal.

Katherine also came to know her own cousin, Sylvia Payne, during this period, meeting her first through the Swanwick Society. I had known Sylvia since the age of seven, when we started together at Queen's College School. She was a year older than I. With our sisters we met constantly and were much in each other's houses. The Paynes lived in Wimpole Street, the next street to us. Sylvia was a strange child, with long, bright, red hair; she often wore spectacles. If her appearance had not drawn attention to her, her irrepressible high spirits would certainly have done so. She enjoyed being naughty. She seemed to revel in gathering 'conduct marks', and since she was always in a hurry, she could never be bothered to formulate an explanation to put everything right. When frustrated she would murmur to herself something like 'jug jug' or 'tch tch', which gave her the name of 'Jug'. Though very fond of her, I often found her exasperating, especially because I was the 'good conduct girl' responsible for the class. Solemn, also wearing glasses, with no sense of humour, I never could see the point of being naughty: a horrid child, once described by my governess as 'a little block of stone'.

But Sylvia was clever and full of artistic sensibility, and after wading through five years of discipline at the school she entered the college.

Sylvia Payne being a day girl had little to do with No. 41 and her friendship with Katherine was rather different from the others, being mostly expressed in letters. Antony Alpers, who found these letters in the safe keeping of Sylvia's sister, quotes them in his book. But they were not evidence of a great new friendship, as he states. Katherine had need to express herself and found in Sylvia a sympathetic soul, for Sylvia was also an artist. In this way they were drawn together. I think that theirs was that true, reciprocal exploration of mind and soul which is part of the experience of living and loving. The exchange of letters went on for some time until after Katherine had returned again to England from New Zealand, in 1908. Katherine was then, as always, a great letter writer.

I remember a letter from Sylvia, given me to read by Katherine, in which Sylvia told of an experience of hers and sought advice. Someone had tried to kiss her. Katherine was not concerned; she felt that such a mundane consideration reduced their relationship, and consequently it changed. I do not think the letter was answered.

I only saw Sylvia once after her father's death in 1910. She had established herself in a studio, where she intended to paint. I think I was too full of other thoughts to pay it much attention, though I remember wondering how she would get enough to eat when she confessed to me that she had never broken an egg into a basin before in her life. Katherine's letters may have stopped by then, but the writer's affectionate feeling towards her cousin will live for ever in the gentle, teasing picture of Jug in *The Daughters of the Late Colonel*.

Perhaps these few short years were too full and hurried for all that Katherine needed to do: music, reading and friendships, apart from the usual college activities. The professors were all well-known, clever and, in some cases, even brilliant men, and demanded full-time attention and study. Many times later on Katherine grieved at what she called her neglected opportunities, and her missed chances of education. Looking back I feel I must have abandoned many friendships during that period; but that was because Katherine absorbed all my time and thought.

Life then was not always easy for Katherine. She suffered many frustrations, usually on account of the control of an over-zealous young aunt, Bell Dyer, her mother's younger sister. This aunt had come to England with the three Beauchamp girls and taken the post of assistant to old Miss Wood, the head of the hostel. Bell was young and hard and more interested in her own affairs than in attempting to understand an evolving artist. In consequence there were frequent clashes. She was one of the family clan who, when troubles beset Katherine, ostracised her completely from the family circle; at least until she had come through and become well known as a writer.

Katherine also had a great-aunt and uncle who lived at Bexley and with whom she spent some of her holidays. This great-uncle, the 'Dee Pa', had long since returned to England after sixteen years in New Zealand, where he had made a fortune. He was a fine-looking old man with a long white beard, and Katherine must have heard much of the early life of Elizabeth his daughter, when she was visiting them. (This was the cousin who first achieved fame with *Elizabeth and her German Garden.**)

Old Mrs Beauchamp, his wife, was a very charming old lady; I must have been several times to her house when Katherine was paying her duty calls. They had three sons, two of whom were on the staff of the Academy of Music; one, de Monk Beauchamp, was a sober, quiet little man always called 'Guardy' by the Beauchamp girls, as he was their official guardian when they were in

---

* Elizabeth achieved immediate success with her first novel *Elizabeth and her German Garden* in 1898 and since then published another twenty novels until a year before her death in 1941. She married Count von Arnim and after his death in 1910 married, in 1916, the second Earl Russell.

England. The second son was professor of singing at the Academy, and the third was a doctor. Another relation was Connie Beauchamp, a cousin of Katherine's father.

These relatives made up a wealthy, old-fashioned and formal generation, and Katherine fretted against being no more than the little girl from New Zealand in their eyes. There was no understanding between her and them and I have always felt bitter towards them. How much they could have helped then, and how little I was able to do.

CHAPTER II

In Between: Back to New Zealand
1906 – 1908

The three years at Queen's College were drawing to a close. Katherine was just seventeen. She longed to stay on in England, but when her parents came to collect the three girls, she failed to persuade them to leave her behind. She was unhappy and rather desolate. I was seeing more and more of her as the time for departure approached. I went every evening to the French class-room upstairs, where I knew I would find her changed for the evening meal and practising the 'cello; she would be playing her heart out. We talked of everything but chiefly of her hopes and plans to come back to London as soon as possible. I remember that during those last two or three weeks each of those secret meetings – secret only against the noise and laughter of the rest of No. 41, but precious beyond all things – seemed like pearls slipped on to a string, to be counted and treasured; for how many years, we could not say.

Sometimes Katherine came to our flat at Montagu Mansions and, curling up in the corner of the sofa, bewailed the fact that she had no one on her side, that no one understood. 'You are the only person in the world who really believes in me.' And indeed I did, with my whole heart. She needed that faith and it was to be justified.

In the spring of 1906 before they were to return to New Zealand the three sisters were sent abroad for two weeks as further education. The place chosen was Brussels, where the young Trowells, Arnold and his brother Garnet, were studying music on a grant from the New Zealand government. The girls' escort was their young aunt, Bell Dyer. It was a great occasion and Katherine wrote me several letters. I remember her account of one 'daring' episode, when she and her two sisters went down to a sheltered seashore and bathed naked, having no bathing dresses with them. Such behaviour, unusual for those days, seemed to fit the romantic bohemianism of student life in Brussels.

They saw much of the two boys and their friend Rudolf, also a musical student, going for bus rides through the town with them, Arnold and Katherine seated side by side. The rest of the party could not guess at Katherine's elation at passing through that beautiful foreign city in the close companionship of her idol. I do not expect there was much conversation. Arnold was a thin stripling, with red hair and no pretensions to good looks. Katherine had a charming post-card photograph taken there, of which she sent me a copy inscribed *mes mains dans les vôtres*; a little flourish of French to convey the taste of the journey.

Then shortly after their return Rudolf committed suicide. This was a terrible shock for the boys, and through them Katherine also suffered.

Katherine had known the Trowells in New Zealand since she was thirteen. She had first seen Arnold at a party in her parents' home, when he had entertained them with his 'cello. Inspired by his example, she took 'cello lessons with his father, characteristically throwing all her passion into music and even dressing in brown to be at one with her instrument.

Mr and Mrs Trowell had two sons, Arnold (christened Tom, but called Arnold) and Garnet, and a much younger daughter. Not at all wealthy, they were an artistic, homely middle class family to which Katherine felt drawn: they had an aura of real life, bohemianism and musicianship. Arnold became the focus of all her girlish aspirations and emotions; she called him 'Caesar'.

When Katherine had left for England in the January of 1903, six months before the two boys, she kept up a steady correspondence with 'Caesar', perhaps more eager on her side than his. Later, when the two boys came over to London for their holidays from the Brussels Conservatoire, Katherine would go to concerts with them and walk through London in their company, feeling herself to be a part of the bohemian musical world. It was this atmosphere which she discovered again when she visited Brussels, and which she so bitterly regretted having to leave behind in England.

At the end of October 1906 the Beauchamps sailed to New Zealand. I waited, and lived on Katherine s letters. They came irregularly at first, posted at stopping places on the way, with photographs of the group: boys and girls happy on board the slowly moving ship. The favourite amongst the boys was called Adonis. Katherine's grand despair at having to leave London inevitably dissipated and she began *seeing* things again, but with a more mature eye.

After her arrival at her home in Wellington letters to me came fast and regularly, at least one a week for those two years of absence. I had a parcel of them which I kept by me for many years. They were the outpourings of all her thoughts and experiences during the time she was away.

I read of Katherine and her beloved brother struggling down an embankment along the sea's edge to where rows of palm trees stood with tousled, wind-torn heads of bunched leaves, rattling in the wild air . . . Katherine clasping her 'cello on her way to a music lesson with old Mr Trowell . . . returning to her room, wildly elated by all she had seen and heard, only to find a bundle of stockings on her bed, put there by her mother to be mended! . . . refusing to join in all the social activities of the family.

For Katherine was restless and impatient with the provinciality of New Zealand. She yearned for that freedom she felt she could find only in England; the freedom to be herself, to be with people who understood and saw as she did. She was what most modern parents would call a problem child. Certainly, her own parents found it increasingly difficult to understand her.

By now her family was depleted; her beloved grandmother, who had always nursed her in childhood, had moved to live with a friend nearby; Bell Dyer had stayed in England to marry a rich husband; Vera was courting and soon to leave and Leslie, the young brother nicknamed Chummie, was at boarding school. Only her parents, Chaddie and her youngest sister, Jeanne, remained at home.

Katherine's father, though a prosperous and influential merchant, was in many ways careful, even mean. (I did not hesitate in my condemnation later on.) Katherine told me of the family trials each time the weekly accounts had to be submitted to him. Her mother, who called her husband 'Mr Businessman', had a weekly allowance which made a torture of each reckoning day.

Mrs Beauchamp was in many ways like her daughter, imaginative and creative. I did not know her well, but she probably understood Katherine better than any of the rest of the family. She was sensitive, delicate and fastidious: her tea was never hot enough unless the cup had been heated first. She had an inner life of her own, and somehow did not quite belong to her husband and the family. She had a habit of wrinkling her forehead and lifting her heavy eyelids when giving her attention to something of interest. In a photograph I have of her, which she gave me herself, she is wearing a black ribbon round her neck as our mothers did in those days, and she looks a little surprised at finding herself there instead of in a cameo or miniature resting on velvet. Later, when Katherine had ended her desperate struggles for freedom, she grew to understand and appreciate her mother, and had a true love for her.

Despite her restlessness there was much that gave Katherine happiness in Wellington. Her father had taken a small holiday house by the sea at Day's Bay and this, with her love of the sea, was a great delight to Katherine: the sea smells, the white sand and the joy of running from the house for the early morning bathe.

Katherine enjoyed rare moments of closeness to her father. Sharing something of his mind, she could talk to him and understand much of his way of thinking. He was very proud of his country, which she appreciated, and she described to me how, when walking with him one day, she watched him cut an apple in half and, turning it round, examine the beautiful red streaks running down its skin, and the black pips inside, exclaiming with justifiable pride, 'Now, there's an apple that can't be beaten anywhere in the world'. Katherine understood that.

In the holidays she had the companionship of her much loved brother, Chummie, and also of her sister, Jeanne, who was devoted to her. Both were much younger, but Chummie became a true friend, and the tie between brother and sister, who felt and thought alike, was strong in those years.

She was growing up rapidly and writing a great deal. A friend of hers called EKB (Edith Bendall) was a gifted artist, and together they planned a book. Katherine's love of children produced child poems and stories which EKB illustrated, but the book came to nothing.

There was one long silence in her letters to me, during which nearly a month passed with no news. I was terribly anxious, fearing an accident. Then I got a frantic letter from Katherine. She had had no news of 'Caesar', nor, I gather, had his parents, and, remembering Rudolf, she feared the worst. Had he too killed himself? What had happened? She begged me to find out anything I could and let her know. What could I do? I did not even possess the boy's address.

It was at this time that the Trowells decided to sell up in New Zealand and go to England to make a home for their two sons.

According to the Journal, *on 28th August 1907 Katherine had news of Arnold from LM, and felt 'First, so sorrowful, so hurt, so pained . . . but now only old, and angry and lonely . . . Now, which is it to be? Shall I applaud his manner of living? Shall I say, Do as you please, live as you like, see life, have experience, increase your outlook? Or shall I condemn it? . . . It's a great pity that artists do live so. But since they do – well . . . but I shall not.' It was probably this incident – whatever it was – that decided the Trowell parents to leave for England.*

Their decision reduced Katherine to despair. Since the age of thirteen, the Trowells' home had always been for her the open door to music, friendship and unconventional spontaneity. They were simple and free from the social bonds of the rich Beauchamps, and provided the only link available to her with the life that she craved. Their departure in August 1907 made her determined to gain her freedom and gave her the courage to face her father. He provisionally gave his permission for her to return to London at the beginning of the new year, 1908. I think that the acceptance of some of Katherine's stories by an Australian magazine publisher may have influenced his decision.*

It was at this time that Katherine's parents decided to send her

* E. J. Brady, the editor of *The Native Companion,* accepted three of Katherine's stories in the autumn of 1907: *Vignettes, Silhouettes* and *In a Café.* They were written in the manner of Oscar Wilde with the heavy exoticism of the 'nineties' which Brady admired; from their style Katherine was mistaken for a mature woman of thirty.

for a trip into the hinterland of New Zealand to see something of her own country before she should leave it. She kept a notebook and was enthralled with all the new experiences and people she met. She wrote poems describing the country; there is one called *In the Rangitaki Valley*:

> O valley of waving broom,
> O lovely, lovely light,
> O heart of the world, red-gold!
> Breast high in the blossom I stand;
> It beats about me like waves
> Of a magical, golden sea.
> The barren heart of the world
> Alive at the kiss of the sun,
> The yellow mantle of summer
> Flung over a laughing land,
> Warm with the warmth of her body,
> Sweet with the kiss of her breath.
> O valley of waving broom,
> O lovely, lovely light,
> O mystical marriage of Earth
> With the passionate sun!
> To her lover she holds a cup
> And the yellow wine o'erflows.
> He has lighted a little torch
> And the whole of the world is ablaze.
> Prodigal wealth of love!
> Breast high in the blossom I stand.

You can feel the hotness of the broom's colour and the strength of its sweet scent. Katherine kept a number of poems in a green notebook and drew large designs of curving, half-open fern fronds on the cover.

She returned to Wellington in December. At Christmas an unfortunate incident occurred which caused the Beauchamps to reconsider their decision about her departure. They were disturbed by a description, which Katherine had written of something that had happened at a ball when she had sat out one of the dances with her partner, and which her mother discovered. In her usual fashion, Katherine had embellished the facts when writing them down, and her parents, taking them seriously, not unnaturally thought twice about letting her go to London.*

However, they finally relented and took steps to ensure that she would be well cared for. Her father found her a room in a students' hostel called Beauchamp Lodge, an old-fashioned house overlooking the canal at Paddington. Her great-aunt, Mrs Beauchamp, was asked to keep an eye on her. The old lady would willingly have mothered her, but Katherine did not want this and her visits to her great-aunt were to be few and far between. There were also old Mrs Beauchamps' sons, but though Katherine knew them all well, there was, as before, no common ground for friendship with them.

Her father made what I considered to be one fatal mistake; he gave her very little money, only forty shillings a week: thirty shillings for the hostel and ten shillings for everything else – writing paper, music lessons, bus fares, clothes and all other necessities. This led her into many real difficulties. Katherine had had no financial experience and came from a very comfortable home. Her new poverty infected her with a constant anxiety about money, that dogged her all her life.

She was to fetch her allowance monthly from the manager of the Bank of New Zealand, Mr Kay, a friend of her father, who was supposed to 'keep an eye' on her. He did so, extending his protection to an invitation to visit one of his London haunts, where he gave her a glass of sherry and chatted of his latest amatory adventures. He could not help himself and was basically a very kind man. I had occasionally to go and collect the allowance myself if Katherine could find a convincing reason for not going.

But none of these people could really help Katherine on her dangerous first steps in freedom and experience. I myself was much slower to reach maturity, life having so far lacked any but the most sheltered experiences. Even much later I sometimes felt like those small yellow water-lilies with their long stalks firmly fixed at the bottom of the river but their heads always floating below the hurrying surface. The big waves and little ripples went over me. I did

---

* LM learned of this from Katherine at the time; but the letters were later burnt at Katherine's own request, in 1918. LM mentioned the incident to Antony Alpers when helping him with his biography in 1947–1951. He quotes it in his book (p. 99) and John Middleton Murry, editing KM's *Journal* in 1954, refers to it again, quoting Alpers.

not notice them, but the roots of friendship were quite firm. At
the bottom in my still waters, I was doing my own growing.

Finally, when all the arrangements had been made, Katherine
sailed for England in July 1908. She made friends on the boat, but
only one was of any importance, a rather charming man, Sidney
Hislop, who fell in love with her and loved her well enough to
continue to be a good friend for several years. It was he who called
her Sally, a name which she used for herself later. He encouraged
her with her work.

    When she arrived in London in August I went to meet her.
I cannot remember any of her relations being there. Originally,
she was to have gone to Miss Wood of Queen's College for a few
days, but instead came to stay with us at Montagu Mansions
before going on to Beauchamp Lodge.

CHAPTER III

Beauchamp Lodge – Carlton Hill: 1908

Katherine's room in Beauchamp Lodge was on the first floor at the back of the house with a French window leading on to a tiny balcony that overlooked the canal. The room seemed so very gloomy that it made me anxious. I well knew the despair and frustration to which she was prey and felt that such surroundings would not help her. However, the room could also be cheerful, and on sunny days she spoke of the flowering tree hanging over the water and the life on the passing barges. Later she moved down to a smaller and cheaper room, on the ground floor, overlooking the road at the front.

She made many acquaintances among the students and one or two became constant companions in her small room. They were too constant, their attentions suffocating her and preventing her from working.

Very soon after her arrival, as might be expected, Katherine found herself in financial difficulties. She had only ten shillings left each week after paying her rent. Her father should have realised this. I then had very little money myself, about twelve pounds a year till I reached twenty-one, and in those days the idea of selling securities would never have crossed my mind; however it was some help, and spending it was always a fine adventure – until it was exhausted. Fortunately, Katherine was able to use her great gift for recitation, mimicry and music, as in those days hostesses often provided entertainment for their guests. When Katherine's gift was discovered through the friends she had made at the lodge, she was soon offered professional invitations, at a guinea an evening. These were tempting propositions and she accepted a number of them.

Such small sums were useful in her straitened circumstances, but the engagements necessitated new clothes, for Katherine was young enough to feel she must look sophisticated. I remember a grey silk dress reaching down to the ground, and swathing her young figure. This was made by an acquaintance and many engagements went to pay for it.

During this time I was studying the violin at an academy of music in Prince's Street and living with my family in Montagu Mansions. I used to go and see Katherine nearly every day. Sometimes when I arrived for my usual visit, I was sent post-haste to some house where she had an engagement, with a note or my own explanation to say that she would not be able to come that evening. How I disliked that task, though I did not, as far as I can remember tell Katie so. I stood by, to help whenever I could, and never asked questions or criticised unless she invited me to do so.

I would help her dress – giving my opinion, which I knew she trusted, on how to place a flower or a riband – and then watch her go out to join a friend. Afterwards I went home, feeling anxious or uncomforted, to hear the next day, probably, of a fresh triumph. Sometimes she would tell me that she had a friend with whom she wished to spend the afternoon, or that she was engrossed in some particular work, and on that day I would not go to Beauchamp Lodge. Or on some occasions when I arrived we would go out and walk through the little garden in Paddington Green, where Mrs Siddons sits like a beautiful marble queen, or wander down the London streets to Soho, Leicester Square or the National Gallery.

At this time she wrote what later became her first published work in England, the poem *November* which appeared in the London *Daily News* of 3rd November 1909.

> Dim mist of a fogbound day . . .
> From the lilac trees that droop in St Mary's Square
> The dead leaves fall, a silent, shivering cloud.
> Through the grey haze the carts loom heavy, gigantic
> Down the dull street. Children at play in the gutter
> Quarrel and cry; their voices sound flat and toneless;
> With the sound like the shuffling tread of some monster
> I hear the trains escape from the stations near, and
>   tear their way into the country.
> Everything looks fantastic, repellent. I see from my
>   window
> An old man pass, dull, formless, like the stump of a
>   dead tree moving.

The Virginia creeper, like blood, streams down the face
   of the houses . . .
Even the railings, blackened and sharply defined, look
   evil and strangely malignant.
Dim mist of a fogbound day,
From the lilac trees that droop in St Mary's Square
The dead leaves fall, a silent fluttering crowd –
Dead thoughts that shivering fall on the barren earth.
Over and under it all, the muttering murmur of London.

Katherine rarely told me when she had no money. I had to
guess, which was not too difficult. One dreadful day, when she
was particularly short, she told me that as she had now finally
decided to be a writer instead of a musician she had made up her
mind to sell her beloved 'cello. I think we both felt the tragedy
of this, and it was not lessened by the fact that when she came out
of the shop at which it had originally been bought for a large sum,
they had given her only £3 for it. Her need must have been serious indeed for her to let this happen.

In those days the bite of poverty was something new, a little
shameful and, therefore, difficult to mention. Later, we decided
that one would never hesitate to ask a friend for a cup of tea, so
why make such a fuss over money. Tea or 'T' became our expression for money. The lack of it haunted Katherine all through her
life until she went to Fontainebleau in 1923. From there she
wrote sending me a 100-franc note, saying I could take it quite
freely and spend it without anxiety: she was cured of her worry
over money.

All through the autumn of 1908 Katherine lived and worked
at Beauchamp Lodge. But she complained that she was being
constantly overwhelmed by the students, who would sit for hours
on end in her room with or without invitation. The social life of
the hostel was thus proving irksome. She met undesirable men,
and was unable to refuse invitations, although she was afraid to
keep the appointments; being young, she made many mistakes.
It was becoming increasingly impossible to get on with her task of
writing.

Soon after her arrival in London Kathrine had made contact
with the Trowells. They were already settled in a house in Carlton
Hill, St John's Wood, with their young daughter, and were await-

ing the arrival of their two sons from Brussels after the completion of their studies.

When the day came for the two boys' arrival, Katherine went to the station to meet them. She looked at Arnold, a smallish, thin, quite ordinary boy. This was not her 'Caesar', 'Caesar' had died before her eyes: this was just brash young Arnold Trowell. And for the first time she noticed his brother Garnet, gentle, sweet-tempered, quiet Garnet.

A few weeks later – it must have been before Christmas – Katherine told me that Mrs Trowell has been talking to her of their family's difficulties; they had no money coming in and their resources were almost at an end. So Katherine decided that the best thing she could do was to leave Beauchamp Lodge, give the Trowells her thirty shillings a week as a paying guest, and thus also find peace and quiet for herself.

I wish I could give you a picture of those early days at Carlton Hill. I had been there often with Katherine, and came to know the family well. The house was quiet, with a small garden at the back and flowering bushes and trees in front; a pleasant place. I remember sitting on the doorstep with the Trowells' young daughter, looking into the garden, the spring scented air drifting in, the large room with Arnold thundering on the piano playing consecutive 6ths – then very unusual and modern – or drifting into delicate Debussy melodies; old Mr Trowell talking to Katherine, which he always loved doing, and Garnet tall and pale passing in and out while 'Mother' was bustling and talking, getting tea for us all in the kitchen.

Katherine was very happy during that period. She and Garnet got to know each other. There were walks and talks and always a background of music. After a while Katherine and Garnet were in love and made airy plans for getting married. He was nineteen, and Katherine just twenty and there was no money, but that did not matter. It was first love, with Garnet practising the violin and she working furiously. She had found a little typist, who could decipher her writing with some help, and who enjoyed doing the work for a small sum. It was during this time of happiness that she wrote *The Tiredness of Rosabel*,* and these two poems:

* First published, posthumously in *Colliers*, February 1924.

Sleeping together . . . how tired you were . . .
How warm our room . . . how the firelight spread
On walls and ceiling and great white bed!
We spoke in whispers as children do,
And now it was I – and then it was you
Slept a moment, to wake – 'My dear,
I'm not at all sleepy,' one of us said. . . .

Was it a thousand years ago?
I woke in your arms – you were sound asleep –
And heard the pattering sound of sheep
Softly I slipped to the floor and crept
To the curtained window, then, while you slept,
I watched the sheep pass by in the snow.

O flock of thoughts with their shepherd Fear
Shivering, desolate, out in the cold,
That entered into my heart to fold!
A thousand years . . . was it yesterday
When we, two children of far away,
Clinging close to the darkness, lay
Sleeping together? . . . How tired you were. . . .

                          *

'It is cold outside, you will need a coat –
What! This old Arabian shawl!
Bind it about your head and throat,
These steps . . . It is dark . . . my hand . . . you
        might fall.'

What has happened? What strange, sweet charm
Lingers about this Arabian shawl . . .
Do not tremble so! There can be no harm
In just remembering – that is all.

'I love you so – I will be your wife,'
Here, in the dark of the Terrace wall,
Say it again. Let that other life
Fold us like the Arabian shawl.

'Do you remember?'. . . . 'I quite forget,
Some childish foolishness, that is all,
To-night is the first time we have met . . .
Let me take off my Arabian shawl!'

I seem to remember that after Katherine and Garnet had fallen in love I went less often to Carlton Hill. It was some distance from Baker Street, where I lived, and in any case I was not much help to her, since I am sure that neither of us had any idea of what the responsibilities and obligations of married life might be.

Quite soon an opportunity came for Garnet to get paid temporary work with a small touring opera company. He could obtain a little part for Katherine in the chorus, but, because of accommodation difficulties, only by saying that she was his wife. They discussed the matter. The deception did not seem to be really important; after all they expected to be married very soon. So why not? And they would both be making money for the family. I do not think the family itself knew anything of the supposed relationship. They went. Alas, it was not long before it became apparent that the arrangement was not going to work. The squalor of theatrical life offended Katherine's fastidious tastes. (She told me later, she could not really bear to see the way that Garnet ate his egg.) The company was tiny with very little financial backing, and she soon became redundant. Besides, in that environment she was not able to write – her one urgent need. And so, sadly – it can only have been a fortnight later – she returned to Carlton Hill.

It is significant that both KM, in a letter written to Dorothy Brett in 1921,* and LM now, recall this period as a lengthy one, and at the height of spring. In fact, KM must have left Carlton Hill and returned to Beauchamp Lodge by the end of January 1909. Thus the whole period away from Beauchamp Lodge could not have amounted to more than three months at the most. It could be an indication of how happy and how much in love she was.

---

* 13th December, 1921: '. . . I lived there in Carlton Hill for a long time when I was young and very very happy. I used to walk about there at night – late – walking and talking on nights in Spring with two brothers. Our house had a real garden, too, with trees and all the rooms were good – the top rooms lovely.'

CHAPTER IV

Beauchamp Lodge – Marriage and Separation: 1909

I come now to a very difficult time in Katherine's life: difficult both for her to live and for others to understand. Arriving back at Carlton Hill she was still deeply in love with Garnet Trowell, from whom she was separated. To stay on there indefinitely seemed impossible. The Trowells would not consider a marriage between them; the difference in their social backgrounds precluded any such arrangement. She, the daughter of wealthy parents, must not be allowed to ally herself with an impecunious musician.

So Katherine felt she must return to Beauchamp Lodge. Young and heartbroken, she had ample time to review the break-up of her life. Away from Garnet, with no prospect of marrying him, and aware of the possibility of a child by him, she hated Beauchamp Lodge, where life was hectic. With no peace of mind for work and no other possible home, she became desperate.

It was at this time that she began to show me the long letters she had been receiving from George Bowden, whom she had met the previous autumn through Margaret Wishart, a friend at Beauchamp Lodge. He was a singing teacher who also sang at small concerts.

I had been once to the little flat near Paddington which he shared with a friend; it was in a bare street with the usual prowling cats and, a little farther down, a high wall hiding either a railway or a factory. The street was empty save for a barrel-organ playing a tune popular at the time: 'Mabel dear, listen here, I'm afraid to go home in the dark.' That tune still makes me shiver. Once in that road I passed a drunken man, stumbling and clinging to a lamp post: a sight more common then than now, but none the less printed indelibly on my memory.

Bowden was a kindly person, and, I believe, very much in love with Katherine. His letters were full of humble devotion and understanding, really beautifully expressed. I think he knew she did not love him, but he seemed to understand her and her needs, and offered security and a place where she would be sheltered and able to work without anxiety. As an artist she was always impelled in the direction of what would help her writing and, if she had doubts, she saw them as a sacrifice in its cause. Young and frightened, she must have been looking for a safe anchorage; I don't think marrying Bowden seemed very important and he was extremely persistent.

So they wrote to her parents – it must have been about the end of January – and, as the mail took five weeks to New Zealand, they had to wait some time for a reply. When it did come, by cable, it told of immense anxiety in her home; Mrs Beauchamp was coming to England at once to look into this young man. The correct procedure must be followed. At once the two young people decided, even though Mrs Beauchamp was on her way, to get married in a registry office. Was their haste due to Katherine's fear of possible opposition from her mother, now that she realised she was to have Garnet's child? She did not tell me. She only announced that she was going to be married on 2nd March 1909.

Her conduct made her relations in England very angry. Why had she not told them? Or even taken the young man to see them? I feel sure that if she had even considered such a step, she rejected it in the certainty that he would not have passed their critical judgement. Life in those days was far more correct and circumscribed than today.

The day came for the marriage, and when I reached Katherine's room I found her dressed completely in black, with a dreadful shiny black straw hat on her head. She said that the hat gave her courage; it had cost us all our spare pennies. I was to be a witness. So I went with her to a horrible little place, where we met Bowden, a small room with what looked like a long counter such as one would find in a cleaner's and dyer's. I suppose it was a table. The room was otherwise almost bare and very dirty, with an uncleaned window. We waited till a small fussy man came in. No other witness? Oh, he'd get one.

And there my beloved friend was married.

Katherine had had no suitcase in which to pack her things, so I had lent her my twenty-first birthday present dressing-case. As I packed her things I had put into one of the pockets of the case a little note of hopefulness saying 'Bear up', to cheer her when she unpacked.

After the ceremony I said goodbye to them and went sadly home. Katherine had promised to meet me the next afternoon to go to a concert.

When we met, she said quite quietly that she had left her husband, for good. She was not going back. I don't think that we went to that concert. That night she returned to Beauchamp Lodge.

The next few weeks were probably the culminating point of her unhappiness. Beauchamp Lodge, being a young students' hostel, could not allow a married woman to stay on indefinitely, and so we had to find some place where she could live until her mother arrived. Looking back, I cannot understand why she could not have come to my family, but I suppose I took it for granted that my father would have been too prejudiced to have allowed it. Anyhow, he was not asked.

Katherine was in a great state of despair and anxiety and neither of us had much money. Finally, I found an unfurnished top-floor room in a small house in Dorset Street, almost within sight of my family's flat. It belonged to a young Swiss couple who were making their living at hairdressing, and were most friendly and co-operative. We obtained a bed and the barest of necessities in the way of furniture. Katherine went there and tried to make life bearable. I do not remember what she had to cook on, probably a small gas ring; electricity was a fairly recent innovation, so I expect she had a lamp or candles. Water and all such conveniences were, of course, downstairs and had to be shared with the young couple. We were very worried when she developed an unexplained rash and felt ill. But a friend from my childhood, Miss Good, who had kept the nursing home next door to us in Welbeck Street days, sent one of her nurses to advise and give her some treatment. She gradually recovered but decided it was unwise to continue there, especially as her mother would soon be arriving and could not possibly find her in such quarters.

The hunt started again, and this time we found a small flat in Maida Vale, a part of London then of questionable reputation. Still, it was a self-contained flat. It has left in my mind an impression of unpainted wood, bamboo furniture – the sort that tumbles over – and cotton curtains. Bravely hiding our apprehension, we thought that it would 'do' for Katherine's mother to come to stay with her. Alas, how far we had fallen!

However, the sun shone in through the windows with their gay cotton curtains and Katherine touched things here and there and they began to assume a life of their own. But she was desperately unhappy. She realised now that by her own action she had finally lost Garnet, or perhaps she hoped still they might come together? She knew then definitely and told me that she was going to have his child, and her whole being cried out for her lover.

She wrote and wrote begging him to come and see her or to answer her letters and every morning woke again to the knowledge that he would not come. It became more than she could bear and it was at this time that she began to suffer from the fears which came to her when she was alone at night and which tormented her for the rest of her life. Being unable to sleep, she went to a chemist and bought some veronal. It made her sleep! Therefore she procured some more, until she could not give it up. I used to go to her early in the morning to be sure of finding her in and sometimes had breakfast with her of coffee and stewed fruit (an innovation in those days of eggs, bacon and porridge). One morning I knocked and knocked in vain. Feeling sure she could not have gone out so early, I returned a little later, to find she had drugged herself so heavily to get through the long, empty, frightening night that my knocking could not wake her.

I may have made Katherine appear much younger and more lacking in self-control than she was in truth. Perhaps her values were unbalanced by the depth of her feeling and the intensity of her imaginative creativity, but her way of living was never light or careless.*

At last on 27th May Mrs Beauchamp's boat train arrived. The platform was crowded with relations to greet her. Katherine was there too, at the farther end of the platform, wearing her shiny black hat and quite unacknowledged by any of the family. Mrs Beauchamp got out, was surrounded, embraced and talked to for a

* It would seem from the *Journal* that KM went to Brussels this spring, though LM cannot remember it; a visit which probably inspired the two stories *Journey to Bruges* and *Being a Truthful Adventure*, completed in 1910 and published in *The New Age* in August and September 1911.

little. Then, as though suddenly remembering her, she turned to look for her daughter.

I had never known, and I think Katherine had forgotten, the unquestioned assurance, security and authority of the rich, represented by her mother. There was no question of where she was staying: it must be at the dignified private hotel in Manchester Street where they always stayed. She swept Katherine away and established her there as a matter of course. Presently, she looked at the black hat.

'My dear child! The chambermaid can have that.'

Then she went out and bought a charming fluffy tulle hat for Katherine.

I only went two or three times to the hotel, but I saw Katherine now and again. I felt that she was glad of any occasion to get right away for a while.

It would seem that Mrs Beauchamp wished to separate us. She felt our friendship was not quite 'wise', and one day she came to see my father and had a long talk. Soon afterwards I heard that she was taking Katherine abroad. She had found a pleasant convent in Bavaria, where Katherine could – as she put it – recover from all her adventures while she herself returned to New Zealand. But in fact, for her family's sake, she could remain hidden and out of the way until all the scandal and shame had been forgotten. I do not think she knew that Katherine was going to have a baby.

Before Katherine was taken to Bavaria she told me she would not go as Katherine Mansfield, but under her married name, Mrs Bowden. A wedding ring would create a safer position for a young woman alone on the Continent. And thus it was she went.

About the same time my father said that he would give my sister and me the treat of a fortnight's holiday in the Canary Islands. I did not mind. As Katherine was abroad and out of reach it did not seem to matter where I was. The Canary Islands were as good as anywhere, and Bavaria was no more inaccessible from them as from England. I was quite unaware at the time of how much our parents were doing in trying to help their wayward children.

The story of Garnet and of KM's subsequent marriage to Bowden is hard to clarify. LM was the only person to know of it at the time. She described it in general terms to Antony Alpers, as can be seen from the relevant chapter in his biography. Alpers says that after Katherine had left Bowden, the morning after her marriage, she went to live above a hairdresser's shop, and from there went to Liverpool to join Garnet, who was playing in the orchestra of a travelling light opera company; that her mother had been told of both wedding and separation and that when she arrived neither she nor KM were aware of the coming child.

John Middleton Murry, editing Katherine's Journal for the definitive edition in 1954, quotes Alpers and says that Katherine fell in love with Garnet, then a violinist in travelling opera, and stayed with him in November in Hull; that she then married Bowden on 2nd March, left him the next morning and returned to Garnet, now at Liverpool; that KM's mother arrived to save what she could of the marriage and that she did not know of the pregnancy though Katherine herself must have known.

Ruth Elvish Mantz, writing her biography in 1933, and Sylvia Berkman, writing in 1952, both before the Alpers biography do not describe the affair in any detail; though Mantz adds that KM had cabled, not written, to her family about her marriage, and Berkman says that the news of the separation was cabled to them.

LM states that Katherine never saw Garnet again after her ill-fated marriage to Bowden in March and that this caused her great desolation and the recourse to drugs. According to LM Katherine joined the touring company with Garnet before her marriage, and it was at this time that she conceived his child. She says too that news of the proposed marriage was sent to New Zealand by letter, and that when the answer was received by cable, although Mrs Beauchamp was on her way, the couple decided to marry. This would push the date of the original plan to marry back to, at least, the end of January. In any case it is certain that when her mother arrived in May Katherine knew she was at least four and a half months pregnant, though her mother did not realise this.

CHAPTER V

Worishofen – London – Rottingdean – Bishop's Flat: Summer 1909 – Spring 1911

Katherine arrived at the convent in Bavaria in June 1909 but she did not stay long. Her next move was up into the mountains to a 'cure' village, Worishofen. There she was able to rest and recover a little from the strain and anguish of the past months. She led the simple life of the place, going barefoot, wading in the health-giving waters, living on fruit and taking long walks in the beautiful wooded country, and was presently able to break herself of the habit of taking veronal. This period is always connected in my memory with Katherine's joy in the trees, mountain forests and transparent air; strangely, too, in the lilac flower. For years the scent and sight of lilac brought back some deep emotional experience for her.

Her poem *The Storm*, most probably written at Worishofen, expresses her new attitude:

I ran to the forest for shelter,
Breathless, half sobbing;
I put my arms round a tree,
Pillowed my head against the rough bark,
'Protect me,' I said, 'I am a lost child.'
But the tree showered silver drops on my face and hair.
A wind sprang up from the ends of the earth;
It lashed the forest together.
A huge green wave thundered and burst over my head.
I prayed, implored, 'Please take care of me!'
But the wind pulled at my cloak and the rain beat upon me.
Little rivers tore up the ground and swamped the
    bushes.

A frenzy possessed the earth: I felt that the earth was
   drowning
In a bubbling cavern of space I alone –
Smaller than the smallest fly – was alive and terrified.
Then for what reason I know not, I became triumphant.
'Well, kill me!' I cried and ran out into the open.
But the storm ceased: the sun spread his wings
And floated serene on the silver pool of the sky.
I put my hands over my face: I was blushing.
And the trees swung together and delicately laughed.

What I know of this time came to me through her letters and
later from our conversation. She had a room in the house of the
postmistress and one day, on coming in, she began to tidy it.
She tried to lift a travelling trunk to the top of a cupboard: it was
too heavy, and she hurt herself badly. She suffered great pain
and was ill for some time. It must have been then that she lost her
baby. She did not tell me this in so many words, but from several
things she said I realised that this was how it must have
happened.

After this Katherine was forced to be inactive for some time
and, as often happens with young women in this state, she became
depressed and miserable. Hearing from her and suspecting her
loss, I did not know what to do until Miss Good told me of a small
boy, Walter, aged eight, who was very delicate, and desperately in
need of clean, pure air as he was just recovering from pleurisy.
I suggested that he convalesce with Katherine and she jumped at
the idea. All Katherine's mother love flowed out to this boy.
Arrangements were easier in those days; we got him a ticket,
tied a label on him, and sent him across to her. She cared for him,
loved him and kept him for two or three months, until he was able
to return, healthy and well. She made him call her Sally, the name
given to her by Sidney Hislop.

In the meantime she was making many friends. Some were
good friends, like an Austrian family she was to meet again later
in Geneva: people in whose company she was gay and happy.
Also she was writing. Most of the *German Pension* stories came
then; and some of the bitterness and ugliness that she had been
through must have been exorcised by them.

There was a Polish literary man, Floryan Sobieniowski, with

whose quiet tastes she found much in common. He was probably in love with her.

There were other people too, the not-so-good, once more ready to pounce and grab. One must remember always her extraordinary charm, gaiety, humour and vivid loveliness. These not-so-good friends became demanding and troublesome, and I think also a little frightening. One was a rough bully from whom she wished to escape.* She was still only just twenty-one, a married woman without a husband. The paradise of the mountains was being spoilt and she was restless. She made plans with the Pole, Sobieniowski, to travel to this country and then to see, perhaps Russia . . . perhaps. . . . She thought she had made it clear that they were to be only travelling companions. The Pole left Worishofen, arranging to meet her in Munich, where he was to have found two bed-sittingrooms in which they could study and read and work. She wrote to him after he left – letters we were to hear of again many years later. They must have been enthusiastic, happy, loving letters, looking forward to meeting him. When the time came she left Worishofen and started on this new adventure. But on her arrival she found only one room and a very different plan for living. Quite natural, probably, from the Pole's point of view, but Katherine was not Polish, and so she ran away and came back to England.

She arrived in January 1910. At her request, I had hurriedly taken a room for her at the new Strand Palace Hotel, where she had heard you could get a bed and breakfast for eleven shillings. This was true; but that eleven shillings a day was more than she could afford or, I imagine, actually *had*, and she was always turning over in her mind what she could do to earn something more, since there was no market for her stories. I am sure she deceived me constantly about what other meals she had besides that 'breakfast'; it was never easy for her to say when her purse was empty, because she knew mine was also very thin.

Somehow we managed that she should stay there for a while. We met and talked. Another guest, a most bizarre and strange woman, soon made Katherine's acquaintance and tried to persuade her to join her in fortune-telling and I know not what else. Katherine played with the idea for a little and then, quite suddenly,

---

* Described in one of her *German Pension* stories, *The Swing of the Pendulum*, published in 1911.

in February, told me that, partly for the sake of the family, she would go back to her husband and try to make it work,

So the next step was taken, but not with gaiety, rather with determination and apprehension. They must have been in correspondence as she knew where he was living.

I did not know then that George Bowden thought I was KM's lesbian friend, and the cause of her leaving him in the first place. Indeed, I did not know then what a 'lesbian friend' meant. But Katherine decided that Bowden must not know that I was still about, and when she joined him in a small flat in Gloucester Place, I was only able to go and see her when he was out. I had to ring up, using the name 'Lesley Moore' that I had decided to use professionally should I need one.

Katherine was with Bowden in Gloucester Place for several weeks, meaning to work when he was out singing or teaching, but she was not happy and was much distressed by his lack of delicacy. Then, towards the end of March, Katherine told Bowden to send for me. I found her in a second-rate nursing home, where they told me that she had been operated on for peritonitis. She asked me to take her away at once as the surgeon was displaying an unprofessional interest in her body. I immediately called a (growler), the horse-drawn four-wheelers we had in those days, and, as the wound was still unhealed, told the driver to go slowly over the uneven roads for the springs were very poor. This he did; alas, only prolonging the pain. I took her to my sister's flat where I put her to bed. Our friend Miss Good kindly came and dressed the wound daily, and between us we cared for her until she was well enough to travel. Unfortunately, this by no means meant that she was well.

A few months previously in the spring of 1910, LM's father and brother had emigrated to Rhodesia to start a farm. Before leaving, her father had established LM and her sister in a small flat in Luxborough House off the Marylebone Road. It was to this flat that LM had brought Katherine when she was so ill.

Though Katherine's attempt at reconciliation with Bowden was unsuccessful, it had one important outcome. For, on Bowden's suggestion, Katherine contacted A. R. Orage, the editor of The New Age, *a well-informed weekly dealing with current issues in politics,* *religion, literature and art. It was the liveliest intellectual periodical of the day. Orage enjoyed promoting controversies in its pages and was well known for the encouragement he gave to young writers and their ideas. His meeting with KM was an immediate personal success and he liked her work. Four of her pieces were published in* The New Age *before she became ill:* Bavarian Babies: The Child-who-was-Tired *and three of her satirical pension sketches:* Germans at Meat, The Baron *and* The Luft Bad. *These were all written in Bavaria; some ideas were taken for them from stories by Chekhov which KM had been reading – possibly in German translation.* (The Child-who-was-Tired *is an adaptation of Chekhov's story* Sleepyhead, *which had in fact already been published in English in 1903 with* The Black Monk *and other Stories.)* A link had been established with Orage and, although Katherine was to leave London for a while to convalesce in Rottingdean, Orage and his editorial assistant, Beatrice Hastings, went to visit her. A friendship developed and KM became one of Orage's protégées.*

In April I took some rooms over a grocer's shop in a little street leading to the shore at Rottingdean. Here Katherine could hear the sea sometimes and smell it always. She continued to suffer pain and the local doctor was sent for. After a long time she was patched up, although the trouble was not correctly diagnosed nor was she fully cured until many years later in 1918 when Dr Sorapure took charge of her. He told her then that the pains that she had suffered from almost continuously since this time in Rottingdean, and had always called her 'rheumatiz', were the result of a disease that she had contracted before she was taken to the nursing home.

With doctor's fees to pay money was again short, and, as she had done what the family expected of her by trying to live with her husband, she felt that she could write to Mr Kay, the manager of the Bank of New Zealand in London. He came down and saw the doctor and made himself responsible for all his fees. This was a tremendous relief.

As soon as Katherine was able to move about I took a cottage for her nearby where she gradually got better.

That convalescence was a peaceful and, I think, happy time. We took in a small stray dog which she loved. The meadow beside the house was full of flowering grasses and large white daisies. I used to go to Brighton to get books from the library and if not always successful in my choice of books, I did at least bring back some lovely, soft, silk scarves for her. It was in that little house that she put on the black and silver Egyptian shawl which I photographed. The sun shone and the sea breezes filled the house, and Katherine was able to walk about again. She had not been able to sit on the shore and listen to the sea since she left Day's Bay in New Zealand, and now she wrote several poems to it:

> The sea called – I lay on the rocks and said:
> 'I am come.'
> She mocked and showed her teeth,
> Stretching her long green arms.
> 'Go away!' She thundered,
> 'Then tell me what I am to do,' I begged.
> 'If I leave you, you will not be silent.
> But cry my name in the cities
> And wistfully entreat me in the plains and forests;
> All else I forsake to come to you – what must I do?'
> 'Never have I uttered your name,' snarled the sea.
> 'There is no more of me in your body
> Than the little salt tears you are frightened of
>   shedding.
> What can you know of my love on your brown rock
>   pillow? . . .
> Come closer.'

*

> Into the world you sent her, mother,
>   Fashioned her body of coral and foam,
> Combed a wave in her hair's warm smother,
>   And drove her away from home.
>
> In the dark of the night she crept to the town
>   And under a doorway she laid her down,
> The little blue child in the foam fringed gown.
>
> And never a sister and never a brother
>   To hear her call, to answer her cry,
> Her face shone out from her hair's warm smother
>   Like a moonkin up in the sky.

> She sold her corals – she sold her foam;
>   Her rainbow heart like a singing shell
> Broke in her body: she crept back home.
>
> Peace, go back to the world, my daughter,
>   Daughter, go back, to the darkling land;
> There is nothing here but sad sea water,
>   And a handful of shifting sand.

Bowden came down once or perhaps twice to see her, but Katherine had decided not to try the experiment of living with him again. She made me take him away on the plea of showing him the village, and when we reached the church, I suggested he should go in alone, as I had no hat. Bowden snatched off his bowler and clapped it on my head, expecting me to enter into the spirit of his pleasantry. He did not come any more; and I think Katherine did not see him again until a few years later when he came to ask if she wished for a divorce.

As Katherine got better at the cottage, so she began to get in touch with people again. Orage and Beatrice Hastings came down to stay,* as well as a number of other writers whose names I have forgotten. If there were too many visitors I would return to London to stay with my sister, as the cottage was so small.

During a walk with some of these friends, we climbed to the top of the cliffs, where a lonely house had been railed off as dangerous. The cliffs were being gradually eaten away, and the house was on the edge with half its garden already gone. We climbed over the railings – I, very reluctantly – and found our way into the lower rooms. I have never forgotten the strange, eerie feeling. The house was breathing its doom and every now and again it shivered with the thunder of the waves breaking far below. I could not rest till Katherine was safely out and once again on the road. As for the others, if they were stupid enough to play with death, it was their affair. I was too anxious really to care: too frightened by that poor Andromeda waiting, waiting.

Another day we went down to the shore and Katherine stood and looked intently out to sea. Then she turned and asked what I was seeing, but I could think only of the colour of the sea and the balloons the children had been playing with. This brought no comment.

* They published her poem *Loneliness* in *The New Age* in May 1910.

One night Katherine had not been feeling well. She had gone early to bed when a terrifying thunderstorm broke over the village. We leaned forward, looking out of the window at the majesty of the forked lightning and shivering a little at the blasts of thunder. Then looking round, I saw that Katherine had fainted Terrified, I wondered what to do. Should I rush out into the storm and blinding rain to try and find a doctor? I had never seen anyone faint before. I laid her back on her pillows and covered her with sheets and stood there whispering: 'Katie, come back! Come back, Katie!' And so she did, after about ten minutes.

Soon she was well enough to go back to London and was told of Henry Bishop's flat in Chelsea.

Henry Bishop was a painter Katherine knew through Orage. She moved into his flat in Cheyne Walk, Chelsea, in the August of 1910 and stayed there for five months while he was abroad. She was twenty-one that October and a new life was opening for her in the literary circles of London. She met writers and people of her own kind; four more of her pension sketches from Bavaria were published in The New Age *through that July and August. She also joined the Correspondence Column, where* The New Age's *fiercest battles were fought, with a biting attack on Fleet Street for its treatment of Crippen and with a review of an American and a Canadian writer; these were especially cutting when she collaborated with Beatrice Hastings.*

Beatrice Hastings was nine years older than KM. She lived with Orage, and appeared at least two or three times in each issue of The New Age *– under a variety of pseudonyms – writing with acerbity on poetry, women's rights, Christianity. The two women's styles were similar and could easily be confused; KM's Marriage of Passion, ridiculing the aesthetics Mr and Mrs De Voted, is closely allied in spirit to Beatrice Hastings'* The Lady, *written two years previously. In each other's company they seem to have incited each other to extremes of sarcasm and malicious wit. They were even alike in appearance; so much so that LM claims that the photograph in Alpers' book (opposite page 144), used again as the frontispiece to the 1951 edition of the Letters, is in fact Beatrice Hastings, and should not be mistaken for KM.*

At the end of August KM temporarily stopped writing for The
New Age, *and, after four months, in December she sent* A Fairy Story
to The Open Window, *a new, poetical and slightly whimsical
magazine started by Locke Ellis.*

Katherine loved being in Bishop's flat. It had two rooms: a large
front one, with a little bedroom behind, and a small cooking space.
Situated on the Embankment, it was close to the end of the King's
Road, where there was an old public house called the World's
End. In the summer evenings an old man used to play his instrument outside it and his music, mixed with the sounds of the river
and of the gently moving barges, trailed into her windows. At
night the plane trees along the wide Embankment were sprinkled
with light from the gas lamps. Katherine drew a picture in charcoal of one of these trees slashed with falling rain, which I kept
for many years.

Katherine had quickly decided to sleep on a low sofa in the large
front room, where the light from the street lamps dappled the
walls and ceiling until late at night. This, I fancy, kept her night
fears at bay.

By then I had drifted away from my academy of music, and I
visited her every day, sometimes staying overnight. I remember
how, when she was hungry, we would have midnight tea and
hard-boiled eggs. One night after I had gone to bed in the little
room, she called out to me that she was thinking of going to Japan.
I was startled and cried: 'Oh, I shall be so lonely!' She at once
comforted me and promised not to go. I cannot think why this
stayed in my mind except that later I was very conscious of my
selfishness in expressing my pain and so throwing a cord about
her feet. The visit was a lovely thought but she gave it up at once.

Of course, one or two undesirable people found her even there,
but there was not much annoyance. One man was very persistent,
until one day I was sent to guard the door and send him away. He
came as it happened on a day when an old college friend, Gwen
Rouse, was visiting Katherine. He had evidently watched the house
for some time to make sure she was in. I went down to say she was
not 'in' and that I could give no information about her movements.
He then started to come in and said he would wait. I had to think
quickly. No, I said, he could not do that as she had lent the room

to a friend and me, and we were dressmaking. This was partly true because Gwen was sewing. He said *he* did not mind, he would come in and help us. I steadily refused, preparing to shut the door quickly. He looked me up and down, and then gave up. I was not worth it. He did not try again.

There is one thing which I must try to explain. So often people have passed judgement on the way Katherine behaved to me, saying 'She made use of you'. But if she did make use of me, it was because I saw to it that she did. 'She must have been terribly difficult to live with', they have also said. Katherine believed that one should try to live perfectly, down to the smallest detail. No human being could always maintain that standard, and though I entirely approved of it and attempted to do so, I fell below it very often, even in the simplest things. Katherine failed too, as she often acknowledged, but through all the difficult later years of her life she held bravely to her faith and succeeded far better than it is possible to relate. If she asked much of others she asked far more of herself, and felt strongly that, if you wished to be a fine artist, you must discipline yourself and learn to live finely.

It was while Katherine was in Chelsea that she found her treasured dressmaker in Redcliffe Road. It was she who made all those small coats of lovely colours and soft velvet materials that Katherine wore for so many years; warm, full skirts for the winters; and dresses with long fitting bodices and pleated skirts. Life was an orgy of dressmaking at that time.

Katherine also met the woman who lived in the flat above: Madame Alexandra, who trained opera singers. She had heard Katherine singing and, coming down like a ship in full sail, had tried to persuade her to train for the opera. Katherine started lessons but then found that it meant giving herself completely to Madame Alexandra and later stopped the lessons. It was at this time that we arranged to buy Madame Alexandra's grand piano so that Katherine could practise. I shared in the payments for it by instalments and this was later to lead to trouble when Katherine suddenly decided to sell the piano before the payments had been completed. Luckily I was able to lay my hands on some money quickly and pay off the balance.

At Bishop's flat we had a very happy time. Katherine seemed well again and was in a place that suited her. Life was flowing in and the dread of the past was no longer with her. She was able to live with real enjoyment once more. It was a time of ending and beginning, or perhaps a pause between the two.

Katherine met and knew many people in these days. William Orton was one of the most important for her. He was a young school teacher who longed to be a writer, which he later became; his autobiography *The Last Romantic* gives a picture of the time when he knew Katherine. There was something mystical about their relationship, strangely special, a place of safety for them both. Katherine spoke to me about it and I understood that its essence was expressed in her poem, *There was a Child Once*.

> There was a child once
> He came to play in my garden;
> He was quite pale and silent.
> Only when he smiled I knew everything about him,
> I knew what he had in his pockets,
> And I knew the feel of his hands in my hand
> And the most intimate tones of his voice.
> I led him down each secret path,
> Showing him the hiding place of all my treasures.
> I let him play with them, every one,
> I put my singing thoughts in a little silver cage
> And gave them to him to keep . . .
> It was very dark in the garden
> But never dark enough for us. On tip-toe we
>   walked among the deepest shades;
> We bathed in the shadow pools beneath the trees,
> Pretending we were under the sea.
> Once – near the boundary of the garden –
> We heard steps passing along the World-road;
> O how frightened we were!
> I whispered: 'Have you ever walked along that road?'
> He nodded, and we shook the tears from our eyes. . . .
> He came – quite alone – to play in my garden;
> He was pale and silent.
> And when he went away, we did not even wave.

She gave her beautiful, square, black opal ring to Orton. It had been given to her by the Maoris, and had some strange significance and occult power.

Other Queen's College friends came too, including Walter Rippmann, the German Professor. But Katherine would not start with him the new relationship that he seemed to want.

A frequent visitor was a young man, hardly more than a boy in appearance, and very handsome. He brought her lovely presents and I remember particularly a tiny painted Russian village. Complete in every detail, with small houses and churches, it was a great joy to her. He would lie on the floor in the firelight playing with it. At Christmas he brought a beautiful, tiny, decorated tree which was illuminated by minute lights. Katherine was much attracted by him, and he fell in love with her. They were young and happy, intended to marry and soon became lovers. However, the affair was short lived: his family disapproved. They looked on Katherine as a potential danger, a married woman who was living alone. They must have forbidden him to see her for he did not come to her again.

The happiness of this relationship and the emotional security it gave KM may have been the reason she turned away from the clever and sometimes bitter world of The New Age *at the end of August, and chose to submit* A Fairy Story *to* The Open Window.

Early in 1911, Henry Bishop wanted to return to his flat and we had to find a new home. There had been so much happiness and laughter there, it was sad to leave. It was, as I said, an ending and a beginning: a new chapter.

CHAPTER VI

Gray's Inn Road – Geneva:
1911 – Easter 1912

The new flat was in Clovelly Mansions, Gray's Inn Road. I cannot remember which of us went to see it first, perhaps we went together. It was a top-floor flat in a solid red-brick building, with cement stairs and an iron balustrade, cold and forbidding. It towered above the neighbouring roof-tops and one had the impression of sailing out over all London. Far below one could hear the clanking of the trams.

The flat consisted of four rooms: a bedroom, a kitchen and two others. Katherine had no furniture, so we covered the sitting-room floor and part of its walls with pale yellow bamboo matting; this was cheaper than anything else. People sat on the floor on cushions, so not much else was needed. There was a roll-top desk, an armchair, a large basket chair which came from my mother's sitting-room, and many cushions. On those nights when I was not sleeping there, for I could not always do so, this furniture was piled up against the sitting-room door against Fear, with Katherine sleeping behind it.

Katherine wanted to decorate the kitchen with large travel posters and I hunted London for them. We made the walls so gay that the kitchen seemed to sail happily away. The other room was also covered with bamboo matting and contained the piano we had bought from Madame Alexandra and a much-loved stone Buddha brought from India by my father. The Buddha had pride of place, with a dish of flowers standing before him.

Soon after moving there Katherine realised that she was again with child. She wrote repeatedly to the young man and begged him to come and see her, but she never had any reply. I went to his office to try to persuade him, but despite his promises he did not come. So he never knew of his child. His desertion was, I think, softened by the joy she took in the thought of the child itself; she seemed to have found security.

She was making a new home and she loved the new flat. I spent

63

a great deal of time with her there in the first three months. We passed many happy hours with Katherine practising her marvellous impersonations, walking about the rooms singing, or playing on the grand piano.

In the sunny kitchen she cooked with an absorbed smile and it was here that she showed me how to mix flour for the stew as she had been taught by the Waters, her relations in New Zealand, when a young, inquiring child. In her present contentment she remembered many small happenings of her childhood and described them in vivid pictures for me. It was a time of colour and light for us; the flat floating calmly in the sky over the chimneys and roofs.

Quite often during the day I would go back to my sister at Luxborough House, to leave Katherine more free to get on with her work. When I returned in the evenings, such was our relationship that she was able to continue with her writing while I sat at peace, dreaming. As often as possible I stayed the night, for Katherine was still sleeping badly; and on these evenings we frequently stayed up late, with Katherine sitting in front of the fire weaving her thoughts into words, the light of the fire reflected in her shining eyes. But as midnight slipped by in the warm room, I found it more and more difficult to keep my eyes open. She was on a plane higher than mine, absorbed and full of beauty and light – while I just slept.

One evening I was deeply conscious of a great happiness and peace and knew quite clearly, at that moment, that I should never be so completely, peacefully happy again: a strange experience that I have never forgotten. It was indeed the flowering of our young friendship.

Katherine now seemed quite secure and settled, so when an urgent demand came from my father in Rhodesia in April 1911 for my sister and me to go out to see him there for a few months, Katherine and I decided that I should go. She was expecting the child and happy at the thought; she was older and more capable of managing things now and to provide for her I opened a bank account with a sensible sum for all she might want whilst I was away. Even so, in retrospect I cannot imagine how I could have left her at that time; it was a foolish thing to do. However, I went and Katherine gave me a bunch of carnations as the taxi drove me away from her.

I was gone for about five months and when I returned in the autumn I found no baby and a closed bank account. We never discussed the matter; obviously it had all been horrible. I am sure that Beatrice Hastings had been in some way responsible.

Orage and Beatrice Hastings had become much more prominent in Katherine's life, especially so whilst I was away. Through them she saw much of their circle of young literary friends. In her customary way Katherine could appear to give all of herself to a given situation as it demanded, until suddenly she withdrew into herself to meet some other contingency. Now it was stimulating to be clever, amusing and even bitter and cruel with Beatrice. As she herself said, Beatrice brought out the worst in her. Perhaps she took on the worst of Beatrice?

Katherine's passion for understanding life was still dangerous: she must know all, feel all, and above all understand all. Life was absorbing and was there to be translated into her one profound preoccupation: her work. She once said that even in moments of most intense living there was always a part of herself which stood aside, looking on, noting all. Though I found this hard to understand, it was true for her.

In June 1911 KM had returned to the New Age *with the last of her pension sketches,* The Modern Soul, *also,* The Festival of the Coronation (*not collected*). *In August and September her two stories* The Journey to Bruges *and* Being a Truthful Adventure *were printed and in October a derisive poem:* Love Cycle (*not collected*). *This and two stories published in March and June of the next year were highly satirical, much in the vein of Beatrice Hastings.*

While I was in Rhodesia, Mr and Mrs Beauchamp came to England in May for a few months bringing their son Chummie, who was to study here. After many years' separation, Katherine and he came together with great happiness. They were wholly at one with each other and spent much time together in the flat. Katherine wrote to me in Rhodesia saying how complete their love and understanding were. I believe that her feeling for him was one of the greatest joys of her life. Many years later I had several letters from Chummie; he loved me because Katherine and I loved one another.

She also saw a good deal of her parents during their visit, and it was now that she discovered that her relationship with her mother was very real and precious. In some ways the two women were much alike: sharing a delicately fastidious nature and a sense of humour that was coupled with a certain aloofness.

During their visit Katherine became seriously ill with pleurisy or bronchitis for which in those days there was no quick cure. At the time I knew nothing of this, but later Katherine described how, while she lay there alone, she experienced the strange power of levitation and found herself floating up to the ceiling. When the fever was high she would watch the little red elephants on the edge of her Indian cotton bedspread waving their trunks and processing solemnly round and round their limited pathway. As soon as she was a little better her parents persuaded her to go abroad to Geneva for a change of air. But they did not take her or even provide her with a companion for the journey. Nor did they see that she had enough money; so how she was able to manage I do not know.

Meanwhile I was on my way home from Rhodesia through Paris. Since our journeys would cross, I wrote telling her where I would be spending the night there. But at my hotel I found a telegram asking me to meet her at another hotel. Of course we missed each other. When I eventually arrived back in London, Chummie came to see me the same evening – he explained about Katherine's illness and her journey, and was very sweet, understanding how worried I was – though he knew nothing of her earlier troubles and illness. During the next few days I saw Chummie two or three times. I managed to scrape together £5 and my fare – the African trip had all been paid for, of course, by my father – and told Chummie I was going off to Geneva to find Katherine When I eventually reached the address he had given me, Katherine's first anxious question was: 'Have you brought any money with you?' The poor child had barely £1 left. Luckily I was able to get a little more money sent out to us. Her father's meanness made me very bitter against him.

At the pension the time passed quietly, with lovely, sunny days. We had to share a charming room at the top of the house, looking out over the clean, tree-planted street. Each morning the windows up and down it were filled with white puff clouds, with the *duvets* airing in the fresh sunshine, while the sweet, clear air blew in from the distant mountains. This air was doing her all the good in the world and she was getting stronger. Of course she was putting her newly found strength into some new stories.

Very early one morning there was a slight earth tremor. I sat up quickly, surprised by the strange sensation. Instantly Katherine was up to comfort and reassure me, imagining I was frightened. *She* 'knew all about earthquakes', and explained it was nothing, nothing at all! Her instant, *active* concern made a vivid impression on me which has never faded.

I think it was during this stay that Katherine had a chance meeting with the delightful Austrian family first encountered in Worishofen and now also staying in Geneva. They spent many happy hours together. I did not feel part of their company and therefore, as my money was running out, I decided to return to London. I was not anxious at the thought of leaving her, for I knew she was happy with her friends.

Whilst I had been away in Rhodesia, I had realised that Katherine had been meeting people with a mental capacity nearer to her own, and through them had achieved an even wider intellectual freedom. She had grown and I had not kept pace with her. I began to know the almost physical ache that comes with the realisation of being inadequate. This came to colour our relationship in the ensuing years and I made poor Katie suffer for my mistakes. A sense of inadequacy has, indeed, haunted me throughout most of my life, and it is only quite recently that I have learnt to accept, and offer, myself for whatever I may be: the only thing that matters is to be oneself – nothing can kill that germ of truth in a person.

Soon after I had returned to London, Katherine, who was much better, began to be restless and wanted to return herself, as much to her brother as to her flat. When she came home in the September of 1911 I did not see so much of her as before, for she was occupied with her parents. Before they went back to New Zealand later in the year, Mrs Beauchamp wrote me a charming letter and gave me a photograph of herself, which I kept for many years.

In the autumn of 1911 KM's ten New Age *stories and three others,
collected under the title* In a German Pension, *were published by
Stephen Swift and met with critical favour (especially in America
where they received six reviews though KM earned only £15 from the
publication).*

At this time Katherine was writing a good deal. She moved away
from *The New Age*, but I do not know much about her work then
for she did not often talk to me of it. There was no reason why she
should do so; in all likelihood I should not have understood and
she had by now many more intellectual friends with whom to talk.

The W. L. Georges asked her to dinner occasionally, which she
enjoyed. It was at their house that she first met John Middleton
Murry, then still an undergraduate, when one evening he was also
a guest. They talked and he came to see her at Gray's Inn Road.
On these visits he would bring his work to discuss with her, lying
on the floor surrounded by MSS – 'like a little boy playing with
his toys' was Katherine's description.

She was much impressed by him: his mind, his looks, everything about him. When he suggested that she should join him in
editing his magazine *Rhythm*, she was both pleased and excited.
Soon Murry tired of Oxford and, against the advice of his friends,
left the university. He found life at home with his simple, working-
class family wholly uncongenial. He told Katherine how much he
was misunderstood, so earning her sympathy, and of his need to
find somewhere to live, in order to push ahead with his writing.
She offered him a room in Clovelly Mansions, the Buddha room.
He was anxious to start a new life and Easter was coming; why not
begin right away?

I did not know anything of Murry's plan and was happily
looking forward to that week-end, as I was free to spend the whole
of it with Katherine. Alas, on my arrival I had to help Katherine
fill his cupboard with good things to eat – hiding a £5 note among
the provisions, since we knew that he was penniless. Then,
forlornly, I returned to Luxborough House. Katherine came with
me part of the way, on top of an old London omnibus. It was a
very rare thing for us to speak of our relationship, but realising
my disappointment at the happiness I had lost, she wrote a poem
for me, inscribing it inside the cover of a small book of occult
widsom, which was always one of my treasures.

The Secret

In the profoundest Ocean
There is a rainbow shell,
It is always there, shining most stilly
Under the great storm waves
And under the happy little waves
That the old Greeks called 'ripples of laughter'.
And you listen, the rainbow shell
Sings – in the profoundest ocean.
It is always there, singing most silently!

CHAPTER VII

From Murry's Arrival to LM's Visit to Rhodesia: 1912 – 1914

After Easter *1912* KM became involved in a life with John Middleton Murry and his magazine Rhythm. *The idea of the magazine had germinated when Murry was in Paris in the winter of 1910 on vacation from Oxford. He had wandered into the bohemian world there, meeting the French writer Francis Carco (who later wrote of this period in* Boheme d'Artiste *and* Monmartre à Vingt Ans, *and who was to be the model for Raoul Duquette in KM's* Je ne parle pas français) *and John D. Fergusson, a Scottish painter who had a studio in Paris. Fergusson talked much of rhythm in art and when he heard that Murry and a friend of his from Oxford, Michael Sadleir (then Sadler) were thinking of starting a magazine, Fergusson picked up the idea with enthusiasm, insisted that it be called* Rhythm, *and that it should express in literature the exciting new ideas which had just burst upon the art world with the Fauves. The magazine's first number stated that its aim was to 'seek out the strong things of life . . . to provide an art, drama, literature, criticism which shall have its roots below the surface and be the rhythmical echo of the life with which it is in touch. Both in its purity and brutality it shall be real.'*

The first issue appeared in the summer of 1911 and thereafter the magazine was published quarterly. It was well printed in Caslon type on fine quality paper with many woodcuts, decorative headings and illustrations. Contributors to the first issue included Frederick Goodyear (another friend of Murry's from Oxford) on the aim of the magazine; Sadleir on Fauve and Fauvism, and JMM on art and philosophy. There were drawings by Othon Friesz, Jessie Dismorr, Peploe, Anne Estelle Rice and Picasso. Rhythm *was the first magazine in England to publish drawings by Picasso.*

In December KM, who had left The New Age, *sent a fairy story to this new periodical; this was returned but another story asked for.*

She sent The Woman at the Store *and this was published in the spring number of 1912. By Easter Murry had moved into her flat in Gray's Inn Road, and they were working together on the magazine.* Rhythm *shows immediate signs of Katherine's arrival. The June number was the first they published together. There were more contributors than usual: articles by Laurence Binyon and W. W. Gibson, among others, drawings by Mauguin, Dunoyer-Segonzac, and with reproductions of works by Henri Marquet and Lionel Helpert. Also the addition of short reviews and advertisements, for which Katherine and Murry themselves had to canvas.* Rhythm *became the focus of their lives; those friends who had helped found it, together with other writers and would-be writers of the day, were the magazine's contributors and their circle.*

Anne Estelle Rice was a young American painter who lived in Paris and had made her name there as a book illustrator and mural painter; she worked in the new Fauve style. As a person she was warm and generous hearted and was to become a firm friend to Katherine.

Gordon Campbell was another close friend of this time, though he was never a contributor to Rhythm. *A young Irish barrister, interested in all forms of art and literature, he had come to London in 1911, and had first met KM through W. L. George. She introduced him to JMM and the two young men soon began to see each other regularly. They found they had a common approach to metaphysical problems and would discuss these at length together.*

After the week-end when Murry moved in I did not go to see Katherine for a week or so. She and Murry worked hard and talked much, so that gradually *Rhythm* began to develop.

Katherine told me that things were going well. If their breakfast times coincided she would cook an egg for him: otherwise one was left on the table, with a note saying it was for him to deal with. Then they worked and went about their business independently till the evening, when they met and often went out together for a frugal dinner, sometimes to the eel shop at the corner. Katherine told me that in the end she quite enjoyed eels. Sometimes they went farther afield and joined other friends. I learnt to know many of those friends by name and occasionally met a few at the flat. Gordon Campbell I knew almost as a human being, not an intellectual or literary figure. He was a very understanding and kindly person, a great friend of Murry. Once he came to my place of work to help me with advice over some business trouble.

As *Rhythm* took shape, Katherine and Murry inevitably mixed with many literary and artistic people, and she began to feel the need of new clothes: the things that had come from New Zealand with her must somehow be supplemented. With great difficulty she saved £4, enough to buy a new suit. She then made herself, without much stitching, a waistcoat from a piece of tartan taffeta silk, and with a single flower pinned to the coat, the outfit was complete. I gave full approval before she went out to meet someone 'important'.

I remember an occasion at that time when I had been washing her long, wavy hair. As it was being dried, it became so tangled and matted that we had to cut it all off. She was delighted with the result and after that always wore her hair short, always well groomed and pressed close to her head, which made many people insist that her hair was straight.

Occasionally we went out together, and I recollect how one afternoon we were speaking of Murry. As we mounted the steep platform of a bus (they were horse drawn then) she continued: 'Yes, he has beautiful style and language, but I have to . . .' I cannot recall the exact words but they suggested that she had to keep a very firm hand or there would be bad mistakes in values, I gathered, in choice of subjects and in general form. She always kept that unseen firm hand when they worked together. I was informed on some occasion – or I may have seen it stated – that Murry claimed to have 'edited' Katherine's work for her. I was up in arms over this, because I knew she never allowed anyone to alter her work by so much as a comma.

Another day Katherine and I went down Tottenham Court Road for lunch at one of the large vegetarian restaurants which used to be so good there. Sitting down, Katherine glanced around, then turned to me and said: 'Look, who is over there. I shall go and speak to him.' It was that young man who had made her pregnant – I expected to glimpse the fine, handsome lad of a few years before, but I saw nothing but a short, rather stout, full-faced youth with very ordinary clipped hair – one of many thousands. Katherine came back, murmuring quietly, 'See what

I've been saved from.' He still did not know that he had lost not only Katherine but his child.*

I was no longer worried about Katherine's night-fears, now that she had another human being always within reach, and therefore I did not see her so often. Having time on my hands and hardly any money left, I decided to join our family friend, Miss Good, in a venture she was starting called the Parma Rooms. We set out to provide scientific treatments for skin and hair, a field in which Miss Good had first-class knowledge and experience. She was to be called Miss Rinsberry and I used the name Lesley Moore. Out of my dwindling resources I paid the rent of a large room in South Molton Street, and we opened in June 1912. I found I was expected to pay the rent for the second year also and had nothing left. I spent sleepless nights trying to think of ways to find the money and in desperation turned to my sister, who came to my assistance.

So, while Katherine was becoming more and more absorbed by *Rhythm* and all the activities it entailed, Miss Rinsberry and I were trying to live on ten shillings a week out of our earnings. I was often very hungry, and more than once I stole from the Parma Rooms the oatmeal we used for face-packs, so that I could make some gruel. I became thin and rather down-at-heel in the mauve uniform we wore at work, and was very unhappy in the job I was doing.

On one of Katherine's visits to the Parma Rooms she was grieving that she badly needed a new hat. Miss Rinsberry picked up a length of wide moire silk ribbon and tied it round Katherine's head, with a large stiff rosette at the side. Katherine was delighted with this clever creation and indeed looked charming in it.

Katherine tried to help us when we started evening sessions of manicure for men. She inserted a splendid advertisement in *Rhythm* and sent the obedient W. L. George along to us on a night when I was on duty. I felt I had no flair for this work, and was terrified. I wished I could push my foolishness aside, but even now I feel I could not really cope with such a task.

I do not remember feeling too worried over Katherine's

* This incident may have inspired the short story *A Dill Pickle*, first published in *The New Age* for October 1917, and later included with *Bliss and other stories*.

troubles. The literary ones were beyond me and I expect she kept the worst of the others to herself or rather made so light of them that I was deceived; her brave spirit always worked like that, and I was, in any case, seeing less and less of her. Life at the flat in Gray's Inn Road was increasing both in complexity and pace. *Rhythm* was all-absorbing of time and energy, but it was perpetually causing them financial difficulties and each number left them more and more in debt. The constant want of money and the weight of unpaid bills must have been almost intolerable.

Katherine and Murry had by now become lovers and at the end of April 1912 they had written to Katherine's husband, George Bowden, to ask him to divorce her. He arrived one day to see her and there was much talk; but in the end he did nothing. So Murry and Katherine decided to live as man and wife without legal consent. But there had been so much coming and going at Gray's Inn Road, perhaps Bowden had also been indiscreet when asking for Katherine, that the owner of the flat below began to suspect the presence of an unmarried couple; this was against the rules and they were asked to leave.

The Murrys were now forced to abandon their home and the office of their paper. What was to happen? Katherine, I knew, was leading a life which was no longer hers. Doubtless there were aspects of it that she enjoyed, and she was working with Murry, but it was not her kind of life and she was becoming restless and tired.

They felt, in these circumstances, that they were justified in taking a short holiday, and went to Paris in May. Murry wanted to introduce Katherine to John Fergusson and his other friends in Paris, and they spent a short time there with him, Anne Estelle Rice and Carco.*

On their return, the problem of the magazine's increasing financial losses had to be faced. Katherine approached Stephen Swift, who the year previously had published her collection of short stories, *In a German Pension*. He offered to take over the responsibility of *Rhythm* with all its debts and to pay them both a monthly salary of £10 as co-editors. It was a great relief to them to put their worries into what should have been trustworthy and

---

* This visit was most probably the basis for *Je ne parle pas français* written later in 1918, and published in 1920 with *Bliss and other stories*.

more experienced hands, and to feel they would have the security of a regular salary.

The June number of 1912 was the first to be published under Swift's imprint. To mark this bold new beginning on a firmer basis the wrapper was changed to bright blue, the magazine was to be published monthly and inside the wrapper was stated: John Middleton Murry Editor, Katherine Mansfield and Michael Sadleir Assistant Editors, J. D. Fergusson Art Editor and Julian Park American Correspondent. New contributors came in throughout the next five issues: Gilbert Cannan (then a short-story writer and playwright, later better known as a novelist, who became a personal friend of the Murrys and nicknamed them the Two Tigers), James Stephens, Frank Harris, W. H. Davies, Haldane McFall, William Orton and Lord Dunsany; and drawings by Gaudier Brzeska which first appeared in the September issue. In August six more foreign correspondents were added; Francis Carco, Tristan Dereme, George Banks and Anne Estelle Rice for Paris, Michael Lykiardopoulos for Russia, and Floryan Sobieniowski, KM's acquaintance from Worishofen, for Poland.

So it was with high hopes that they set off in July 1912 for Runcton near Chichester, where Katherine had taken a cottage. I have no idea how she found it.

It was a lovely little house, full of light and sunshine, and with enough money under the new arrangement they were able to settle down happily. I went there once or twice and Katherine seemed contented. Certain parts of the house I can picture clearly; the room where we took meals, for instance, which looked out on to flowers and green trees. But I was not at ease there. There was somehow a sense of tension. Murry considered me as a blank wall, uninstructed and unintelligent. I never could make a direct approach to Katherine's friends, partly, I think now, owing to a sense of divided loyalties and also because Katherine did not mix her relationships. Her friends were my friends but only *through* her. So it was natural that Murry found, as he said later, that I could never have any real relationships with people. I remember how once at Runcton, while we were walking by the marshes, he was swinging my African walking stick in his hand. It had been a personal extravagance of mine and its polished smoothness was very precious to me. He understood me so little that when he swung it so carelessly that it flew from his hand into the reeds, he made no attempt to find it or make me an apology. In later years, he came to accept me up to a point, and even in some ways to depend on me. And I was fond of him, even if often angry at his treatment of Katherine, though I was so often to fail her myself.

While staying at Runcton, I mostly sat and talked with Katherine, enjoying the lovely, simple living and the long walks by the marshy waters. I came back to London glad for her and doubtless much refreshed, though not at ease.

In the comparative peace and quiet of the cottage after Gray's Inn Road, Katherine had time to sort out her thoughts. She was both a creator and an extrovert. She looked out at life and saw it; then she took it into herself and created.

Murry was, I always felt, an introvert, looking inwards, probing, questioning, insecure, always trying therefore to establish himself by some outside help or posture whether as a God-worshipper or as a devil, it did not seem much to matter which. There were in him dark, turbulent, unresolved problems. Katherine got to know him, and she learnt from her knowledge a truth she once confided to me. She had spoken of the 'dark' places in him, and said she had come to realise that if a person we loved had a weakness – something out of tune, perhaps evil – it was quite wrong to cure it by force or argument. It could only be cured, or resolved, by love. Gather up the whole personality, just as it is, and our love, if it be true love, will neutralise, transmute and cure the evil.

Unfortunately Katherine was not allowed to enjoy her happiness at Runcton for long. Trouble followed her even there, and everything seemed to go wrong. The man they had engaged to work in the house and who she thought would be all they could wish for proved to be a thief, and also extremely dirty. This latter trait offended most, I think.

At Runcton, too, the friendship with Gaudier Brzeska and his 'wife' Sophie was severed, Katherine and Murry inadvertently making enemies of them. Gaudier Brzeska had submitted drawings to *Rhythm* while the Murrys were still living in the Gray's Inn Road, and in this way they had come to know each other. Both couples discovered that they were living together unlawfully and had no money, and soon the Gaudier Brzeskas asked if they might share the Murry's cottage at Runcton. The Murrys felt forced to accept this unwelcome suggestion – Katherine did not find Sophie congenial – and they were unwillingly preparing for them when Katherine, putting up some curtains, made a remark about Sophie which Gaudier Brzeska overheard as he walked up the garden path. He was bitterly hurt and returned outraged to London.

Then came the terrible blow in October of 1912. They heard that Stephen Swift, who had taken over *Rhythm*, had absconded. He had in fact left the printing order in Murry's name; and Murry found himself saddled with debts to the printers amounting to £400.

Everything was in ruins: they had to give up Runcton and go back to London. I was told afterwards that some friends came to their rescue and that in November they made their home in a vile little flat in Chancery Lane. There they set to work harder than ever to carry on with the magazine.

Against perhaps more prudent advice, the Murrys determined to persevere with Rhythm. *It was the venture that had begun their life together and they had had to defend themselves against ridiculing attacks from* The New Age *which KM had left to work for it. They now no longer had their monthly salaries; moreover, KM pledged all her allowance for the next four years to go directly to the printers. However, Martin Secker volunteered to take over the publishing for them, Edward Marsh offered a guarantee of up to £150 and Wilfred Gibson was invited to come in as permanent assistant editor. The contributors increased both in number and importance, including Drinkwater, Lascelles Abercrombie, Rupert Brooke, Walter de la Mare, Frank Swinnerton, J. D. Beresford and Richard Curle with O. Raymond Drey (later the husband of Anne Estelle Rice) as art critic. The old format was kept but the decorative tail and headpieces were all eliminated and J. D. Fergusson was no longer art editor. The most important innovation was a literary supplement which appeared twice, in December 1912 and March 1913. H. G. Wells wrote for this, and in the March issue D. H. Lawrence appeared with an essay on the Georgian poets.*

Meanwhile, the Chancery Lane flat proved to be really horrible. It had a sitting-room, bedroom and kitchen. One large cupboard with no window at all became Murry's office. The front room looked over Chancery Lane, through thick windows that kept out more light than they let in. The back room had a view of the gloomy houses behind. Some kind but misguided friend gave Katherine a canary, to bring a little cheer. The poor little bird died, and Katherine, for all her brave façade, was fading away too. I think that that place must have been the origin of the pleurisy to which they both fell victim later on. But Katherine did not show what she felt. She furnished the flat on the hire purchase system and bravely made light of their difficulties.

One evening when I went to the flat after work, she met me with a smile and a little grimace. It was the *chair*, she said. Could I take it away?

This chair had suffered a chequered history. It came originally from my mother's sitting-room in Welbeck Street, when as children we first came to London. After my mother died and we came back to London, we moved into a large flat in Montagu Mansions and the chair came along with all the other furniture. I remember it was there when Arnold Trowell came one morning at 9 and startled us with the crash of his piano playing. He had come to see me, and I shall never forget the look of formal astonishment on my father's face on finding the red-haired boy, smoking a cigarette in *his* drawing-room, and running his fingers all over the piano as though the house belonged to him!

After this the chair went through several vicissitudes before it came to Gray's Inn Road, where it was the only chair in Katherine's room and had to accommodate any visitor who could not sit on a cushion on the floor. It carried many people including J. M. Kennedy, one of Orage's two permanent members of *The New Age* editorial staff, who almost broke its back when he emphatically told Katherine that he would probably shoot himself for love of her. Poor man, I should not make fun of him for he was sad and very devoted; but any chair had to be strong to carry him.

From there it travelled to Runcton and then, escaping the crash in some mysterious way, it reached Chancery Lane.

'You must take it *tonight*, because the men are coming from Maples tomorrow to fetch the furniture: we can't pay the deposit. They might go off with the chair. . . .' So, the chair in my arms, hoping to be inconspicuous, I crept down the iron staircase of the fire escape at the back of the mansions, and then I must have climbed to the open top of a bus. I have transported a cabin trunk that way, swinging it outside the handrail as I climbed up the perilous stairs.

Seeing the sorry condition that the Murrys were in at Chancery Lane, Gilbert Cannan suggested they should take a small cottage near him and his wife at Cholesbury in Buckinghamshire. The Gordon Campbells would share it with them and so halve the costs, and Murry would continue working in Chancery Lane and come down at week-ends.

This they did, but Murry was not happy working alone and was also alarmed by the increasingly threatening letters he was receiving from Gaudier Brzeska. In this situation, and as the magazine was constantly losing money, Rhythm *could not go on. The March issue was the last under this name. After two months planning it appeared again in May as the* The Blue Review. *It was still under Martin Secker's imprint, the art side directed now by Albert Rothenstein. Max Beerbohm, Marcel Boulestin, E. J. Dent, James Elroy Flecker, Oliver St John Gogarty, Edward Marsh, D. H. Lawrence and Hugh Walpole came in with contributions.*

It was also in May 1913 that Gaudier Brzeska finally broke into Murry's office in Chancery Lane and physically attacked him at the same time demanding payment for those of his drawings that had been published in Rhythm.

Murry then gave up the struggle to find some way to pay the debts, none of which was his fault, and became a bankrupt. Katherine told me how really dreadful he felt about it, almost as if he himself had actually absconded. But it must have been a haunting burden gone, and they took refuge in Cholesbury.

I have no very clear recollection of the cottage, although I must have been down there at least two or three times. I seem to remember that often the company, which used to be a rather fluid mixture, consisted of the Gordon Campbells, Gilbert Cannan and his wife, who had previously been married to J. M. Barrie, and one or two casual visitors. There were many emotional cross-currents of love and grief at that cottage.

Katherine, writing to me on one occasion, said that they had all painted the outside of the cottage bright blue. This I can well understand, as Mrs Cannan was very interested in 'home decoration', and the Cannans owned the cottage. Katherine took me to see the house in which the Cannans themselves lived, an old windmill, wonderfully transformed. The big floor had been turned into a splendid circular living-room, the walls of which Mrs Cannan had decorated with great flower patterns, cutting out and pasting up each flower and leaf and branch to her own design. It was an impressive piece of work and most ingenious, but it was not Katherine's taste.

Another time Katherine took me over to meet Vivian Locke Ellis at Selsfield House, East Grinstead. He was greatly troubled, as his wife had just died; I seem to remember seeing cupboards full of her rather delicate, beautiful clothes. I think KM felt I could help him in some way with his farm, and tried to make plans, but in the end it came to nothing.

One incident at Cholesbury stands out clearly. The household was on the point of settling down for the night and Katherine had seized the chance of the first bath. The bathroom was an extension to the house on the ground floor, with a window looking out on the garden. For some reason the young men decided that they would play a trick on Katherine. They would send Murry through the pitch-dark garden to startle her, suddenly, as a stranger at the window. I was torn between being a spoilsport and loyalty to Katherine, but could not believe they would really do it, until I saw Jack slip out of the room. I was so angered, knowing what a shock Katherine would get, that I hurried to the bathroom door with a warning 'Look out Katie'. I had not imagined that Jack would allow such a thing to be done. But perhaps she had hidden all her nervous fears from him.

Gordon Campbell was an intimate member of the Murry's circle. Katherine had a very warm feeling for him, although he was understood to have been more Murry's friend than hers;

but after Campbell's marriage to Beatrice Glenavy in the August of 1912 the tie loosened. Beatrice was gay and kind, but of different clay. Katherine did not have the same affection for her as she always seemed to have for Gordon before he married.

When the Campbells took a house on the little island outside Dublin near Beatrice's home and invited the Murrys to stay with them that summer of 1913, Katherine confessed that she did not want to go but had accepted because Jack wished for it so much. She went so far as to persuade me to go too. I was to take a room at some small house and she would meet me each day for a walk and a talk. This was partly because she did not want me to be lonely during the holiday, but also because she was glad to have an excuse to leave the party and come to me where she could be 'alone' and herself. I in turn visited the Campbells' house on several afternoons, and remember playing card games of chance, of which I knew nothing. I took appalling risks in consequence and then won, which rather annoyed Jack. Not a very good idea.

During these two crowded years from 1912 to 1914 when Katherine and Murry were working on *Rhythm*, I seemed to live three lives at the same time: the long hours of work at the Parma Rooms, family life with my sister at Luxborough House, and the constant visits to Katherine.

Then in May 1913 my sister decided that she ought to go out to Rhodesia to care for our father and brother. So we gave up the flat and packed or stored the furniture. I remember the day that she left so well. She was lame from early polio and mother had said I must always look after her, although by then she was possessed of a brave, adventurous, pioneering spirit. I helped to dispose her things in the cabin, then said goodbye and watched the ship go out. On my way back to stay with Katherine at Cholesbury I looked for a quiet field where I lay on the ground and wept. I felt so lonely and alone: up till then we had always had a home together which formed my refuge and base.

Without our home, I first stayed with Miss Good in her Nurses' Home in Welbeck Mews. Then, when she had to leave, I shared rooms with her elsewhere. But this was not at all satisfactory and eventually I settled into an empty room above a pub opposite a small eating shop in Dorset Street, off Baker Street. A street very like the one where Katherine had stayed in Maida Vale, before her mother came to inspect the son-in-law-to-be. My room, which cost me six shillings a week, was furnished with a mattress on the floor, a wash-hand-stand and a chair. In a little cupboard were knives and forks and the necessities of a kitchen. It was bare and poor and unpainted but I hope tolerably clean. I know I had a broom somewhere.

During this whole time I was impoverished and tired, and often really exhausted, and only the most striking of Katherine and Jack's activities come back to me now. I was *in* a great deal of what was going on, but not *of* it, unless it personally touched Katherine. In between the crowded times, she and Murry were getting to know each other and building up a relationship which was often stormy but also happy and strong. Katherine, I believe from what she told me, understood and loved him as he was, almost in spite of him, though she often had to throw him off and escape, to get on with her own urgent inner life. Murry in turn loved her and was guided through his clouds by her vivid, glowing flame. Unconsciously he leaned on her strength and the reflected light helped him to live and integrate himself. Alone, his eyes turned *into* himself, and often were dim. Physically, he often had an 'inward' look in his eyes, especially if he was frightened.

Later on I felt that her love became imbued with the tenderness of mother-love, with which her heart was always full. So, constantly, when she had escaped, she pitied and let him come back. And then she would forget the frustration and they would be happy. Katherine, of course, depended on the man she loved. But often, so often, in her greatest need he failed her, until in those last few days at Fontainebleau, I think she was happy, both *in* and *for* him. But this I can only guess by what they told me, and by one little note of pleasure when she wrote how glad she was to see him happy in the life and work of the group there.

At the beginning of 1913 D. H. Lawrence sent a story (The Soiled Rose) *to* Rhythm *which was subsequently published in the May issue under the new cover of the* The Blue Review. *The next month, June, Lawrence and Frieda met the Murrys. This first meeting was auspicious and successful. Lawrence was rising on a crest of enthusiasm; he had just completed his third successful novel* Sons and Lovers (The White Peacock *had been published in 1911,* The Trespasser *in 1912), and had that previous spring persuaded the high-born German, Frieda von Richthofen, to leave her academic English husband and three children in order to join him.*

From the time of this first meeting with the Murrys, Lawrence took an immediate and personal interest in them, which led to a close yet difficult relationship between the two couples. Lawrence's prophet-like intensity, kindled by his recent successes, took hold of Murry especially. With KM it could not be the same, for she was Lawrence's equal in spirit. However, through the tie between the two men, Lawrence was able to exert a strong influence on the lives and movements of both the Murrys during the next three years.

In July The Blue Review *finally collapsed after three issues. Lawrence, unsympathetic to the Murrys' loss, encouraged them to go abroad. He and Frieda were going to live in Italy – why not join them? So the Murrys were persuaded but, as Murry had no possibilities of reviewing from Italy, they decided on Paris; this time it was to be 'for good'. To economise they gave up Cholesbury and Chancery Lane and worked from a new flat in Barons Court. Murry was to concentrate on reviewing in order to save the necessary money.*

The flat at Barons Court was small but quite comfortable; a suburban flatlet with communal gardens at the back, where the flat owners played tennis. Murry had the sitting-room for his study. There was also a living-room where they had meals; Katherine was obliged to use the table there for her work. Her writing was irregular and spontaneous, and so somehow she must manage. They furnished the flat simply and I gave them the remainder of my share of our family furniture, which had been put in store when my sister left for Rhodesia.

But it was not a happy place. There was a feeling of tension, of waiting, as it were, for something, and I could tell by Katherine's behaviour that things were not all they should be. Here, too, she suffered a recurrence of the curious aches and pains she always spoke of as her 'rheumatiz'; gradually they came to trouble her more and more.

I was a good deal at Barons Court and Katherine did not seem to be working much whenever I went. We made her some new clothes and I think she was glad to have something practical to do. I sometimes stayed there until very late, and was always rather conscious, when Jack was also present, of being a visitor and only just tolerated at that.

One night I had mistaken the time and realised when I left that I had missed the last 'bus. It was quite six miles to my own place and it was after midnight. I decided I must walk. I could not go back to the flat and disturb them, putting them to the trouble of arranging somewhere for me to sleep. I started to walk and in those empty streets was suddenly overtaken by a man in a car. He stopped and asked if he could give me a lift. We argued a little. I think now that he was a genuinely kind man with no ulterior motive; but when he had gone my heart failed me and I returned to the Mansions to spend the night on the stone staircase outside Katherine's and Murry's door. I was away well before any porter could find me in the morning, and I don't think I ever told Katherine.

I took some small photographs at Barons Court. Not one of them was like Katherine and she would have been annoyed had she known that I did not destroy them. The only ones that are like her, of all the photographs I ever took, are those taken years later at the Villa Isola Bella in Menton which show her sitting at her table drinking tea and talking to me. And for those, poor dear, she had to keep still for sixty seconds in the middle of a sentence!

I must have had many meals with Katherine at the Barons Court flat, but I remember none of them. She was a good cook and so quick and neat and graceful in her movements that things got done so easily that one barely noticed. The Barons Court flat gave me no sense of home, though Katherine was a great maker and lover of home at all times. Wherever she was, even if it was only some place where she paused for a night or two, Katherine made and kept her 'home' as beautiful and expressive as possible. There was no untidiness or any kind of confusion, so that however poor and sparse her possessions, her sense of order and form always imparted a feeling of space and beauty. Of course this was the expression of her inner self, for ever discarding extraneous matter and imposing form and order.

Katherine hated 'fuzzy edges'. This appeared so clearly in an incident when, possibly before she met Murry, she was caught up briefly in an odd group of people. I think they had formed a small society, experimentalist and extravagant, with an interest in the occult.* Katherine was invited to an Evening, during which the participants set about exploring the 'inner truth' of their beings. Hashish was taken, which apparently caused them to become unaware of their surroundings and therefore completely un-inhibited. Katherine was persuaded to take part (unwillingly, I believe) but from their point of view she proved to be a total failure. Instead of showing herself to the expectant gathering as some unmasked and extraordinary female, it appears that she spent the whole time arranging and rearranging with the greatest exactitude the matches from a box which she had in her hand, making patterns on the floor.

While they were at Barons Court Katherine would come to my attic room in Dorset Street in order to have some time to herself. It was completely quiet and 'lost' above the teeming crowds of London; there she could work or dream, remote and safe from everyone. She had the key and came and went as she wished, and I generally tried to leave some food in the cupboard.

I don't know how often she came, but I am afraid that her visits did not help her to make money, and the lack of her independent income, small though it had been, must have added to her financial discontent. She became particularly anxious to earn. I remember going with her for an audition to some agent who was offering small walking-on parts in the films. It all seemed very sordid and I don't think Katherine even tried it; the pay, too, would have been negligible. I waited for her at the entrance and when she came out she was discouraged and tired and her description of the man at the desk made him sound utterly unpleasant.

In many ways, therefore, I was glad when the tension broke and she and Murry decided to go and try to make a living in Paris. It was my loss, of course, but I was sure that Katherine would be better and happier in the air and light and life of the city she loved. Murry had the promise of reviews for the *Times Literary Supplement*, and their friend Francis Carco from *Rhythm* was to find them rooms.

In the December of 1913 they set off. Since the furniture I had lent them for Barons Court, added to their own few things, would be useful in Paris, it was all packed up and taken over. One small addition, not so small in reality, was a pair of grotesquely carved

* The leader of this group was Aleister Crowley.

figures, made for my father by the inmates of an Indian prison of which he was at one time the medical officer and governor: strange ornaments, but Katherine and I both prized them.

On the day they left, I and a pleasant woman who had worked for them and loved Katherine took over the flat for final clearing and closing. I had one of my really dreadful colds and coughs, a legacy from my early life in Burma, and that and the sadness of farewell had brought me low. Then occurred one of those charming incidents, which happen now and again, and which I shall never forget. That kind woman, the work being finished, firmly put me to rest in the last remaining bed, went out and returned with a strong dose of hot rum and lemon. I, never having taken spirits, drank it up and slept soundly until late the next morning when she came back and cheerfully took over the keys and the responsibility.

At that time my life and work were really in the doldrums. I was terribly run down and shabby both inside and out. My partner and I could no longer bear the sight of each other; something had to be done. Our enterprise was hardly established in London, but she suggested that we should open a branch in Brighton and I was to go down, find the rooms, advertise for the necessary furniture and do all the arranging. Anything more utterly foreign to my nature I could not imagine. My heart failed me and turned to jelly at the thought. But I went down, engaged the rooms and visited a few distant friends, all in my old-fashioned and worn clothes, which took what was left of my courage away.

Then suddenly I had an urgent letter from my sister, begging me to go out and take her place in Rhodesia, as she wanted to get married. This seemed to me an ideal way out. Katherine and Murry were happily settled in Paris and independent of me. (I had had letters from Katherine telling me of their lovely little flat at 31 Rue de Tournon.) So I spoke to my partner, cancelled the rooms I had taken in Brighton, came back to London and made my plans to sail. In the midst of all this preparation, without any warning, I received a frantic letter from Katherine: could I possibly send some money *immediately?*

Apparently everything had now gone wrong. Murry's work in Paris had suddenly ended; they had no money for the rent and had even had to sell all the furniture to pay for essentials.

I raised all I could, about £5. Rushing from the Parma Rooms, I found all the post offices shut, as it was after six o'clock. Down to Charing Cross I then raced, where I knew there was an office open all night.

'No, the Post Office could not insure money to Paris – only as far as the coast.'

What could I do? The man was concerned and helpful:

'Well, if you tear the notes in half and send the halves in separate envelopes they will not be stolen (what trust we had in the French officials!) because one half would be of no use to anyone!'

Rather anxiously – since it seemed a dreadful thing to do: tear up English money – I followed his advice and posted both letters. Poor Katherine! She received the letters by different posts and was more frantic still, if that were possible, thinking I had gone mad.

I have learnt in old age that, given time, everything resolves itself. Desperation is not necessary. I gathered more money for them, or someone else did, and soon they were lent a flat in Beaufort Mansions, off the King's Road, Chelsea, which belonged to a friend from *Rhythm*, Richard Curle.

I can never remember Katherine complaining. This last really serious loss of job, money, furniture, everything, seemed only to make her more determined. Of course she had Murry to fight for, and I hope, to share her struggle. I heard later that Murry had previously been recalled to England by the courts and had been cleared of his bankruptcy charges, and that while in London he had obtained, through Stephen Spender, a permanent post on *The Westminster Gazette* as art critic. So he had this to return to, and Katherine planned to find some small place in Chelsea to rent in which to try again.

Meanwhile it was too late for my plans to be altered. I was to sail to Rhodesia on 27th March 1914, so I only went once or twice to see Katherine at Beaufort Mansions, before my last visit to say goodbye. I was by now utterly worn out, with the rush of last-minute arrangements on top of everything, and I can remember well the luxury of sitting quietly with her while the outer tensions dropped away in the silence by the flickering fire. There was nothing to say, though the sadness of a long parting lay ahead and filled the room.

I could not stay long and hurried away with the raindrops staining the pavements, to catch a bus, arrange the last things for storage and get my trunk ready for the station. I remember now with amusement how, the next morning, accompanied by a friend who had even less time sense than I had, I almost missed the boat train. Met by Evelyn Payne, Katherine's cousin and our friend from Queen's College days, I was rushed down the platform and hurriedly pushed into the compartment where my cousin Olive was waiting for me. I was very touched that Evelyn had come to see me off. Perhaps, being old friends, she suspected I would need a guiding hand. There were other friends too, but I felt too numb and dazed to notice them.

And Katherine: she was probably hunting for those cheap rooms in Chelsea.

CHAPTER VIII

LM in Rhodesia:
1914 – 1916

While I was away in Rhodesia from 1914 to 1916 I had only Katherine's letters to fix my memories, and these were later burnt. But I followed her in my thoughts from place to place. They found two rooms off the Fulham Road, and then in July a charming top-floor flat in Arthur Street, Chelsea, which turned out to be bug-ridden. Murry, I knew, had some work to do on the *Westminster*. I gathered, too, that Lawrence and Frieda were coming more into their lives. It seemed to me that Lawrence was always a disturbing spirit. Then, of course, in August, war broke out.

With the declaration of war in August 1914 Murry had immediately enlisted, then saw his doctor who pronounced him unfit, adding 'Query T.B.'. He and KM went to Cornwall for a short holiday, returned to London and then proceeded to Udimore near Rye, looking for a house. They were then persuaded by the Lawrences, who had returned to England in July, to take a cottage near theirs, at The Lee, two miles on from Cholesbury near Great Missenden, Buckingham-shire. They moved into Rose Tree Cottage in October and stayed there for four months. It was a time of unhappiness for both couples; the war seemed incomprehensible and Lawrence and Frieda, whose marriage in July the Murrys had envied, were now quarrelling violently. The Murrys felt alienated by Lawrence's vehemence in general and his preoccupation with sex in particular, which, for JMM and KM, had no relevance to their own simple acceptance of love. (Later, they were astonished to learn that Gerald and Gudrun in Women in Love *was Lawrence's portrayal of their relationship.)*

Lawrence seemed to demand in a personal way, from Murry especially, an impersonal affiliation to his fundamental idea or 'cause' that, as he put it, 'each should be an angel of himself, so that

*the animal in him might be reborn'. Murry could not comprehend
this, and turned more towards Gordon Campbell, who was a frequent
visitor, and with whom he could discuss metaphysical concepts. This
intellectual stimulation led him to flights of, what he later called,
'intellectual mysticism'. Katherine was unmoved by both these ways
of thinking.*

After a short period when I think there were no letters, Katherine
wrote that they were in a cottage near the Lawrences in
Buckinghamshire, at Lawrence's request. Katherine said that Rose
Tree Cottage was small, ugly, damp and cold. Murry, I think,
was away all day, probably in London with his job on the
Westminster, and she found it depressing to be alone; also they were
very hard up for Katherine's allowance was still going to the
printers. The housework seemed to take all her time, and the
cottage was difficult to look after: she could not settle down to
write. Murry, of course, had the only room fit to work in, while
Katherine went upstairs to the upper floor. She did not put it like
this, and I may be wrong. Perhaps she insisted, for his work had
to be written regularly and on time, but I was often to be
annoyed later at his lack of consideration when it was a matter of
her comfort and well-being. Here, too, her 'rheumatiz' became
very bad again, and she was really miserable. Jack and Lawrence
were not really of her kind and neither were their friends; so she
was doubly lonely.

The one fortunate and important happening of this time was
the meeting with Samuel Koteliansky. He was a White Russian
Jew, who had left Russia and come to England, where he had a
scholarship, in 1911. He stayed for the rest of his life. He translated Russian into English, and later worked in collaboration
with Murry, Katherine, and Leonard and Virginia Woolf.
This meeting was the beginning of a lasting and true friendship.
Katherine had complete trust in her new friend, though of course
she did not agree with all his judgements. All through the subsequent years he was probably her most staunch, trusted and
loyal supporter. Dear Kot. To him an enemy was always an
enemy, but nothing could shake his faith once his friendship was
truly given. He always seemed to me like some fine old-time
prophet, denouncing fiercely what he thought was evil. Katherine

sent his name and address to me in Rhodesia as a safe deposit for
my letters, saying that I could always rely on him.

Katherine and Kot met at the Lawrences' cottage. Koteliansky
was visiting Lawrence, when suddenly Katherine appeared at the
door, apparently blown there by the wind. She described how
Kot would come often to visit her, cheering her loneliness and
bringing cigarettes and delicacies quite out of her reach and,
indeed, difficult for anyone to procure in those wartime days. I
think his visits were comforting also in the unspoken knowledge
they brought her that he understood so many of her problems and
the prowling anxieties that beset her restless life.

Gradually the unhappiness and dissatisfaction grew too much
for Katherine and the next I heard was that she was in Paris.

*The situation at Rose Tree Cottage had gradually worsened.
Gordon Campbell, Murry and Lawrence would discuss endlessly the
contrast between what Lawrence phrased as the 'male knowing,
mental, self conscious principle' and the 'female principle of being,
self mortification and "blood-law" '. They planned to escape to a life
of harmony on a desert island. Murry, as he describes himself in*
Between Two Worlds, *became completely wrapped up in his own
mental probings, discussing things out of existence. Katherine felt
estranged and repudiated by this; she longed for immediacy and life
and by Christmas 1914 it was decided that they should separate. She
was receiving loving letters from Francis Carco, now at the front, and
determined to see him. In February 1915 her brother Chummie
arrived in England and he lent her the money which enabled her to
go to Paris. She went the same month and stayed in Carco's empty
apartment in Paris.*

The letters she sent me from France always carried with them the
light of the early Paris mornings. Carco's apartment, I gathered,
almost overlooked the river, near the Quai des Fleurs. She gave
a wonderful picture of the market-place, full of great baskets of
flowers in charge of the old French women.

She was living once more, happy in the clear Paris sunshine,
enjoying the early morning light on the bowl of flowers and the
smell of fresh coffee and milk and the little French rolls – all so

vivid, the flowers almost waved me a greeting as I read her description of them. Francis Carco was with the army and his apartment was entirely at her disposal. With his help she was able to make a much wished-for visit to the front; his influence obtained a permit for her to visit 'an elderly relation who was sick'. She described the journey, which I remember as being constantly shadowed by the colour of violets, in an account that gave me the feeling that her excitement was touched with a quiver of fear at what she was doing and seeing. 'Pleasurable apprehension' is possibly the best phrase to sum it up. Carco met her and guided her through the crowds of uniformed men to a house where he had found a room for her. It all seemed to be an anxious, organised, disorder.

Katherine always seemed happy and more free in France, and hoped for peace to do her work in this land of her adoption.

Katherine's visit to the front is described in An Indiscreet Journey. *She came back to England in March disillusioned with Carco, but invigorated by Paris. In March and May 1915 she returned to Paris to write. She completed* Three Spring Pictures *and* The Little Governess, *and, as JMM states in the 1951 edition of KM's* Letters *to him, she began her first drafts of* The Aloe, *a picture of her childhood in New Zealand. She again stayed in Carco's flat (he was still at the front), and she saw Beatrice Hastings who had left the staff of* The New Age *and was now living in Paris, though she continued to send weekly articles back to England.*

On 19th May KM returned to JMM in Elgin Crescent, and then, in June or July, again influenced by Lawrence, they took a house in St John's Wood at No. 5 Acacia Road. The Lawrences were then living in Hampstead and had started a group, which met every Thursday to explore the nature of the human psyche.

They insisted that the Murrys should live nearby to attend the group and help them edit a periodical, Signature, *to further their ideas. Lawrence was to expound his philosophy, JMM to write on freedom for the individual, and KM to 'sugar the pill' with her stories.**

* Only three numbers were issued (4th Oct., 18th Oct. and 1st Nov., 1915). KM contributed three stories in October under the nomme de plume Matilda Berry: *Autumn I,* later called *Apple Tree Story* and

Katherine stayed at Acacia Road for five months and they were some of the happic st and most poignant of her life. Chummie, who was still in England training, came to see her there constantly. She was so content in his company that she did not write to me often; but when she did so it was to give me an impression of happiness and beauty. She described the radiance of the pear tree in the little garden; the same pear tree that she put into her story *Bliss*. And she told me that she and Chummie had long talks about New Zealand, and how very happy they were together there. Chummie brought Katherine memories of her childhood and family, which she had not shared since she left home in 1908. He had to leave to go to the front in September.

Then in October 1915 I received a letter telling me of Chummie's death, apparently caused by a hand grenade which accidentally exploded. I really think that this was the greatest grief of her life. A great friend of Chummie wrote to her after his death telling her how Chummie had kept Katherine secretly in his heart. It was not till his death that this friend heard him use her name, as he called out 'Lift me, Katie, I can't breathe, lift me'. Then only did the friend realise what they had meant to each other.

Katherine turned to me for understanding and sympathy but I could send her nothing better than she received from everyone else. In Rhodesia life was quiet and happy and I felt remote. I did not experience Chummie's death as a personal loss and tragedy to myself, but merely as a terrible blow to her. Not having known Chummie intimately, I could not offer an understanding of him as a solace for her grief. In great sorrow, after all, one finds comfort only in the company of someone who also feels that sorrow personally. I did not know what to write and finally sent a letter of conventional 'sympathy', ending with an account of what was happening to me. Katherine herself, a little later, wrote this poem for Chummie:

---

never collected; *Autumn II,* later changed slightly and called *The Wind Blows:* and *The Little Governess.* These two latter stories were published in *Bliss* in 1920.

L. H. B. (1894–1915)

Last night for the first time since you were dead
I walked with you, my brother, in a dream.
We were at home again beside the stream
Fringed with tall berry bushes, white and red
'Don't touch them: they are poisonous,' I said.
But your hand hovered, and I saw a beam
Of strange, bright laughter flying round your head
And as you stooped I saw the berries gleam.
'Don't you remember? We called them Dead Man's Bread!'
  I woke and heard the wind moan and the roar
  Of the dark water tumbling on the shore.
  Where – where is the path of my dream for my eager feet?
  By the remembered stream my brother stands
  Waiting for me with berries in his hands . . .
  'These are my body. Sister, take and eat.'

In turning over the memories of that time of Katherine's bereavement, I feel again and again my sins against the Almighty Spirit of Love. I had nothing to offer but a dumb sense of inadequacy. This inadequacy was the real cause which Katherine and I looked for *later*, in trying to understand why our friendship had never flowered, and why so many buds on the tree had remained closed. My insecurity and immaturity made me fear to reach up and grasp the full flower, though it was there for my plucking.

Many years earlier, at Gray's Inn Road, I had told Katherine she was many planes of life beyond me and she had laughed. But it was true. I am nearer now, but still catching up; which makes me wonder if I can hope to give even a glimpse of the true Katherine.

Meanwhile, Katherine could no longer bear to be in Acacia Road with all the memories it held for her; so she left the house to some Russian friends of Kot, the Farbmans, and Murry escorted her to the south of France, and settled her into the Hotel Beau Rivage in the little town of Bandol. It was perhaps necessary for Katherine to suffer alone, because it was through this spiritual unity with her brother and the loss of his physical presence that she turned to memories of their past and formed her mode of expressing it. She told me once that she was determined to write a book, not just short stories, about their country. She felt she had so much to say and so little time in which to say it. Her brother's death brought clearly and fully before her mind all the pictures of their homeland which she had already begun to write down that Spring as *The Aloe*.*

In December 1915 Jack joined her and they lived in a little house called the Villa Pauline in Bandol. They stayed there three months and were deeply at peace and happy together. Murry was writing a book on Dostoyevsky† and both worked hard during the day, sitting either side of the same table to write, and in the evenings they would relax together. In an atmosphere of such harmony and felicity Katherine was able to come to herself in peace and complete *The Aloe*, that perfect picture she drew of her homeland.‡

Then I heard that they were leaving the south of France, against Katherine's wish, but once more it was Lawrence's doing. He had taken a cottage in Cornwall and was now writing repeatedly that there was another close by, to which they *must* come.

The letters from Cornwall spoke more of the Lawrences than of any other subject: Lawrence enjoying watching Frieda at her washtub on the hillside, the wind blowing her bright coloured clothes and covering her with the flying froth of the soap-suds; or Frieda running up the hillside to escape from Lawrence's furious chasing, till she took refuge in the Murrys' cottage. Katherine spoke of how she and Jack were turning away from Lawrence's constant preoccupation with sex. Another time she wrote that she had had a letter of violent abuse from Lawrence. Finally it was too much for them and they left the stone cottage, and found a pleasant little home in Mylor, called Sunnyside Cottage, where I was to join them when I returned.

* His death was also the source from which Katherine wrote six and seven years later two of her most important stories: *Six Years After*, which was unfinished (*The Nation*, April 1923) and *The Fly* (*The Nation*, March 1922).

† Commissioned by Martin Secker to cover the loss, of approximately £30, he had made on the *Blue Review*.

‡ Later revised and published as *Prelude* by Virginia and Leonard Woolf at their Hogarth Press in 1918, and with *Bliss and other stories* (Constable) in 1921. (*The Aloe* in its original version was posthumously printed privately by Constable in 1930.)

At Mylor Katherine was restless and found the countryside bleak. In consequence, she would go up to London as often as possible to see her friends. It was at this time that she became more closely acquainted with Lady Ottoline Morrell whom she had met already, and she would stay either with her at Garsington or with the Campbells in London. In the early autumn Murry was called up by the army for re-examination, and through friends made at Garsington obtained a post as translator in military intelligence.

In September the Murrys moved up to London and stayed with the painters Dorothy Brett (Lord Esher's daughter) and Dora Carrington, the friend of Lytton Strachey, in J. M. Keynes' house in Gower Street. J. M. Keynes had vacated his house, and it was planned that in his absence KM and JMM would share the first floor, Brett lived on the second and Carrington in the attic. It was here that LM found them when she returned to England in the autumn of 1916.

CHAPTER IX

Gower Street – Church Street – South of France – Paris – Redcliffe Road: 1916 – 1918

In those days in Rhodesia travelling and communications were slow and news seemed to filter through dimly. We had one paper a week and no radio; letters took over three weeks to reach us. My father could not understand my eagerness to snatch at the post-bag delivered to him by one of our 'boys'. 'A few more hours can't matter, now can they?' he teased.

I loved Rhodesia and the lazy yet vibrant life of the untouched land with its few people and miles and miles of peace. In the moonlight the plantations of eucalyptus trees shone like still moonstones: in the early dawn the tall grasses swayed in the light breeze, heavy with dewdrops, till suddenly the sun rose and in one half hour the world was once more a hard, dry gold. Then, dotted all over the fields, fine spirals of blue smoke began to curl up from the fires of the early workers, while across the wide valley soft, white blankets of cloud rolled up and toppled over the slopes in a hurry to get down to the river before the hot sun licked them up.

But far away in Europe the ghastly war raged. The remote peace of Rhodesia made it all seem somehow unreal. However, my two years had now come to an end and I was to go back to England. My father returned home with me to escape loneliness, I think. We travelled on a troop ship bringing South African gunners to England, and came to know one of their officers Robert Gibson, particularly well; I found him to be an admirable person.

Then the boat train was puffing into the grey station, and I found myself on the crowded platform, awkward and strange, looking for Katherine: rather apprehensive too, because of the veil of misunderstanding which Chummie's death had thrown between us.

I said goodbye to my father rather sadly, promising to see him again soon, and went with Katherine. She and Murry had suddenly come to London feeling Cornwall too remote. They were staying in Gower Street with Dorothy Brett and a woman called Carrington, who had some plans to share the house with the Murrys.

The atmosphere there was somehow uncomfortable and it was quite impossible for me to be with them. So I went to stay with my old friend from my childhood in Burma, Dolly Sutton. She was now married and lived in Chiswick. She at once gave me the address of an office where women with some college background were being recruited to work as charge hands in the factories. I was taken on for an intensive six weeks' training in metal work, and then became a tool setter in an aeroplane factory in Chiswick, run by a Mr Gwynne. I enjoyed my work there very much. Mr Gwynne was extremely kind to us, and I met there Stella Drummond (later Lady Eustace Percy) who became a great friend, and Lady Mary Hamilton.

Whenever possible I went to see Katherine; but this was not so often. She wanted to be alone. This was a period in which she was withdrawn from most people. Also I was visiting my old father at the Strand Palace Hotel. I would find him wearily walking up and down the passages and staircases, unable to decide what to do. Life was all so changed. He looked up some of his old friends and tried to persuade one of them to marry him and go back to the easy life of Rhodesia; but, failing, he finally went home alone. I was the only one who could tolerate and manage the occasional fierce outbursts of temper from which he suffered, a legacy of long years of service in India. We were fond of each other, and when a few years later, in the temporary absence of his son, he had a fatal 'accident' with his gun, I could only blame myself.

Katherine had found a home for me on Holly Mount in Hampstead, in the rooms of a man they knew slightly, who had been called up. Poor man, he was so kind, and came to supper there with me once in his own flat and gave me books; but he never got back to his home with good old Mrs Butterworth, the landlady. She was so kind and I was very comfortable there. She considered looking after me her 'war work', and she performed it most efficiently, providing a warm room and solid breakfast soon after

5.30 a.m. ('of course, Miss, I go back to bed'), and a nice fire and supper when I came back, in the little sitting-room where I could rest and read.

As the winter progressed Katherine became more restless. She could not bear the proximity to Carrington and her circle in Gower Street, though Murry did not mind it. I knew that she wished to withdraw from her present surroundings and be alone, and again she and Murry parted in the spring of 1917. She found a studio in No. 141a Old Church Street, while Murry had rooms at 47 Redcliffe Road.*

Katherine wrote asking me to meet her the next night at the studio in Church Street in order that we could look at it together. However, when I got there after my work, she had for some reason been prevented from coming, and I could only peer over the high wooden partition which screened the small yard and the path leading to the front door. There was a damp and ominous air about the place.

Later, when Katherine moved in, I saw that the building was rectangular, filling the space between two normal houses with a locked door joining it to the one on the south side, and its own front door set in a blank wall with one large window high up above it, suitable for an artist's 'light'. The rectangular room which it lighted went right through to the glass doors at the back of the house, which opened on to a communal garden, and on sunny days it was rather lovely with the large leaves of a tree tapping on the window. Half way through this main room, on the right, a bedroom was curtained off, with a bathroom to the left of it. Above this was a staircase leading up to a deep balcony, like a minstrels' gallery, which stuck out over the bedroom into the studio. Behind this was a small kitchen. Katherine slept in the big main room on a wide settee. I always felt this studio was rather like a well, with only the high window to give it light. Katherine had few visitors at first and since I could only get to her late in the evenings, after 'clocking in' my night workers at

* From his autobiography *Between Two Worlds*, Murry seems to have isolated himself in his work at the War Office at this time, and also to have turned for friendship to J. W. N. Sullivan the scientist and writer on Beethoven whom he had just met. Sullivan had been attracted by JMM's book on Dostoyevsky and had asked Dan Rider, of the Bookshop, to introduce them. Through JMM he also obtained work at the War Office.

the factory, she was usually by herself all day. I think she was experiencing her dreaded 'night fears' alone in this rather queer room, with no outlook to see who might be at the door.

My rooms at Holly Mount were both far from the factory at Chiswick and from Katherine; several times I found it difficult to get home after my visits to her. Once I even had to spend the night in the crypt of the church of St Martin-in-the-Fields, on my way home. To make the long journey to Chiswick by 7 o'clock, I had to get up at 5.30 every morning.

So presently Katherine and I decided it would be better if I joined her. I gave up Holly Mount, and the 'Minstrels' Gallery' at Old Church Street became my home. If there happened to be a visitor I lay on my bed very silently, since, though Katherine and I were content, it might have been inhibiting for the visitor to know that an unseen third person was present. In the end I made an arrangement with Katherine that I would not be back till 9 o'clock. I was often busy or visiting Dolly Sutton who was always my kindest friend in need.

In June of 1917 my sister came home from Africa, to have her first child in England. The midwife said she could not take charge alone, so I spoke to Katherine and she instantly agreed that I must go and stay with them, though both she and I knew she dreaded the nights alone. I went to my sister at Ravenscourt Park for three weeks. When I returned, Katherine confessed it had really been rather dreadful. She had spent nearly every night, after a struggle to be 'sensible', walking about the streets till early dawn. I think the haunted hours were from midnight till about three in the morning.

I have spoken of communal gardens behind the house, where the windows were much larger and looked on to grass and trees that were really green. On sunny days Katherine would go out of doors and sometimes watch her neighbour's small son at play. This neighbour was Mrs Maufe, whose husband, Edward (later Sir Edward Maufe) was subsequently to be the architect of Guildford Cathedral.

At this time the Maufes were both working for Heal's, as designers and interior decorators. Mrs Maufe and Katherine became very friendly and when Katherine eventually went on a visit to her, she described to me some of the beautiful furniture Maufe had designed and made himself.

By now Katherine was receiving several visitors and one day I heard that Murry was also coming. After that he came regularly; of course he knew that I was there too. I think Katherine felt he was not getting enough to eat and so saw to it that he had a good meal every evening. One evening they had a fierce argument and Katherine disappeared out of the front door. I, as usual anxious about her, made the mistake of not understanding that she was better alone, and set off to find her, in spite of Murry's discouragement. She was not very far away, and probably my appearance altered her attitude of mind because we soon returned to the studio. I felt, however, that she was not particularly pleased with my intervention and therefore disappeared hurriedly and left them to finish their argument alone.

So the summer of 1917 passed, with Katherine visiting and being visited by her chosen friends, and working when the silence fell; but I cannot now remember what she achieved there precisely. After so many years, recollection seems rather like looking through either end of a telescope – one period so short and clear and another so long and dim.

KM returned to The New Age *in the April of 1917. She appeared in* Pastiche *and had* Two Tuppenny Ones, Please, Late at Night, The Black Cap, In Confidence *(not collected)*, The Common Round *(collected as* Pictures*)*, A Pic-Nic *(not collected)*, *and* Mr Reginal Peacock's Day *published between April and June. These, except for the last, were written in dialogue form, in a resumption of her brittle, satirical style. After a short break she appeared in September with her translation of* M. Séguin's Goat, *by Alphonse Daudet, and again in September and in October with her more serious stories,* An Album Leaf *and* The Dill Pickle.

She was also working on The Aloe, *finally calling it* Prelude, *at JMM's suggestion. She sent the manuscript to Leonard and Virginia Woolf that September, to be printed at their Hogarth Press.*

Katherine also saw more of Lady Ottoline Morrell. As a child I had often looked fascinated through the broken gaps in the high fence into the garden behind their mansion in Cavendish Square. She was a remarkable and astonishing woman, tall and striking to look at, with a complete disregard for all ordinary rules and regulations of behaviour. I have in my mind's eye a picture of her at the seaside in a long cloak with the end thrown across her shoulder and a high plumed hat. She wore beautiful clothes and owned beautiful things and collected round her a crowd of brilliant and gifted young, and not so young, people. She had found Murry and now was charmed with Katherine, the newest lion in her net. She had a lovely garden and a generous gesture of giving. She would send Katherine great baskets of lovely flowers; not so much a bunch of flowers, as a whole picture of a garden. She said she walked round her garden picking anything beautiful to smell. I can hear now her deep, almost cooing voice as it must have sounded, floating through the evening air as she wandered among her night-scented stocks. Katherine wrote this poem, *Night Scented Stocks*, about her garden.

White, white in the milky night
The moon danced over a tree.
'Wouldn't it be lovely to swim in the lake!'
Somebody whispered to me.

'Oh, do-do-do!' cooed someone else,
And clasped her hands to her chin.
'I should so love to see the white bodies –
All the white bodies jump in!'

The big dark house hid secretly
Behind the magnolia and the spreading pear tree,
But there was a sound of music – music rippled and ran
Like a lady laughing behind her fan,
Laughing and mocking and running away . . .
'Come into the garden – it's as light as day!'

'I can't dance to that Hungarian stuff,
The rhythm in it is not passionate enough,'
Said somebody. 'I absolutely refuse . . .'
But he took off his socks and his shoes
And round her spun. 'It's like Hungarian fruit dishes
Hard and bright – a mechanical blue!'
His white feet flicked in the grass like fishes . .
Someone cried: 'I want to dance, too!'

But one with a queer Russian Ballet head
Curled up on a blue wooden bench instead.
And another, shadowy – shadowy and tall –
Walked in the shadow of the dark house wall,
Someone beside her. It shone in the gloom,
His round grey hat, like a wet mushroom.

'Don't you think perhaps . . .' piped someone's flute . . .
'How sweet the flowers smell!' I heard the other say –
Somebody picked a wet, wet pink
Smelled it and threw it away.

'Is the moon a virgin or is she a harlot?'
Asked somebody. Nobody would tell.
The faces and the hands moved in a pattern
As the music rose and fell,
In a dancing, mysterious, moon bright pattern
Like flowers nodding under the sea . . .

The music stopped and there was nothing left of them
But the moon dancing over the tree.

Katherine was rather fascinated by Lady Ottoline and enjoyed
her, but she was an interruption: so that when Murry stayed at
Garsington in the October of 1917 and caught a bad chill and
Ottoline begged her to go down and succour him, she went
unwillingly. The weather was treacherous and probably her coat
was thin, for there she too caught a terrible cold. She returned to
Old Church Street and promised to rest and be careful all day,
but presently complained of a slight pain. 'It's nothing,' she told
me, 'just a touch of pleurisy. I've had it before, it will go.' But it
did not go.

She said she would stay in bed; that her 'daily'* was coming in
regularly and would see to everything, and that I must certainly
not stop away from work. So I lit her fire, gave her a hot water
bottle and tea and left for what I thought was my *duty*, trusting
to the 'daily'. Later I learnt she had lied to me to allay my
anxiety. The 'daily' was not coming. Katherine got up and
fetched in her own coal and did all the necessary work. So again I

* This was Ma Parker, the source of KM's story of this name.

had failed her in her time of need. I had not enough imagination to do the right thing, though perhaps it would not have saved her. She was so independent, yet so helpless.

She told me later that a careless and extravagant remark of mine as I came in one night, hungry after a hard day's work, exclaiming 'I'm so hungry tonight, I could eat the table if it were a loaf of bread', had so shocked her that she had been almost unable to eat for several days.

It was left to Mrs Maufe to visit her and beg her to go to a nursing home; but Katherine would have hated this and in any case she probably felt she had not enough money. Mrs Maufe finally found a doctor. He was called Ainger and he and Katherine soon made friends. He told her she must get out of England *at once* as she risked 'galloping consumption'. If he had specified Switzerland and insisted on this many things might have been different. But at that moment, in the middle of the war, Switzerland was practically impossible for us. So Katherine turned her thoughts to warmer places and longed again for her beloved France and Bandol, where she had been so happy.

Murry came and they talked of Bandol. Yes, she would go there and soon be well. Neither Murry nor I could get permission to go with her: the war ordained we should not. So on 7th January 1918 I packed for her, and persuaded her to dress as warmly as possible. I seem to remember a large fur muff owned by one or other of us. Then Murry and I anxiously saw her on to the boat train, swaying a little with weakness as she walked.

The anxiety was well justified. She wrote that the journey had been terrible. It had taken three days. The French train was full. She only just managed to secure a seat by the window (which was broken) and cold air rushed in and snow rested on her fur muff. There was no food to be had, not even a hot drink. I think a kind woman, seeing her condition, helped a little: it was a dreadful journey, though in the end she reached Bandol.

But Bandol! What a final disappointment after her previous visit two years before. The hotel Beau Rivage was quite changed, all the friendly staff had gone and it was coldly severe and un-welcoming. She obtained a room and went to bed, and presently made friends with the new *femme de chambre*, a type of woman whose heart she always won. In London, we hoped for an improve-ment. But none came. Bandol was, of course, a quite unsuitable

place for her to go to; the warm, relaxing sea air engendered a low
fever.

When Katherine left Old Church Street I moved into a large
and comfortable house on the Embankment, Eyot Villa, which
had been turned into a Y.W.C.A. hostel for the workers at
Gwynne's factory. I must have been seeing Murry, for suddenly
I heard that he had just had a wail from Katherine: she was no
better, feeling worse and indeed quite ill.

I decided instantly that I must go to her. Jack warned me: 'No,
don't go, she will be furious.' But the decision came from within
me, not from common sense. So I stuck to it and obtained permission from Mr Gwynne to take a few weeks leave. Then I boldly
tackled the passport and permit office, but met with blank refusals.
I sat down and wept. My tears seemed to soften somebody's
heart and I received permission to go. The journey was a nightmare, ending with a night train from Marseilles. The train was
packed with all the local folk from the coast; crammed in the
corridors, we were lucky if we could even get room to sit on our
cases. All the stations were in pitch darkness, and I had not the
least knowledge of their names, even if we could hear what was
called out. We crept slowly along that beautiful, hidden coast,
and I cannot now remember if I spent the night on the train
or in the station or how I found the Hotel Beau Rivage at
Bandol.

Katherine met me in the courtyard by the front steps with
'What *have* you come for?' My heart sank to the uttermost
depths. All that struggle and effort and anguish of mind and body
was wasted – thrown away – and useless. I was not welcome, I
was intruding in that country of her grief and joy. But I was there,
and must fit in with the order of Katherine's day. She rested in
her room all the morning. We met at lunchtime: after that she
worked or otherwise occupied herself, and I walked or sat in the
gardens.*

We had supper together and then perhaps chatted a while in the
salon, where by now Katherine had made acquaintances. Starved
of sugar in our rationed England, I was thankful to find sweet

* KM wrote *Sun and Moon* and her two important stories *Je ne parle
pas français* and *Bliss* during this January and February at Bandol. In
a letter to JMM that February she says: 'I am still in a *state of work* –
you know, my precious: dead quiet and spinning away.'

things and fruit in the shops. Katherine, I think, disapproved of my craving for dates. Perhaps I was greedy!

Of course we met occasionally during the day and I saw Katherine in her room, but she did not want her daily routine and privacy broken into, even by me; perhaps, at that moment, particularly by me. However, she took me to the small shops and showed me where she had bought things when she and Murry had stayed at the Villa Pauline.

One night there was a terrific thunderstorm. Remembering the incident when Katherine was ill at Rottingdean and we had watched just such a storm with the wildest lightning playing, I left my room and found my way to hers and stayed till the storm died down. But this time I discovered that she thought that it was I who was frightened and that she was comforting me!

One day, wishing to prove to me how well she really was, (as though I had not eyes to see), she suggested she should take me for a walk through the beautiful country with its grey-blue olive trees and feathery fern-like undergrowth on the hills. I agreed unwillingly, for I did not feel that she was really fit enough, though I could not say so. She remembered the way from the past, and hurried off. But now it was more than she could manage – as she realised when we had still a long way to go round a high hill. We stopped and she thought she knew a short cut. It may have been one, but it was long enough none the less and we got back with Katherine thoroughly exhausted.

The next morning she sent for me. She had been at the window, had jumped back into bed and had then started coughing. Her handkerchief was stained with blood! The realisation that this could really mean tuberculosis terrified her. I sent for the only English doctor in the place, and a dreadful little man came, who drank and was quite useless. Katherine was really frightened: her one wish was to go home to England and Jack, and get help from the doctor who had seen her there.

So in the middle of March 1918 we started back, but after what difficulties! The endless journeys I made to the Mairie, the long waits in the little office with walls festooned with great trails of flowers and baskets overflowing with fruit!

Why should Madame wish to leave the south? She would get better here, travelling was very difficult, it was impossible to get permission, etc. I suppose it did seem mad to want to leave the

sun and warmth of the glorious south to go back with chest
trouble to that cold and damp island, England. 'But of course if
Monsieur le docteur said it was necessary and desirable, well. . . .'

So back came the little doctor with his tipsy smile and smell of
drink, and Katherine used her charm and feminine wiles to get
him to write the necessary letter. Triumphantly I carried it to the
rather worn little office, and got the permits, but only I think as
far as Marseilles, because I remember Katherine had to be left
sitting somewhere while I spent interminable hours at the consulate, up and down stone passages and stairs, always waiting till the
last case had been dealt with.

Katherine could not have made that long return journey alone,
and my money as well as hers was running short. But at last we
got to Paris, and there we stayed at the Select Hotel in the little
Rue de la Sorbonne. There could be no more travelling to London.
It was March 1918, and the Germans were making their last big
offensive, the line at Amiens bulged dangerously near and Big
Bertha was dropping her bombs every fifteen minutes.

We had to eat all our meals out, which was a tremendous effort
for Katherine. Generally, we went to Duval's restaurant. The
waitresses were elderly women for the pretty young people were
all at war work, but I remember the dainty clothes of these
women with their crisply frilled caps and aprons and always a
smile of welcome as they carefully turned the salad leaves over
and over before serving them. But by their faces you could tell
when the moment for the bombing drew near. Big Bertha was
very regular and the old faces lost their smiles, the wrinkled
cheeks puckered with fear, till – bang! and suddenly all was
bustle and smiles again – for another fifteen minutes.

The big gun did not really do very much damage, it was more a
question of morale. It completely demolished everything in its
way as it came nearer, but seemed to have very little explosive
power, and some people began to get careless. If it hit you directly
– well – phit! But if not, it did little harm. I saw one house in a
street with the whole front wall cut straight down as though with
a knife, but still standing with no other visible damage.

At first, obeying orders, Katherine and I crawled down to the
cellar when the siren sounded for a raid. The cellar was icy, and
the stone steps hard and chilly, so we decided it was better to be
bombed in our beds than to suffer miserably in a dark hole below

ground, and from then on we listened unperturbed to the little cars with warning sirens screaming down the streets.

For three weeks we were held prisoners in Paris. No travelling was allowed till the tenuous front line was at last held and then pushed back, and all this time our private tensions grew and grew. Katherine, brave as she was, felt apprehensive at the change in her physical condition. She had not yet had time to accept or indeed to understand it. Then one day she complained of a pain in her back and I, gently running my fingers down her spine, came upon a slight swelling, caused probably by some muscular strain. 'Yes,' I said, 'there seems to be a little growth of some sort.' That word! I don't know how I came to use it; to Katherine it suggested I know not what horrors. Her world shivered into fragments. Another enemy was upon her!

One morning, on the way home from a meal, we stopped to rest at a small café; the handsome, buxom *patronne* reminded her of a happier Paris, and she spoke of some of the places she and Murry had frequented. But most of the time she spent resting upstairs in our hotel. Our rooms were on the top floor amongst the attics, but they were somehow comforting with their odd shapes, and every night I crept to her room with my pillows and blankets to sleep quite comfortably, I think, on the floor, slipping back before anyone was about next morning.

This long stay was emptying our purses, until one day Katherine summoned up her courage to go out and see someone she would have given anything *not* to see – or was it feared to see? I suspected it was Carco, but I did not dare to ask her. She came back with enough money for our tickets home.

I did not know then that the consulate would probably have helped, nor did I know that if I had written to my friend Stella Drummond, whose father General Drummond was head of Southern Command, we would probably have been brought home immediately by official orders. By now, however, that weary time of strain and trouble was nearly over. The Amiens line held, and the railways began to work again, and we found ourselves safely on a boat bound for England.

Then a miracle happened. As she sat on a bunk in the cabin, all Katherine's fears and troubles lifted and fell away. The dark cloud of strain between us dissolved and Katherine and I reposed in a wonderful serenity of happiness and understanding. We played a simple game of cards, a Patience I had taught her long before, which she would often use to relax her mind and fill in time on long journeys. And so in contentment and joyful anticipation we journeyed to Redcliffe Road. Murry had taken a large flat there and was waiting for her.

I unpacked and made her as comfortable as possible and attended to all her small necessities. Then I gathered up my possessions – no, not my suitcase! I had left that behind on the station at Bandol, from where, exactly one year later, good Messrs. Cook returned it to me for a ridiculously small fee – and slipped back into Eyot Villa and to my friends at the factory.

Katherine was so happy and thankful to be at HOME – as her letter shows – able to cook her own egg and boil the kettle, or watch Jack doing these simple things, in spite of being so ill.

                                         12 April 18
                                         Redcliffe Road

Friday.

Dearest Jones,*

The little Messenger at the door sent me back years and years. Thank you dearie for the 'goods'. I am glad the box has turned up. What is the next step to take and which of us takes it? I am also glad that Stella† was there as well. I'd like to know what the fights are – I have been wondering about you so . . . .

'Home' looked lovely, and feels so lovely. I never want to go out again. I had to spend a long time casting up my eyes at all the

---

* The name KM and LM both called each other when all was well between them. KM's mother and a friend, whose name also began with B, called each other 'B'. Katherine proposed that she and LM should call each other by the same name too – and chose Jones. (KM liked to change her name: Kathleen, Kass, Katherine, Katie, KM, K, Jones, apart from her various pen-names.)

† Stella Drummond at the factory. The fights were the various squabbles at the factory; another charge hand was rather difficult.

'surprises' and improvements. They really were many. Ribni*
was sitting in the window on the look out on a little box which
held my letters. When he saw the taxi you can imagine how he
began to wave and tap his toes on the glass – and then when I did
come there, said he was only looking to see if the milkman was
coming. He has got rather out of hand and bosses me up – if I so
much as move a thing out of its place.

Johnny† came in last night – God! he gave me such a welcome.
Before I knew where I was we had hugged and kissed each other
and Johnny kept saying 'this is a great success'. It really was!
And you can imagine all the enjoyment he got out of a *fig* or two.
We are dining with him tonight. I feel horribly weak and rocky
now that the strain is over – *blissfully* happy (illegible) happy – but
really ill. I phoned Ainger. He is away until next week. I'll wait
if I can. I weighed myself. Curse it, 7 stone 7. I've just lost a
stone, *alors*. Isn't that annoying. But ever since I came HOME I
have done nothing but eat. I am hungry all the time so perhaps
my last state will be worse than my first and I will put on stones
like I've thrown them off.

But Jones – one's *own* fire – and lighting the gas and making tea
– and Oh! the hot bath which really was hot – and Jack and Jack
and Jack.

Does it gleam to you, too – like a little jewel beyond price –
those hours on the boat when you sat on the floor in a draught
and I sat on the lounge and we put the red on the black and
wanted a seven? I was so happy – were you? Try and forget that
sad and sick Katie whose back ached in her brain or whose brain
ached in her back. It's such a lovely afternoon and very warm. I
would like to turn to you and say 'Oh Jones, we are quite all
right, you know' –

About Saturday – Jack has got the afternoon off and we have to
go and see his Mother – You'll understand. Try and find a
minute to write to me in. Do you want money?

Yours, dearie
Katie.

* A little Japanese doll belonging to KM, named after Colonel
Ribnikov, a Japanese spy, the hero of one of Kuprin's short stories.
† John L. Fergusson.

CHAPTER X

Redcliffe Road – Looe – Hampstead: 1918

On 12th April 1918 JMM and KM were reunited at Redcliffe Road and on 3rd May they were married (Bowden having divorced her by this time), an event they had planned and looked forward to for so long; F. D. Ferguson and the Hon. Dorothy Brett were the witnesses.

Katherine was by now very ill. I was of course, hard at work at the factory and only went to see her when I could and when she was free, but she did not seem to improve at Redcliffe Road. She was very weak from her attack of pleurisy and the hardships of her journey to and from Bandol. The 'rheumatiz' distressed her as well as her lung and at times she could only walk with the aid of a stick. Her letter to me of 18th April explained her position.

18.IV.18
Redcliffe Road.

Thursday.

Dearest Jones,

. . . I saw Ainger yesterday and discovered he was a New Zealand boy. That explains my feeling of confidence. But he's called away to France on Saturday till the end of the war. What a bother!

He said: Yes there is no doubt I have definitely got consumption. He appreciates that a sanatorium would kill me *much* faster than cure me. (It's a 2nd lunatic asylum to me.) I am to try a 'cure' at home. Home is to be either Hampstead or Highgate or further afield. Must live in a summer house (find the summer) eat and drink milk and not get excited or run or leap or worry about anything – You know all the old wise saws. In fact repeat fortissimo with a good strong accent on the second note: 'She *must* lead the *life* of a *child* of *8*'. Can't you *now* hear the oboe taking it up it Oh so plaintive with little shakes and twirls and half sobs? I must not borrow a handkerchief (this is serious Betsy, for you know how they fly from me) or drink out of loving cups or eat the little bear's porridge with his spoon. And so on. But you see I am ever so gay – with long beams coming from my fingers and sparks flying from my toes as I walk.

(As to money – well – I keep on taking taxis for the moment – I can't help it but I will draw in my horns the moment my wings put forth.)

Tell me all about the coat and skirt dearest – Most important. In fact tell me all you can about everything. Bell and Chaddie* called last night in a private kerridge and brought me some oranges and dead roses. Fergusson came to dinner and we talked strangely enough about 'this Art business' and 'What is honesty'. But however I wander in *that* orchard I always find fresh fruits and bigger boughs and loftier trees. So it's an adventure.

Goodbye darling
Katie.

Despite the courage implicit in this letter the shock of finding herself actually in the grip of this dread complaint was very new, and she was not yet able to come to terms with it. In 1918 it was still one of the most feared diseases; there seemed to be no effective treatment and no cure. Ainger had recognised that she would not be able to bear a sanatorium and suggested a 'cure' at home.

She and Murry talked about it and decided that Murry should look for a house high on one of the hills in north London. He eventually found No. 2 Portland Villas, in Hampstead, which they nicknamed 'The Elephant'; perhaps because Murry had to sign the lease before they had quite made up their minds.

---

* Belle Dyer (now Trinder) KM's young aunt; and Chaddie, her sister.

JMM realised that for her sake, and for the sake of their lives together, he must maintain the pretence that this would work – though the very fact of her illness made him despair. In Between Two Worlds *he wrote: 'We were trapped. And I was caught in a world of strange and subtle fantasy. . . . Now between Katherine and me a subtle and impassable barrier had descended. To speak my thoughts to anyone but her was unthinkable; it was the more unthinkable to speak them to her.' It is doubly ironic that this should happen in the very months that they were officially able to marry.*

Meanwhile Katherine could not stay in Murry's cramped rooms at Redcliffe Road, and Murry, who had so little determination or self-control when things were difficult, began to get 'tortured' (as Katherine put it) by her condition. So, though it was anguish for her to be separated from him so soon, she adopted the suggestion of Anne Estelle Rice (now Mrs Drey, for she had married the art critic O. Raymond Drey in 1913) that she should join her for a while at Looe in Cornwall, the so-called Cote d'Azur of England. Anne had found a very good hotel and she took a room for Katherine too. She helped her in every way, arranging all the difficult essential diet that Katherine was ordered to have, despite wartime shortages. She was a wonderful friend and Katherine, who was in dire need of food and comfort and rest, really benefited a great deal. But it was once more a hotel, almost an institution, and Katherine longed with all her tired heart for the security and peace of 'home' and for the company of the man she loved.*

Also at Looe she had another severe attack of the pain she always thought of as rheumatism. The letters she sent me from Looe show her struggles with this pain, and with the dread of tuberuclosis, that she experienced.

---

* At Looe, Katherine wrote *Carnation* (published posthumously in *Something Childish*, 1924,) and *A Married Man's Story*, (unfinished, and first published posthumously in the *London Mercury*, April 1923).

Headland Hotel
Looe
Cornwall
21.V.18

Dear Jones,

Very many thanks for your letter. Do please go and see Jack as soon as you can and find out about his cold – also how he looks and seems. It is *anguish* to be away from him but as my presence seems to positively torture him – I suppose it's the better of two horrors.

I feel a great deal better and my pain is infinitely less – scarcely there. Of course mentally (here I am telling the truth again) I feel just like a fuchsia bud – cold, sealed up, hard. My hatred and contempt for life and its way overwhelm me – and all this beauty – far richer than the South – means – less than nothing. I'd as soon – sooner in fact, hear the rag and bone man. I'm being exquisitely cared for in every way. It is for all the world (and here I can see a grin on the face of life) a perfect sanatorium. But SO EXPENSIVE. So that is that. I wish I could say anything else, but I can't – and be sincere. You know the mood. I implore you *don't* spare me about Jack's condition: that would be *too* cruel.

Yours as ever,

Katie.

Dear Jones,

I can't remember whether I wrote or intended to, to say that 'after all' I am in favour of the Elephant and of us three being there. It can I am sure not only be arranged, but be a great joy. Yes, really.

And did I thank you for tea?* It was a comfort. My bill for a week with my extra cream etc. was £5.13.8, pretty staggering – Jones I don't want any cigarettes – thanks dear. Virginia† has sent me 6 packets of those Belgian ones from Richmond.

* Tea or T; their expression for money.
† Virginia Woolf.

I feel ever so much better – Hate life more than ever – see
MORE CORRUPTION every day – and everybody seems to be evil and
vile. Nearly everybody.

Still, one mustn't think – at least not aloud – But life is a sorry
disappointment you know.

Yours, Katie.

12.VI.18

Wednesday.

Dear Jones,

I have waited until this afternoon's post has come and as there
is still no *sign* from you I am very worried.
You must be ill.
You equally *must* let me know at *once*.
Get Miss Oldfield* or one of your friends to write if you cannot,
dear. But do, please, let me know the full truth about what is
happening – as *soon* as *possible*.
I know you wouldn't have kept silence for any other reason.

Yours ever,

Katie.

14.VI.18
Looe

Friday.

Dear Jones,

I was very glad to get your letter this morning – very sorry
to hear you've been ill I should think it was caused by heat and

---

* One of the women at the factory, also living at Eyot Villa.

rushing and bad diet. Anyhow I rather gather you've seen a doctor and as you're 'out' again perhaps the worst is over. I suppose if I hadn't sent the letter registered I should not have heard at all – You're not just an agency to which I apply for pills and cigarettes, free of charge, though your whole letter was concerned with trying to make me believe that's what I've brought our 'relationship' to. However if it pleases you to feel it, my dear, you must feel it. Lord knows I deserve it enough, according to the WORLD. I thought you were the person I flew to with bad tempers, worries, depressions, money troubles, wants, rages, silences, enfin – but the little bottles, boxes and postal orders, though God knows welcome, seemed to me to be only the trimmings – and not the feast. However you think otherwise – which is humiliating to us both.

Take care of your wicked self.

Katie

22.VI.18
Looe.

Sunday.

Dear Jones,

Thank you for the B.P.s* and the cigarettes. I am 'taking' both.
Jack writes that you have been looking after him most beautifully. He has been, I know, dreadfully needing a kind hand, poor boy, and yours, according to him, was quite of the kindest.
I sit writing to you in an armchair in front of the window. The dreamy vacant sea dreaming by, and castle and mountains in the sky – I am wrapped up in my pink quilt, and hot water bottle for I've got an awful attack of that spinal rheumatism, the worst I've known so far. It has swept me completely off my feet this time. Oh, it's horribly painful! Outside a crowd of children, accompanied by a fiddle and a 'cello have been singing songs for the Devon Hospital or something. Not hymns proper, but tunes

* BiPalatinoids, a strong iron pill.

KM in New Zealand before 1903

The Library at Queen's College, Harley Street

KM with her 'cello at Queen's
College

KM in Brussels, 1906

KM at Rottingdean, 1910

The black and silver Egyptian
shawl, Rottingdean, 1910

LM (in black) in Rhodesia, 1914–1916

LM in Rhodesia

Chummie, Leslie Heron
Beauchamp

Mrs Beauchamp

KM at Barons Court, 1913

KM, JMM and Richard Murry at 'The Elephant', Hampstead, 1918

The Villa Isola Bella, Menton

KM at the Villa Isola Bella, 1920

like enough to hymns to fill me with Sunday Sentiments. One wants to weep; one thinks of death; the seagulls fly into the infinite – and one wonders why on earth one should be cursed with this perpetual ill health! It seems a mockery to be 29 and as Mrs Honey says "nought but a frame" when there is so much that one longs to *do* and *be* and *have*.

(I wish I did not hear you say, in a small voice: But Katie you might be paralysed or pock-marked or an ampute.) For it don't console me at all. I want to run; I want to jump; I want to scramble, and to rush and laugh.

Oh well, there you are. I don't know why I write to you so intimately. For you have quite given me up and thrown me over in such a way, too. Walking out of the house without a word. But perhaps there was someone waiting for you at the gate – Stella – Wenna – Herssey of the Eyebrow – a little Mrs —— and So On. I don't know and I'm sure I don't care. It's only when you are *in* the house that I love you. I never – as it were recognise you when you're dressed and ready to depart. You seem so awfully like everybody else in your hat and jacket. Yes, I only love you when you're blind to everybody but US. That's the truth. I simply hate the person who met Fergusson and *he* recognised me. I was surprised that he recognised me for after all he's not seen me except in the dark when he had his back to me. But I'm glad he recognised me. I should like him to like me – I didn't think he even realized who I was – I never thought he'd have known me again – I wish I could see something more of Fergusson – (ad. lib. take all the repeats). Horrid, horrid, Katie.

27.VI.18
Looe.

Jones love,

Our letters crossed – and yours with the T arrived today. Thank you ever so. Don't forget, mignonette, to tear yourself away from your admirers on Saturday and come to '47' – will you?

You sent such an *astonishingly* lovely letter – I am thrilled about the seeds, and about your coat and skirt – equally thrilled.

The seed that is coming up standing on its head, is particularly engaging – I am so glad that you are seeing your people – and that they are 'good' – I wish you would marry Webb* or Gibson† and have some children. We do seem so *very* short of children, don't we? I simply pine for some but they don't want me (small wonder). Now I feel you would be superbly successful. Lay it to heart, Jones.

Jack has cried blessings on you ever since he came. You know, in him (whatever you may in your black moments think) you have a most loyal, utterly sincere friend. He's *for* you – *for* you and he believes in you – really enough to satisfy even you – I thought I'd tell you. These are the things that are so lovely to know. My back's pretty fairish – not more than that. It all depends on the day – and my wings – well they are *there*. The left one is groggy – and the right one I don't know about. But I have got used to them now and take them in my *stride* as they are no good for my flight.

I have had such a nice letter from Margaret Wishart‡ that was. She heard of me through a notice for *Prelude*. I am going to see her when I come home – she has two almost grown up sons. LY has not come – she always 'cries off' at the last hour, so Eileen says. She has been ill again and she wears her hair short – and Mrs H. is still a very great tartar – Men don't like LY at all – That has made her very bitter (This is the news I glean for you). But the reason for it is that she is "always in love with some woman." She becomes desperately infatuated with women just as she used to with Robin‖ and Poppy Robinson. Devotes herself to them – slaves for them – just as she did when she was a 'little girl'. She sounds to me rather a tragic figure. Won't you try and see her.

My writing is vile today. One of my hands shake so – I am still filling myself with shot in the shape of Bi Palats – and if you held me up by my heels I am sure I would rattle – They are good, I think.

---

* The foreman at Gwynne's factory.

† The Officer LM had met on the boat coming home in 1916.

‡ KM's friend from Beauchamp Lodge (it was through her that Katherine met George Bowden).

‖ Miss Robinson, nicknamed Robin, the assistant Matron at No. 41, the boarding house for Queen's College.

I don't care a button for this place Jones – though I suppose to the unjaundiced eye it is wonderfully beautiful, I don't care. No place is to me. I'd just as soon be in the Mile End Road, sooner really. There are rocks and beaches and shells and pools and flowers and so on – but, don't you know – I'd just as soon let them all fall out of my lap – In fact I don't care about the sea or the country – *or* this town for the matter of that. Oh, she is *very* hard to please. No, dearie, I like books and fibres and cigarettes and flowers and fruit still – and at this moment I feel awfully like you.

I have had a long letter from Mack* today on his way to Pekin to be crowned Emperor of China – inviting Jack and me to go to Canada and on to N.Z. with Vera and the boys. *So* kind.

Then I'll see you on Saturday. And until then don't forget that you have for a friend, in spite of everything, qui s'appelle
Katie.

Murry went to fetch Katherine as arranged and they came back to Redcliffe Road in June, and stayed there till The Elephant was ready. It was here that she received a few weeks later the news of her mother's death. I arrived to find her deeply grieved; she had realised for the first time how strong her feeling for her mother had become. This attachment had first emerged consciously in 1911, in the days of Clovelly Mansions, when the family had come 'home' from New Zealand. Katherine spoke to me of the many things in herself she had come unexpectedly to see in her mother.

One evening that July, Katherine definitely asked me if I would like to go with them to Hampstead to look after things. She had already mooted the proposal in her letters to me at Looe.

My heart sank. I had become integrated in the life of Gwynne's factory and Eyot Villa. I had friends there who shared my interests. Stella Drummond wished me to be with her family when Eustace Percy came down to see her with a possible proposal of marriage; and there were other kindly, simple folk too. I was also making some headway now with my machinists. To go would mean losing all this.

Besides, I knew nothing of housework, cooking or shopping.

* The husband of K's sister Vera.

To be with them both I would become part of the family; but I felt slightly tense with Katherine because of my anxiety that I might not do things quite right. It wasn't easy to ask 'Shall we do this or that at The Elephant?' Katherine saw in the house her last chance of a home of her own. She would say in answer to my queries, 'Oh, we'll see', all the time wanting it to be hers alone.

I hesitated just a little, as one braces oneself before plunging into a river, and that hurt Katherine. She had so wanted me to want to undertake this adventure with her. Of course there was no real question in my own mind. Nothing else would have been possible for us. This letter of hers expresses her attitude:

1. VII 18
47 Redcliffe Road.

Dear Jones,

We are being unfortunate in our meetings. I don't *want* to quarrel though I believe you think I do. The truth is that for the time being my nature is quite changed by illness. You see I am never for one single hour without pain. If it is not my lungs it is (far more painful) my back. And then my legs *ache* and I never can change my position without such a creaking of all the joints as ever was. This, plus very bad nights, exasperates me and I turn into a fiend, I suppose. And when you turn to me and say 'You did have a box of herbs *if* you remember' as though those words of yours came out of an absolute cavern of HATE I realise the 'change'. All the same, and knowing and realising this as I do, I *still* ask you to come to Hampstead – until I am better. For the sake of all that has been I ask that of you. I know I shall get better there and quite well again, but see me through these next few months will you?

I know exactly why you talk of what you are going to do after the war 'Carrie' – 'The Big House' – 'I may be in a factory'. That is because, untrue to my first talk about Hampstead I have never made you feel part of it, and every time you say 'our', I give you a vile look. This is wrong of me but at present I can't control it. I'll try and explain it a bit. You see out of all my external world only the house remains just now. It is all my little world and I want to make it – *mine beyond words* – to express myself all I can in the small circle remaining. And so I am plagued with wicked childish jealousy – lest my last doll shall be taken from me– dressed as I don't want it dressed – hugged by others arms. You won't understand this in me; there is no reason why you should. But you must believe, that, as we live there, things will quite change, and if you are only 'careful for me' it will all be *quite* different and we shall call each other over the stairs.

Oh! it is (yes it is) incredible that one should have to explain all this. I always feel that the great high privilege, relief and comfort of friendship was that one had to explain nothing. But I have sinned against friendship that's why.

Only I do think I am the last person on earth who has undying, unbroken faith. That will really seem to you *too* contradictory altogether. Nevertheless it is true.

If I don't see you before your week-end, I hope you have a happy time, dearie, and take an old *well* Katie in a corner of your heart to think about if you have a moment.

In this imperfect, present world we have failed each other, scores of times, but in the real unchanging world we never have nor come down from our high place.

Yours ever,
Katie.

So I withdrew from my life at the Y.W.C.A. hostel in the riverside house 'Eyot Villa' that had long been my home. My friend Robert Gibson came to tea there, and we walked to Kew by the river. My companions at the factory, true friends by now, were grieved at this break-up of our circle; they gave me a gold watch when I left.

As it was still wartime, it was difficult to leave the factory, but nevertheless I gave in my resignation to Mr Gwynne. After a long and serious discussion, in which he impressed on me the folly of expecting any good to come out of a home-cure for my friend, he let me go. He considered that without the strict regime of a clinic she would not get better; there would be too much emotional stress between individuals. Unfortunately, I told Katherine of this, thinking his advice reasonable and experienced; it was to this she referred in one of her letters later when she spoke of 'you and

Mr Gwynne wanting to put me into a loony-bin'. Sometimes I talked too freely to her without thinking first how she might interpret the meaning of my words

When I explained to my childhood friend Dolly Sutton what I was intending to do, she laughed heartily: '*You*! *You* are going to take care of a house and run it!' It was, perhaps, an echo of my own misgivings. However, we embarked on the adventure. And as July came to an end we spent the next few weeks making arrangements for the move. Katherine was brave and uncomplaining, determined to face the new life. And so a new chapter opened.

CHAPTER XI

'The Elephant', Hampstead: Summer 1918 – Winter 1919

KM, JMM and LM moved up to 'The Elephant' at the end of July 1919. In May her story Prelude *had been published by the Hogarth Press, and in August the English Review had printed her story* Bliss. *Both were well received and brought her work before a wider public.*

At 'The Elephant' life began to take shape again; there were now definite objectives – peace, Katherine's work, making a home.

Before we moved in, when the painters were preparing to paint the inside of the house, Katherine found them just finishing the undercoat – a lovely dove grey. The work was stopped at once and the house remained within always a pearly grey. There was lemon colour too and in my room I remember a pattern of pale green leaves and large golden fruit for all the curtains. The little black and white cat would come steadily and heavily, pad, pad, pad, down the staircase: his name was Charles, and he was specially chosen. Alas! he became the mother of two kittens: Wingley and Athenaeum.

There were many ups and downs at 'The Elephant'. Poor Katherine, what she suffered at my hands! I was bad at getting up in the mornings, as I had nearly always been awake late the night before, and to light Katherine's bedroom fire and then brush and dust all the little house by 9 o'clock was a herculean task. Five minutes for the carpets and floors, three for the dusting, two for polishing – then I could get round; but when the second fire had to be lit, oh dear! I felt that all the house should be done before Katherine came down to a peaceful, charming room, and her work. Of course she had to have her slender breakfast in bed.

As soon as she came down she would move around lightly, either touching the flowers, which always responded, or just pushing things a fraction of an inch this way or that, which for KM made the room come alive. I once remarked on this habit to her, because I always kept the things exactly as I thought they had been the day before, but somehow it never worked. Things needed her presence. She wanted to make 'The Elephant' a perfect and beautiful home, and she did it. But something wasn't born – or was it still-born?

After giving this light touch, Katherine would dicuss the day's duties and meals: then I shut the door and she was at peace to work till lunch time. She would sit at her table that had been painted yellow with a great foot muff underneath it lined with fur and satin, for her feet were often cold.

Lunch, on a tray, would be at 1 o'clock. She hated being kept waiting; the pattern of the day would be disorganised, the thread of work broken. I understand now how the least disturbance, not planned, can break all one's continuity of thought and I sympathise completely with her in retrospect.

After lunch she had tea, often mint or camomile, which I would sometimes have with her, and then back she would go to her concentration till tea-time, when Jack might come in or anything might happen.

That was the rule of the day, but of course it was not always kept.

In the afternoon, if I did not have to go to town to shop or to attend to some household business, I would sometimes go into the little square garden to tidy the leaves and broken stems. I then knew nothing of gardening save that there were 'wild' and 'garden' flowers, and that dandelions were in the first class. One sad day, in the neglected garden, I found a huge dandelion in full bloom. A 'wild' flower I thought, and pulled it up. Katherine's wail of distress when she found it had gone – the single pool of golden glory, throwing up the sunshine to her – has stayed with me all these years.

It was on one of these idle afternoons that I did another dreadful thing. I had always had with me since the break-up of my family home a very large packet, quite a foot square, of all Katherine's letters from the early New Zealand day sof 1906 to 1908, treasured through all vicissitudes. With them also were all her later letters written when I was in Rhodesia between 1914 and 1916.

With an immense effort of self-sacrifice, feeling she would find in them much material for her work, I gave them back to Katherine. She opened the parcel, glanced at one or two letters, and cried:

'What dreadful rubbish – burn them *all*!'

Little trails of transparent smoke from the garden outside drifted, almost wistfully, past her window and were gone, gone for good. Pages and pages of her early girlish enthusiasms, hopes and visions – pictures of her own land and the England of her dreams. I could have cried as my treasured, half-remembered glimpses of those years curled away into the sky: but she would have none of them.

I cannot have been an easy person for Katherine to live with. I was doing a job at Portland Villas for which I was quite unfitted. Our friendship never flowered fully there. I was too immature, too emotionally involved and insecure. Kot told me I was 'afraid of life'. I never gave her the buoyant, unfettered love that she needed, and was often a responsibility which, for a sick woman, must have been exasperating. She needed all her strength for her work. I do not know if it was self-pity, for it seems as if it must have been, but I was very miserable over my many failures.

As a child I had always been terribly upset if I did anything wrong. I tried so hard that it was difficult to accept a failure when pointed out. In college days I needed a lot of sleep and was often late for prayers, running down the stairs at the last minute. Once old Miss Wood called out to me to remonstrate, and began by saying 'I know you don't like being found fault with. . . .' Now, when I was so very often doing or saying the thing which I should have known would distress my sick friend, I found my petals closing and I would withdraw apprehensively. Thus Katherine blamed her poor suffering body and mind for my weakness. If I had only been braver, a little wiser, more of an identity of my own.

There were times, too, especially in Hampstead, when I exasperated her with my constant, constraining care. She wanted to be *free*. If she crept down the stairs to go for a little walk, on her own, without anyone knowing, I would hear her and run after her with a coat, as I knew it was much colder than she expected and she was so very frail. She would then want to throw away even the jacket she was wearing.

When she was ill – and she was often very ill, at one time

existing only with the help of an oxygen cylinder – Murry would come home in the evening from some office, not from real life at the front, and bemoan how terrible it all was, how dreadfully he was suffering, and how he could hardly bear it. He was too full of self-pity to give her any help. I, in turn, crept about quietly, knocking gently at the door for fear of disturbing her. What she needed from us both was some assurance of life and a clear blowing wind filling the room with life and vitality.

I remember on one occasion at New Year's Eve when I deliberately stood aside and was sad, grieving for my personal loss, unable to join in joyfully with her. New Year's Eve had always been one of our particular festivals. Katherine was fascinated by the London lights: the dark blocks of houses, sprinkled at random with golden squares, oblongs or mere slits, behind which she knew others' lives were so busily being lived, and the lamplighter, making his steady progress up the streets, blazing his trail with little yellow fish-tails of flame She and I had for years made a little ceremony of standing at the window to welcome the New Year together. But this year it was too difficult; she and Jack had gone up to their room before 12 o'clock and I could not bear this apparent break-up of our custom. So I went to bed forlornly before midnight, only to repent and be ashamed next morning when Katherine asked me where I had gone. She had called across to me from her window and I had not heard.

It was a short time after she came to Hampstead that Katherine found Dr Sorapure, and was fortunate enough to become his patient. A Roman Catholic, he was wonderfully kind and imaginative. He seemed to understand both her illness and the way in which she, with her character, could best come to terms with it. She told me once, when the treatment he was giving her proved almost unendurably painful, he helped her over it by quietly talking of the immensity and wonder of the universe and the incomprehensibility of space. He showed real and deep understanding in all her troubles, and even eventually discovered the infection that was the true cause of the 'rheumatiz' which had persisted and increased ever since 1910. This he cured within the next year and Katherine was then saved much of her constant nagging pain. Katherine wrote a few words at the top of the manuscript of *Daughters of the late Colonel* dedicating it to Dr Sorapure. I salvaged this MS from her wastepaper basket;

unfortunately when I parted with it I did not copy out the dedication and it was not printed with the story. I think this should be known, as it was the expression of the great debt of gratitude she felt and of her very genuine affection.

There were times at 'The Elephant' that were cheerful and happy. I remember one beautiful day when the windows of Katherine's room were pushed up and the wind blew the light curtains out like transparent balloons. I was trying to make things grow in the garden while she, moving in her room, called out to me to watch the two kittens who were dancing over the grass. Indoors Katherine loved to watch the kittens playing hide and seek under the frills of the sommier. When they were small they lived generally in her room. 'Look!' she said, 'their tiny paws are just like unripe raspberries.'

At Hampstead, the owls often called and Katherine loved hearing them, especially in the night when she could not sleep. To me they always cried, 'trouble to come, trouble to come'.

Katherine loved wearing, and being surrounded by, beautiful colours and materials. I used to make fine linen and drawn threadwork clothes for her and delicate French lawn and lace handkerchiefs. I was delighted when I could find pieces of coloured silk or charmeuse in the sales, which we could then turn into fine things to wear or to furnish the house. Sometimes, when she felt stronger, we would walk on the Heath for a short time.

Gwynne was quite right in one of his arguments in favour of a proper clinic for a sick woman; she would have been assured of proper feeding. When we were still living off our ration books, Katherine was ordered to eat steak every day, of which there was none in Hampstead. So I went down every other day or so to one of the big stores in London, to buy a tiny portion. She tried to describe to me how it should be cooked and I tried to follow; but later she told me that I often produced a tough strip of leather which she could not chew, and to save hurting my feelings she threw it into her fire. Poor Katherine. I could have cooked it beautifully now.

Later, when the work proved more than my experience could manage, we got people to help in the house. One was a small elderly, true London 'char', a fine character. She taught me how to light Katherine's fire with paper balls when there was no wood kindling. Then there was a tall Cockney girl, Gertie. Katherine was very interested in the women and each morning would see them and, after a little chat, would allocate their several duties. We decided they would much rather take their orders directly from her, so I became a member of the staff!

Of course there were difficulties; one of these was the cook. She came to 'live in' while the other help came as 'dailies'. The cook was sent by a registry office and Katherine interviewed her. She was very formal and correct and seemed promising – until she had earned enough wages to enable her to drink. At first it was only a little; but presently there was a tipsy scene and Katherine had to sack her.

By Christmas the household was established and Katherine was feeling better; indeed she planned a Christmas party, which she gave with much enjoyment. There was a small Christmas tree with many lights, and much talk and laughter flowed around Katherine, who looked almost her healthy self of younger days, wearing a rather frilly soft dress of plum-coloured silk embroidered all over with tiny bunches of flowers. It was what John Fergusson would have called 'a great success'. Her devoted staff helped to make it so, and I, strangely enough, was quite content – or so my memory tells me.

In January 1919 JMM was offered the editorship of the Athenaeum, *with the task of resuscitating it after the war years; J. W. N. Sullivan and Aldous Huxley were his assistants and E. M. Forster, T. S. Eliot, Bertrand Russell, George Santayana and Herbert Read were among its contributors. The April issue shows signs of his advent with a new type face and format.*

In the evenings Murry's friends would gather at 'The Elephant'. Some of them became Katherine's friends too – Sullivan, for example, the young scientist from Ireland, who angered me because he smoked vile-smelling tobacco all the evening, making Katherine cough more and more. Though a rough diamond, there was something about him which made him become more a member of the family than the many other literary friends. Like Gordon Campbell – they were both Irish – he was simple and sincere. He had married Evelyn Bartrick Baker, Katherine's friend from Queen's College, and after Katherine died, I too came to know him as a friend. He was kind to me, with a sympathy and gentleness I have always remembered and treasured. He was an interesting talker and a great worker, with a very special interest in Beethoven, with whom he felt he had a close spiritual affinity.

Then there was Milne from the British Museum, quiet and thoughtful. I remember him particularly, because unlike most other visitors he stopped and talked to me when coming in. I think his own life was not a very happy one from what Katherine told me. Eddie Marsh was another visitor I seem to remember from this time.

But by far the most regular were Jack's brother Richard, and Brett – the Hon. Dorothy Brett; they were almost part of the family.

Richard, as he was always called although he had been christened Arthur, was humbly devoted to Katherine and she felt a great, almost motherly, affection for him and would talk to him for long periods. She said she felt she could do so much for him, give him so much – a sense of direction, vision. He used to bring his drawings for her criticism and appreciation. I remember a most delicate, sympathetic drawing he did of a very young baby's head. He was then taking up art as his life's work – I think with some success.

I took a rather charming photo of Katherine and the two brothers one day in the bright dining-room at 'The Elephant'. The boys were both smiling and Katherine was looking very stern – because she told me she was trying hard not to laugh.

Brett played a full part in the life of 'The Elephant'. She had a house in Pond Street which I think she took when the Murrys moved up to Hampstead, so that she could visit them frequently at 'The Elephant'. She could hear practically nothing and had those clear, keen-gazing, almost questioning blue eyes of the deaf. A slim, straight little figure with a small mouth always just slightly open, as though to help her hearing, she was one of the friends to whom Katherine was always the giver. Her wish was to be an intimate member of the Murry household. I remember one particular occasion when she came to see Katherine in the summer. I took cushions and chairs on to the grass in front of the house, and we had tea there outside. Katherine and Brett sat enjoying the sun, while I took some photographs. But it was not a great success.

I think that even then she was in love with Murry; I know that he found himself in some sense entangled with her after Katherine died, and fancied she expected him to marry her.

Another visitor to 'The Elephant' was Katherine's cousin, Elizabeth, Countess Russell (of the *German Garden*). I remember her as small and very upright. I did not know her myself till much later, after Katherine had died, when I understood how much she had felt for Katherine. Elizabeth was very hurt by a remark Katherine had made about her in one of her letters. She spoke of her 'claw-like hands laden with jewels'; but, being a writer, when Katherine saw or lived an incident, she could not resist touching it up till it became a picture. The remark should not have been published, as it was not kind and had probably been made thoughtlessly to amuse a particular reader. I know that Katherine was in fact really fond of her cousin.

Virginia Woolf was another visitor, but I think not a frequent one. Katherine saw her more at her own house, and I believe she and Murry were both very interested in the press on which Leonard Woolf had printed *Prelude* for her. Murry had decided that he must print and produce things, and got a hand-printing press. It was enormously heavy and had to stand in the garden room downstairs where, with terrific thumping noises, Jack worked at it. It was all most intriguing but Katherine was never very interested in things mechanical.*

I went once with Katherine to the Woolfs' house. We waited for a while in the sitting-room, and Katherine drew my attention to a handkerchief pushed into the seat of an armchair and forgotten. There was a note of amusement in her voice, as she said, 'If Virginia was carrying a jelly to the supper table and had dropped half of it, I can see her picking it up and dreamily putting it back on the dish as she went on into the room'; her head was full of other things. Katherine explained that Virginia was one of two sisters well-known for their beauty, so I was not surprised, when she came into the room, to see a tall, slender, rather willowy figure, with a long, fine-featured face, as in a nineteenth-century portrait.

She greeted us and swept Katherine into her own room to talk.

* KM's story *Je ne parle pas français* was printed on this machine in November 1919 by JMM and Richard Murry; their imprint was the 'Heron Press', the name of their dream home in the country, (see page 139).

I always felt the relationship was literary rather than personal, and that during Katherine's visits the conversation was 'erudite' and perhaps even 'intense'. But there must have been something real in the relationship since Virginia sent Katherine flowers.

Ottoline Morrell came once or twice. I remember her tall and gorgeous in stiff sea-green silk, with her strange deep voice and long face. She had lunch with us but I don't remember much about it because it was such a terrible ordeal for me, completely inexperienced as I was, to cook lunch, to serve it, and then to have to sit down and eat with strangers.

Once – I can smile now – my hands were so badly stained with vegetables, that being ashamed and wishing to hide them at that daintily laid table, I passed the dishes with my hands hidden underneath them. Afterwards Ottoline hummed to Katherine, 'M'm . . . Why does the Mountain (her name for me) hold the plates in such a strange way?'

I am sure Ottoline was really fond of Katherine, as a person and not merely as a lion for her social zoo. In the earlier days before Old Church Street, she tried to persuade Katherine to take her to Paris, to see all the small interesting cafés and other haunts – 'quite private and inconspicuous, just us two'. Katherine laughed at the idea of Ottoline being inconspicuous anywhere, with her tall, commanding figure, her sweeping cloaks, strange dresses, and cartwheel hats surmounted with feathers. But Ottoline was innocently unaware of herself; Katherine told me how she would pull her skirts up to fasten her suspender, in any group of friends. Some years later she was ill and sent me a message by Koteliansky asking me to go and see her. I felt I could not, and I never went.

Lawrence had returned to London in the autumn of 1918, and Katherine saw a good deal of him in those months. I think he was staying on Holly Mount in Hampstead, for I remember meeting him one day coming down the stone steps looking grave and with a beard like an old Italian picture of Christ. One day too he came to lunch which I remember was most carefully planned, for Katherine was introducing him to her 'home', of which she was justly proud. I can still see him, upright and forceful, striding up and down the room when I brought in the first course. I think he had as acute a sense of time as Katherine, because I remember clearly the atmosphere of disquiet. Lunch was three minutes late, and they had been so aware of those waiting minutes. I have no sense of time at all and that day I was in the grip of a feverish cold.

'Lunch is late,' said Katherine severely – it was a bad mark against the 'home'. Then noticing the tears gathering in my eyes, she added kindly, 'There's no need to cry about it.' Did her remark make things better or worse? Much worse! I sank out of the room into the kitchen, thankful for its emptiness. Gratefully I remember that the lunch was good.

Both Katherine and I had a great admiration for the actor Gerald du Maurier, whom we had often seen on the stage. He had a house not far from Portland Villas, which I often passed on my way to town. I reported back everything I saw in the beautifully ordered garden. Once, the great man himself came out of the house, looking exactly as he did in a play, and on another occasion I met his wife, richly dressed, buying fish at the little shop (with white, much ringed fingers she handled the fish herself, just like any housewife). I could hardly believe it! When I carried these tales back to K, I think she was amused. But what gave her greatest pleasure, she said, was to hear, on a sunny morning, the light-hearted singing in the house next door, and the tap-tapping on the edge of the kitchen sink of the squeezed-out dish mop – a happy, homelike sound.

Among others who came to see Katherine was Walter de la Mare. He came to tea, bringing some of his children. As this was rather more of a family affair, I had tea with them and helped to entertain the young people while de la Mare and Katherine talked. It was at this tea that the poet noticed Katherine's queer little habit of holding her spoon in the air after stirring the cup. She was in the middle of a sentence, probably, and could not remember to put it down. There is an allusion to this habit in his poem *To KM*.

Koteliansky must have come, but in those days I would only have spoken to him at the door, so I do not recollect. He was then living in the house that Katherine and Chummie had so enjoyed, 5 Acacia Road in St John's Wood.

The *Athenaeum* was proceeding well under its new editorship. Katherine was much concerned with the undertaking and was, of course, a regular contributor; but her most important contribution, I fancy, was the control she had over Murry's work as editor.

When JMM had become editor of the Athenaeum, *KM undertook to review the novels for him. This was an exacting task and was to last for nearly two years; from April 1919 until December 1920 she wrote reviews on two or three novels every week. (These were later collected together by JMM and published in 1930 under the title* Novels *and* Novelists.) *The* Athenaeum *also provided an assured outlet for KM's writing; she worked with Koteliansky on a translation of Chekhov's Letters which appeared in thirteen parts from April to October 1919, and she had her poems – under the pseudonym Elizabeth Stanley – printed from April to August. One short sketch,* Perambulations, *was published in May, and she also wrote three new stories at Hampstead:* See Saw (The Adelphi, *July 1924*), This Flower (Something Childish, 1924), A Suburban Fairy Tale (The Adelphi, *December 1923) and began* Second Violin, *though this was never finished.*

Since Katherine was now an acknowledged authoress, with a house of her own, a staff of servants, and a husband who was earning a substantial amount, the family decided it should know just how she fared. So one day, the doctor son of old Mrs Beauchamp was more or less sent to find out. Katherine had a talk with him, and she hoped for some assurance and advice on her condition. His comment came as he left: 'Well, dear, of course you won't make old bones.' Like much of her treatment by the family, Katherine found this very cold comfort. Did no one but Sorapure understand?

Her sister Chaddie and Aunt Bell, now Mrs Trinder, also drove up to Hampstead in a carriage and pair to see her. They were rich but they only brought small offerings of fruit or flowers; they did not even suggest taking her for a drive.

When she had been so hard up after she first came to England alone in 1908, I had spent almost all of the small inheritance which came to me from my mother, and now I had only an annual pension of £45 so that later in the coming years, when Katherine and I needed to go abroad to Switzerland and France for her health, she had to support me as well as herself. Murry never supported her. When they lived together they shared their expenses and kept strict accounts, though of course they occasionally gave each other presents. To me, when things were going better in Hampstead, they jointly gave a weekly allowance; which was as well, for I was not a careful shopper and often paid more for things than they could afford. At Hampstead, Murry had a good regular salary from the *Athenaeum*;* and he was also able to pay Katherine £10 a month for the reviewing she did for him.

I must mention two other visitors who came to Hampstead. They were friends of mine, Robert Gibson and his friend Marshall. Katherine and I had been out to dinner with them when Katherine lived at Old Church Street and we had enjoyed ourselves. Therefore when they wrote that they were coming home again on leave, Katherine suggested they should come to tea at 'The Elephant'. Unfortunately, Jack also turned up. He and Katherine sat by the fire talking to the two men, while I sat trapped behind the tea tray. I think the men expected the usual long welcome we gave our soldier friends in those days, especially when they were so far from their own homes. But Murry could not for a moment forget himself and enter into the lives and interests of men of such different cultures. The conversation became more and more strained, and I more and more miserable. Katherine seemed to be no better at handling the situation than I was.

At last the men could stand it no longer and got up saying that they must go. An argument started as to the shortest way to the station: 'Yes, to the right and straight on. Goodbye.' But they turned to the left! I ran to the gate calling out to put them right, only to overhear a fierce, muttered exclamation, Oh, for God's sake come on!' I never saw or heard from Gibson again. We had met several times since the voyage home from Rhodesia, and we had been drawn to one another. In a different situation, I might have married him and gone to Africa with him. But I was really leading a double life, my own and Katherine's, and I should not have dreamt of leaving her. She must have understood that that afternoon, but as far as I can remember we never discussed it.

As the summer of 1919 went by and the weather changed, it became clear that Katherine must leave her home and go to a better climate for the winter. She and Sorapure had discussed a summer house in the garden but both of them saw the impossibility of it. He said that she could not survive the winter mists

* He received £1000 a year, as KM indicates in her letter of 21st October, 1920, to JMM from Menton.

and London fog, which in those days crept up even to Hampstead.

So it was decided that she and I should go south and that Jack would accompany us for the journey. This time San Remo was chosen; we fixed on a hotel because it was kept by an Englishman.

CHAPTER XII

San Remo – Ospedaletti – Villa Flora – Menton: September 1919 – April 1920

On 14th September 1919 JMM took KM and LM to San Remo. It was agreed that he would fetch Katherine home again eight months later in May, and that meanwhile he would look for 'The Heron', the home in the country that since the summer of 1916 they had longed to own 'once the war was over'. It was named after KM's brother Chummie (Leslie Heron Beauchamp) and was the dream they had put their trust in when Katherine had to leave Murry to escape the English winters. It became the pledge of their love for each other and hope for their future. The visit abroad this winter, 1919–20, was the first time since they had met in 1912 that KM planned to be away from JMM for a long period, with only LM for companion and with the certain knowledge that she now had consumption. It led to great stress.

Meanwhile JMM stayed on at 'The Elephant', looked after by Violet the maid and with Sydney Waterlow, another Athenaeum *contributor (who had also appeared in* The Blue Review), *as his co-occupant. Murry continued to edit the* Athenaeum, *while KM from Italy continued to write her weekly review.*

We set out in September and all I remember of the journey to San Remo was that it seemed interminable and that I was very worried about Katherine's fatigue. The constant question of expense was also a great burden, and conscious of this I made a stupid mistake on that journey. We three were sitting down to a meal and not being very hungry, I asked for a simple egg at supper, thinking it would not be so dear as the elaborate sounding items on the menu. After a long time, while I sat uncomfortably in front of an empty place and the other two had almost finished, an enormous soufflé omelette arrived costing, if anything, more than the prepared dishes.

The hotel at San Remo seemed clean and quiet, and so after two weeks Jack left us and returned to 'The Elephant' and the two cats, Wingly and Athenaeum.

Katherine's cough was troublesome, and it became noticeable to the staff and guests that she had tuberculosis. Very soon an apologetic manager came to us and said he was sorry but he must ask us to leave; his other guests were complaining, not just because of the cough, but because of the danger of infection. He was distressed, etc. Yet another blow for Katherine, so soon after the strain of the journey: she was an outcast, an undesirable, as well as being very ill. She hardly seemed to know which was the worse; and there was yet another indignity – she had to pay to have the room disinfected.

But the hotel manager proved a friend and help in trouble, though I think he did himself a service at the same time. He had 'a small chalet on the hillside at Ospedaletti; a beautiful view and very comfortable, with a bathroom and all one could desire.' He 'would be glad to let it to us . . . ' The situation with its privacy sounded ideal, so an agreement was quickly reached and, at more cost, we packed and were transported to the Casetta Deerholm at Ospedaletti.

It was all, or nearly all, that he had said: it was high above the sea and the road running round the coast was below and out of sight. But alas the water was not running. This meant no baths, and for days I had to carry all we needed up from a spring by the roadside below us. The furnishing was simple in the extreme and the chalet was really small; Katherine's sitting-room was tiny, with only one other room for meals and daily living. There was a little kitchen, too, with a row of copper pots, pretty to look at, but a real agony to me. They blackened with use and had to be scrubbed regularly; with no scouring powder, I had to resort to sand from the hillside. There was only a charcoal stove; fun, perhaps, if it did not matter how long you waited for meals . . . or tea . . . or hot-water bottles. How did you light the contraption? How did you keep it alight? The humiliating thing was that Katherine could have managed it perfectly, after her experience at Bandol. 'It's really quite easy', she said. For the open fires we had to buy large quantities of wood, which was very expensive and sometimes green and quite damp; and the woodman cheated.

The chalet and the village below it overlooked a smal bay of the Mediterranean surrounded by high hills, as though at some time there had been a terrific landslide of the cliffs into the sea, making a completely sheltered sun trap. Where the bay opened out, the hills sloped back, covered with aromatic grasses and herbs. In the sunshine there was a rich scent of honey.

Our garden – really no more than a terrace cut out of the hill-side beside the house – was quite delightful. A small lawn ran across it and all around were beds of flowering plants. I remember particularly the quantities of cyclamen, with their daintily nodding heads of many shades. The grassy hill sloped away in every direction, and beside the gate to the house stood a cotton bush, the seed pods of which burst open while we were there, covering the whole bush with gleaming white tufts that reminded Katherine of her homeland. She made much use of the little garden and occasionally, very occasionally, ventured out of the gate and down into the town. There on a lower terrace, where one or two hotels stood, she would rest and look at 'the world' before undertaking the wearisome climb back.

The stay at Ospedaletti should have been so enchanting. It would have been a perfect place for a happy young couple, but Katherine was suffering from a low fever all the time we were there, with a good deal of pain as a result. She was frustrated at every turn by her weakness and fighting an always losing battle for her health. Small problems seemed immense. Still, here we were and here we had to stay for several months at any rate.

Katherine was desperately lonely too. Jack would not write or come over, nor, in spite of her request, did he trouble to send her the newspapers he had been reading, with perhaps a comment in the margin on an item which he found of interest. Each day I went down the hill to the little post office, coming back with the same 'No Katie, no letters!'

I could never understand what made Murry so cruel and thoughtless during these months. I don't think Katherine knew either, which in some ways made it worse for her. He was young and, perhaps, not a very strong character, and he suffered not only for Katherine, but for himself when he saw her so ill. He seemed to look into himself and not into her, and perhaps her absence, in what should have been a perfect place, relieved him of some tension which unconsciously he was unwilling to take up again. It is impossible to know.

I was quite unable to provide her with the mental support she needed, and that sense of powerlessness affected me in – well, really in my heart. I became apprehensive and uncertain. It was at this time Katherine found she could not bear the sound of my tired voice calling up the stairs: 'Katie, the woodman has come. He wants seven francs more this time,' or. 'Katie, there are no posts, some trouble between England and Italy.' I had always called her Katie – it was my mother's name, but now it was changed to KM or occasionally Katherine. We both tried to think of someone who could come and take my place to ease the tension, but there was no one. We discussed it – our relationship made this possible.

We did, however, have one wonderful thing which we could share: at certain times the waves of the sea would break at the far point of the bay, low and loud, making a strange orchestra. Katherine said she could distinguish the different instruments, though I could only hear the general music.

Katherine's longing for music was always unsatisfied. In those days there was no wireless, no contact with the outside world; and moreover, at Ospedaletti, no bookshops. Katherine had to make do with her copy of Shakespeare, which she read constantly, making many notes in the margins. (This copy was later sent to her cousin Elizabeth, by Katherine's wish.)

We were at Ospedaletti during just that period of anti-British feeling which followed the war. At its height, it cut off all communication between Italy and England and caused anyone English to be scowled at and counted an enemy. The consequence was, of course, that we were unavoidably forced even closer together and that Katherine felt doubly lonely. Her only other friends were a few English people: a man who had a large rose garden on the opposite side of the bay, a doctor, and a charming household of English women, who paid visits though Katherine herself could never get to them. They had mutual interests and Katherine enjoyed their calls. I was always anxious about Katherine if I had to go a long distance away – to Ventimiglia, for instance. The itineraries were complicated and the buses very infrequent, and Katherine hated to be left alone. Indeed on one occasion when I was away in Ventimiglia someone had come to the front door and, finding it open, had taken an overcoat from the little hall. Katherine had heard nothing.

She always kept a small revolver in her sitting-room which was near the front door. One day when I was out, the Englishman of the rose garden called to see her. He knew the local people well, and on leaving, he glanced at her revolver and said, 'What's the use of that? They'd knock it out of your hand in a minute.' Probably quite true, as her wrist and arm were very frail and weak in her feverish condition. But it was not comforting to be told this.

My room was on the opposite side of the little house from Katherine's and I always slept on the sofa in her room at night for by then she was quite nervous alone. She slept under a mosquito net, as a mosquito bite would have been very serious for her, and often I would get up to track down and kill a 'monster' that had somehow got inside.

One evening she was lying in bed, strangely still for a very long time, so long that I feared she was skipping away across the thin border-line between life and death. But she came back, and in quite a full voice said, 'I have had a most wonderful dream. I dreamt I was dead and was walking in a garden. The flowers were so beautiful, with glowing colours, more lovely than I have ever seen or imagined.' That night she seemed very peaceful.*

We were really isolated up on the hill, and so our fear was quite natural and rather overwhelming when, late on another night, we heard steps on the gravel round the house. The hill rose so steeply behind the house that it was comparatively easy to spring on to the sloping roof of the shed which reached nearly up to Katherine's bedroom window. Katherine was in bed when the door bell rang. With beating heart I went down to the door and asked in my best French, 'Qui va la?' No answer. Again I spoke and there was no answer. So I went back to Katherine and we waited. For quite a while nothing happened, and through the window of her room I kept watch over the roof. About an hour later the bell was rung again. This time Katherine gave me the revolver and I called again and again out of the window, punctuating my 'Qui va la?' with pistol shots. That was the end. We never had an explanation –

* This is probably the dream that KM refers to in her *Journal* for 15th December 1919.

except that someone suggested that a slug might have passed over the electric doorbell!

The next morning we called in the *blanchisseuse*, who had had a good deal of conversation with Katherine, to help us find some boy or man to come and sleep in the cottage. She did: a brother or cousin who took a fantastic fee from Katherine's very slender purse.

The *blanchisseuse* was an attractive, gay young French girl. She lived farther down the hill and came to take the washing and bring the milk and, above all, talk. She was a great comfort and help to Katherine, for she carried her head high and laughed.

Another visitor, however, was completely useless: a French doctor. He spent his visits in outrageous flirtation, perhaps believing that a sick woman needed this to cheer her. But he did say it was totally pointless to stay in the south; she needed the bracing, snow-cleaned air of the Alps.

Each morning I went down to the market to buy our food. The Italian money was difficult to get used to and Katherine was told that I was known as 'the English woman who never counts her change!' Katherine had been forced by circumstances to be so meticulous that she found this outrageous.

The money situation had by now become critical. Legally Katherine was Murry's responsibility and to the official mind he should have been supporting her; but, he never did. By now she had also to support me. And so she decided to write to Mr Kay, the London bank manager, to tell him of her situation and ask if it were possible for her to have any help, or perhaps a loan. Since Mr Beauchamp's other daughters were then receiving large allowances at Mr Kay's importuning, her father raised her allowance to £260 a year, which certainly helped a little.

All this time Connie Beauchamp, a cousin of Katherine's father, and her friend Jinnie Fullerton were staying in luxury at their house the Villa Flora in Menton, just over the border on the French Riviera.

These two women had been converted to Roman Catholicism many years earlier and had become firm friends, running a large and expensive nursing home in Hampstead for a good many years. Connie was an old-fashioned English lady, to my mind sincere and certainly kind. Jinnie, her friend, was tall, slender and commanding. Her great aim was to gather converts for her adopted faith, and since with her gift for nursing, she surrounded her patients with sympathy and the relaxing influence of every luxury, in this she had been extremely successful. Indeed, she was once allowed to kiss the Pope's hand in a special audience as a reward for all her work.

They both came over to Ospedaletti one day to see Katherine, and took her for a drive. Then in November, during one of his periodic visits to Europe Mr Beauchamp went to visit the two friends at Menton, and it was decided that they would all come to lunch with us at Ospedaletti.

That dreadful lunch! Five people squeezed into that tiny room! As cook, I suffered from fright and produced ten times too much onion and not enough chops. However, the stewed fruit with cream was fool-proof. But Katherine had *so* wanted to impress them.

They went for a drive afterwards, and her father related humorously that he had just been robbed of £50: 'Just imagine, the chap just took my notebook out of my pocket. Can't think how he did it.' This had impressed him more than the loss. I had quite hoped that he would be generous and bring Katherine a present, but he went away and gave her nothing – except I believe, the sense of a closer relationship between them. I bitterly counted up how much that lunch had cost!

Some time after that Connie and Jinnie wrote suggesting that Katherine might like to go to Menton to recuperate in their charge. I think Connie was genuinely upset at the obvious discomfort and hardships of Katherine's life at a time when she was so ill. Their villa in Menton was all one could wish for on a holiday in the south; spacious and lovely and beautifully situated among the sweet-scented hills above the Mediterranean.

As winter drew on Katherine became more and more restless and unhappy because of Murry's absence and silence. As Christmas approached she wrote to him and asked if he would come. He said he could not, and she was deeply disappointed and hurt. Just when she had woven his answer into her days, he suddenly changed his mind and decided to visit her. He came, but something had happened, I do not know what, and he brought no happiness. The days of those two weeks were shadowed and, contrary to my expectation, he spent his nights in the little spare room.

Katherine said I must wait till all was quiet and then creep with my rugs into her room to sleep as usual on the sofa. She evidently did not wish him to know of my presence. He often hurt her like this, and the hurt was too deep for a quick cure. In the beginning of January he left.

From her letters, in September 1919, it is clear that, as usual, Katherine at first wrote cheerfully to JMM; after two weeks the mood of her correspondence became lonely and depressed, and by the end of October it had reached a black despair. JMM must have said he would pack up the Athenaeum *and come out at Christmas, for Katherine in a letter at the beginning of November, when she had recovered her spirit, begged him not to. A month later the intense depression returned and on 4th December 1919 she wrote the bitter verses accusing JMM of abandoning her, which definitely decided him to come at Christmas. Again she begged him not to, but none the less he arrived on 16th December. This must be the occasion to which LM refers.*

During the past two years since the beginning of 1918, when she realised she had consumption, and especially during these three months alone at Ospedaletti, Katherine had been acutely aware of death. This had made her cling to her love for JMM and the hope of The Heron. But Murry's letters in response to her poem of 4th December in particular and her bitter despair in general, forced Katherine to come to terms with her situation. In her Journal for 15th December 1919 she wrote: 'After a few days J's letters in response to my *depressed letters began to arrive. As I grew depressed, he grew depressed, but not for me. He began to write (1) about the suffering I caused him: his suffering, his nerves, he wasn't made of whipcord or steel, the fruit was bitter for him. (2) a constant cry about money. He had none; he saw no chance of getting any – heavy debts" – "as you know I am a bankrupt". "I know it sounds callous." "I can't face it." These letters, especially the letters about money, cut like a knife through something that had grown up between us. They changed the situation for me, at least, for ever.' This proved to be the breaking point of her old child-love for Murry: it was to be built anew. A deeper certainty had to be found and it was now that her own work, her writing, came to the fore.*

After Murry's visit to her that Christmas, Katherine wrote

The Man without a Temperament (Arts and Letters, *Spring 1920*) *and began* The Wrong House *which was never completed. These were the only stories she was able to write while she was in Italy, (though two of her poems were published in the* Athenaeum *in January*).

In the New Year, Katherine decided that she would stay with Connie and Jinnie at Menton. I think it was the feeling that everything was impossible for her, that she was bound by her weakness and fever and pain, which made her depend so much on others, even though she loathed this dependence. It became a burden from which she could not free herself. She needed someone from outside, and of course she also needed a little comfort and luxury. Later, much later, we talked of Ospedaletti and noticed how we remembered only the pleasant things.

So, in January 1920 the time came for us to leave the cottage. I went to Ventimiglia, the border town between Italy and France, to get visas, and somehow obtained a hired car for us. Our driver announced that he could not possibly go by the main sea road; that because of the violence of the anti-British feeling, it would not be safe or indeed possible to take English ladies into France by that route. So we had to climb up miles of mountain road to a small unfrequented post to cross the border, then down again the other side; all the while anxiously wondering how much more this detour was going to cost. In the end we got there safely: but not to the Villa Flora, for Jinnie Fullerton had decided to put Katherine into a clinic – a grand hotel for the wealthy sick. She and Connie were expecting a patient from their London nursing home and thought that this woman might object to having a tubercular case with her in the villa. For poor Katherine, exhausted by the journey, her happy anticipation was ended with this blow.

I was taken in at the Villa Flora in Katherine's place. Miss Fullerton came, graciously, to my room in the evening to 'see if I was comfortable' and to make searching inquiries about Katherine and her affairs. No doubt she assumed that someone so unsophisticated and simple would reveal all. But I was always silent concerning Katherine, and refused to be drawn. In consequence, though for the few days that I stayed with them they were politely charming, I was out of favour.

Very soon they discovered how much Katherine detested any form of sanatorium life, and as the London rest-cure patient now gave her assent, she was moved into the Villa Flora. I was placed in rooms in the town. Then Jinnie found a job for me in a nursing home in Menton, which I was glad to take.

When everyone had settled down after these rearrangements, a new rhythm started for Katherine and me. I would go round to the Villa Flora in the evenings, when I was off duty from my clinic, and make my way quickly to Katherine's room. If she were there, we would talk a little. The tensions of Ospedaletti had now all disappeared and she would tell me about what had been happening that day, and about Connie and Miss Fullerton as well. I felt happy to know that she was wonderfully cared for; they were certainly very capable and efficient. They did much for Katherine at a time when her need was desperate, and helped to bring back her strength and spirit.

Later Jinnie Fullerton permitted me to use my experience in hair-brushing on one of her patients, which made me a little money; but her final criticism of me to Katherine was: 'She will never set the Thames on fire.' Quite true: I never have.

At my nursing home I was working for two more ordinary, but extremely nice English women, and I thoroughly enjoyed it. On the staff, in my charge, were two young girls from a Belgian orphanage, whom I suspect were very much alone in the world. They became embarrassingly attached to me and tried to run away to join Katherine and me when we had to return to England. Katherine was interested in my activities and therefore she, no less than I, was distressed by this incident.

Connie and Jinnie took Katherine for long, quiet drives into the country round Menton, and Katherine was happy in the peace and beauty of the place. She and Jinnie had long and intimate conversations for Jinnie was an interesting clever woman and she was trying to win Katherine's allegiance to the Catholic faith. Katherine listened and was impressed and once nearly made up her mind to join the Church. I found this letter waiting for me on the table by Katherine's bed one evening after she and Jinnie had been for a long drive in the hills, spending the whole day in the sunshine.

My dear Jones,

I want to tell you a secret but I cannot when we are face to face.
I feel you know what it is. But the fact is all I can tell you now.
Later on, I'll laugh about it and talk about it and you can make
fun of me but just at present Jones I'm so sensitive that I couldn't
even bear to hear you say you have got this letter. I tremble with
shyness – that is *dead true*, my dear. Later on, I promise it won't
be so, but for the present will you forgive me if I ask you not to
even breathe a word of it to me.

This afternoon when we were lying on the hills (I'll tell you all
about it one day) I knew there was a God. There you are.

One day (before I go back to England, I hope), I mean to be
received into the Church. I'm going to become a Catholic. Once
I believe in a God, the rest is so easy. I can accept it all *my own
way* – not 'literally' but symbolically: it's all quite easy and beautiful. But unless one really believes in a God even though it is tempting to have that great inward gate opened – it is no good.

I mean to make life wonderful if I can. Queer, Jones, I've always
a longing to *heal* people and *make them whole*, enrich them: that's
what writing means to me – to enrich – to give – I want to do it in
life too.

I shall tell Jack this, some time. Perhaps not for a long time.

Perhaps I shall just leave him to find out. But you can't live
near me and not know it and yet I could not bear you even to
refer to a *book* I read. Do you understand this? I am so sorry to be
so dreadfully secret and sensitive.

But I tell you for another reason too – and that's because you're
my 'sworn friend' as they say – Jones, I am not at all well yet –
terribly nervous and exacting and always in pain – But I'll get
over it – But I need you and I rely on you – I lean hard on you –
yet I can't thank you or give you anything in return – except my
love. You have that always.

Katie.

She never did, in fact, join the Roman Catholic Church, and it
was only later, after returning to England, that she began to dis-
count the almost mesmeric power of Jinnie Fullerton and her
surroundings. To me, this letter is one of my most treasured

possessions, for I too have always known 'there is a God', though we never spoke more of this to each other.

In these weeks at Menton KM seems to have reached the crisis in herself, begun at Ospedaletti, and finally accepted. Thenceforth her attitude changes; her letters to Murry become more restrained, more loving, and she speaks in them of LM with affectionate acceptance. Indeed, in her letter to JMM of 14th January 1920 she acknowledges her bond with LM and admits that now she can no longer do without her.

While staying with Connie Beauchamp and Jinnie Fullerton KM wrote The Second Helping *(not collected under this title),* Daphne *(unpublished) and some biographical notes on Chekhov (Athenaeum, January 1920.). She also listed a number of stories for publication, which she was prepared to sell to Grant Richards for £20. JMM was against this and approached Michael Sadleir at Constable. They offered £40 in advance of royalties, and the result was fourteen stories published under the title* Bliss *later that year.*

Grant Richards had visited KM at Menton at the end of February and told her that the writer Sydney Schiff, known as a writer under the name Stephen Hudson, and his wife Violet were also staying there. This was the beginning of a warm friendship for KM, which was to develop when she returned to Menton the next winter.

So the lovely Mediterranean days slipped by, until the end of April 1920 found us back at Hampstead, where Katherine took up life again as before and where we stayed for five months.

The summer of 1920 was the last we were to spend in the beautiful home Katherine had made at 'The Elephant', indeed it was the last time she was to have her home in England at all. She planned to winter again at Menton with Connie and Jinnie, and she did not return to London until the summer of 1922, in the last months of her life.

CHAPTER XIII

Villa Isola Bella, Menton:
September 1920 – May 1921

During the summer in Hampstead, KM had a story published each month in the Athenaeum; *Revelations (*June*), The Escape (*July*), Bank Holiday (*August*) and Sun and Moon (*September*). Earlier in April, a translation of Chekhov's Diary which she had worked on with Koteliansky also appeared in the* Athenaeum. *Her book* Bliss *was published by Constable before she left London in September and the reviews were sent on to her at Menton. There were eight in all, and some were highly favourable, acclaiming her brilliant.*

In September when she returned to Menton with LM, JMM stayed on at Portland Villas, with Milne now for company and looked after by Violet the maid. It was agreed that he would join them for Christmas. From September to December KM continued to send stories back monthly to the Athenaeum.

Murry was busy editing the *Athenaeum,* so this time he did not accompany us to France. We made the long journey alone and without mishap, reaching our destination in the early evening of 13th September 1920.

Connie and Jinnie had by now given up the Villa Flora and were established in a new house on the opposite side of the bay. They rented us the little Villa Isola Bella which lay at the end of their grounds. That first evening they kindly sent down to us Marie, their cook, to see if all was well. Katherine was shaken and tired and we had only brought enough food for the journey. A small leg of chicken was left from our lunch, so I dropped it into a saucepan with some water, hoping to make a soup. It was simmering away when Marie arrived. She spoke briefly to Katherine, and then came into the kitchen to see how things were. She seized my saucepan – 'Tch, tch, how long has this been cooking?' she demanded.

In two minutes the chicken was through a sieve, the stock was thickened and flavoured and a beautiful bowl of soup was ready!

Marie had sized us up, and taken pity on us. Yes, she thought she could get a maid for us; a friend might come. This friend proved to be another Marie, slim and elderly with a fine wrinkled face and dark, sharp eyes that missed nothing. She had a delightfully wicked little smile, a fineness of perception and wit and a genuine gift for flower arrangement. Her dinner table was a joy to look at. Katie delighted in her conversation; she was exactly the kind of woman she liked to have near her.

We found, however, that things in the kitchen had a surprising way of disappearing and her weekly bills would not bear looking into. When I once expostulated that I had only just given out a large box of sugar lumps, she threw up her hands and, almost in tears, went to Katherine to give notice. Katherine knew what had happened and was prepared: she 'would not part with her for anything'. So that was settled and Marie became a fixture. I think in the end she became truly devoted to Katherine and was very happy in her work, especially later on when Murry joined us.

Isola Bella was on the steep side of a hill, so that the property was on two levels, with a terrace at the front of the house surrounded by a stone balustrade. On the east side there was a garden with flower beds and shrubs, shielded from the rising road by a high stone wall. From the west side a curved stone stairway led to the lower garden and sheds, from where there was a small shady path winding up the hill to the big villa. Katherine explored all this terrain gradually, but stayed mainly on the terrace. We bought a chaise longue and a large striped umbrella on a stand. These we put on the terrace, the chaise-longue spread with a big karosse of flying-squirrel skins which my father had brought home from Africa. Here Katherine would sit and read or write most of the day, when the weather was warm enough.

Below the villa and away to the west spread the modern town of Menton, and across the bay the yellow walls of the old Saracen dwellings clung to the steep slopes of the distant headland. Between, the blue sea lay, held in the embrace of the two towns.

Katherine loved her gracious little house; she was at peace there, and so she was able to write many stories. As she was very

feverish most of the time she would go to bed early, sitting up below the looped mosquito nets at her writing. Many evenings and
nights I slept – or rather waited half-asleep – in the next room with
the door open, in case she called. I remember the night she
finished *The Daughters of the Late Colonel*, that gentle caricature
of her cousin Sylvia Payne and me, which she wrote in about three
or four hours with hardly a break or correction. 'It's finished!
It's finished!' She called. 'Celebration with tea!' It was 3 o'clock
in the morning, and we sipped tea in her room with the pale morning light gleaming through the golden sprays of the mimosa trees,
which grew tall and fernlike outside the terrace.

Katherine still struggled with the reviews for the *Athenaeum*.
They had to be done by a certain date, whether she was ill or not,
and she found most of the books so dull, so impossible to write
about with interest. Our life out there was costing a great deal,
and that £10 she received from them meant so much. Then,
suddenly, the money ceased to come. She wrote and still it did
not come. Whether Jack had just forgotten or had not enough to
send I never could understand; certainly, since Katherine's departure, the paper had shown signs of the lack of her controlling
hand. I remember her walking by the garden wall telling me about
it and saying, 'It's too bad'. She loved him, but he gave her a great
deal of trouble. He could not really live alone for long, even in his
beloved England. He got bogged down in his own personal problems, even his critical literary work seemed to become shaky;
that was why the *Athenaeum* went to pieces when Katherine was
not there.

*These three months from October to December were the first period
of an astonishing spate of stories from KM. In addition to the weekly
reviews she wrote,* The Young Girl (Athenaeum, *October 1920*),
Miss Brill (Athenaeum, *November 1920*), The Lady's Maid (Athenaeum, *December 1920*), The Stranger (London Mercury, *January
1921*), The Daughters of the Late Colonel (London Mercury,
May 1921), Poison (*posthumously published* Colliers, *November 1923*)
and possibly also at this time The Singing Lesson (*published first
with* Garden Party, *February 1922*) *and* Life of Ma Parker (The
Nation, *February 1921*).

By the first week in December, KM had seriously overtaxed her strength, and the local doctor, Dr Bouchage, stipulated rest. She wrote immediately to JMM to say that she could no longer continue her reviewing – those appearing on 10th December were the last she wrote. Murry was proposing to resign his editorship in the new year, a plan which they would discuss when he arrived for Christmas.

Just a few days before Jack came, Katherine called me to show me a letter which she had just received from Elizabeth Bibesco.* Katherine was shocked beyond measure, for Princess Bibesco had written a letter blaming Katherine for her treatment of Murry: how could she, a sick woman, away in France and quite unable to make any kind of life or happiness for Murry, how dared she try to hold him, to keep him tied etc, etc. I have quite forgotten the words, but that was the gist of it. It was the letter of a jealous woman, with a suggestion of intimacies which may or may not have been true. Katherine knew Murry had met Princess Bibesco and seen a certain amount of her, but this was a dreadful revelation. She grieved, not that Murry knew her, – this she accepted – but that he had not been open about it, had not told her the extent of the relationship; the furtiveness was what hurt Katherine most.

She wrote to Jack immediately, asking for an explanation. She became ill with the delay and the anxiety, and then Murry came. He went up to her room and was there for a long time. Then as I went up to my own room, I met him coming downstairs, almost slipping down. I tried to speak but he went on past me, and left the house.

Later that day Katherine came to me and said that I must never, never forgive Jack for what he had done to her. She could not have laid such an injunction on me had she not been most desperately wounded. Looking back I can only feel that his behaviour was wholly due to his insecurity, his need for someone to give him assurance, and in choosing Princess Bibesco, he had chosen wrongly.

* Princess Bibesco, daughter of the first Earl of Oxford and Asquith, married to a Rumanian aristocrat. She contributed to the *Athenaeum* (her story *An Ordinary Man* appeared as the main short story feature in the 14th January number 1922.) She was for a time in love with Murry.

From Katherine's letters and journal it seems that JMM came to Menton twice this winter; once from 17th or 18th December until 11th January, and a second time from 19th January to the beginning of February.

KM apparently knew JMM was seeing someone in London (though the person is referred to in her letters as 'A'), and she tells him to feel free, but not tell her about it. Her entry in her journal for 19th December and the few preceeding and just after this, all show her struggling to come to terms with a painful truth; by 22nd December she has obviously learnt to accept and to transmute it.

The second visit was, according to JMM, due to a sudden relapse on KM's part, though the letters published for this time, say nothing. In the course of these visits it was decided that JMM should definitely resign from the Athenaeum. *He went to London at the beginning of February to wind up his connection with the paper, which merged with* The Nation; *JMM continued to write for it weekly. He was back with Katherine again in Menton by the middle of February.*

Jack seemed to come and go at Isola Bella at the beginning of that year. Once he came on what must have been a long visit: they were happy, I gathered, and Marie excelled herself, playing up to Jack and enjoying them both.

There was only one bedroom beside Katherine's, so we found an Italian couple living up the road who could give me a bed and meals. It was a new and interesting experience for me: a peasant home with great yellow pumpkins hanging over trellis-work arches, and wonderful Italian pasta for dinner; I learnt all the names for the many different varieties. The woman of the house made butter in a long hollowed log, pumping up and down with a thick wooden block like a rolling pin. It was fascinating, though all very unhygienic by our standards.

Often Murry and Katherine were very happy together, but frequently he was depressed and his moodiness was sometimes too much for her; then she could only grieve. She once wrote to Violet Schiff from Isola Bella: 'This morning . . . Murry arrived. I feel fearfully sorry for him, overwhelmingly so. I did not realize myself until this morning the extent of his need.'

Katherine had met the Schiffs when she stayed at Villa Flora in the April of 1920. They had a villa at Rocquebrune, not far away, and now that she had come to stay at Isola Bella their friendship was a great delight and comfort to her.

Katherine felt the Schiffs *understood*, and I know their appreciation of JMM meant much to Katherine; she could write of him freely to them: 'My money is on JMM as THE English Critic. I agree, he makes mistakes sometimes; he's rash, he's not steady yet; he leaps before he looks. But there is a sign – a something in what he writes. Hurra for JMM. Murry with all thy faults I love thee still, and I mean as a *critic* please. He's the man of the future I'm sure. He risks himself.' And later: 'Your understanding of Murry is of course simply too amazing. It is your great *gift* – this "finding" the secret of another's being.'*

When they came to Isola Bella, the Schiffs had soon realised Katherine's financial difficulties. They were very well off and accustomed to much luxury, and later on, anxious to do something for Katherine, they left her a sum of money in a Paris bank for her use.

Katherine was very happy with these friends, and they exchanged visits and letters continuously. It is significant that when writing to the Schiffs she always spoke of me as 'Jones' – the private name we used between ourselves. I remember driving with her on one of her visits to see them and while she was at their house I amused myself by exploring the surroundings. The colours of the steep red cliffs going straight down into the blue sea were almost startling, and there was a strange and beautiful tree in their garden. Sometimes, however, although she loved to be with them, she was too ill to make the effort. Then she would have to spend days in bed, in great pain and weakness, with a high temperature, and the doctor would have to be called.

One occasion remains vividly in my mind. We were returning in an open horse-drawn carriage from seeing the doctor at the clinic where she had had some minor but very painful treatment, when it began to rain. The *cocher* put up the hood and fixed the apron over us and Katherine sat back, tired out. Suddenly, as we turned in at the gate, she gave an exclamation. The long grasses by the roadside were trembling with raindrops. She never went out in the rain now and it was a long time since she had seen

* KM's letter to Violet and Sidney Schiff from Isola Bella 1920 and January 1921, published Adam International Review, Number 300 at the Curwen Press, 1965.

such a thing. Her joy was intense, beyond all the pain and fatigue.

At Isola Bella Katherine and I once spoke of our friendship and wondered how it was that it did not now flower. At that period we were baffled, but I think that now, after all these years, I can see more clearly. Those rare moments of joy came when we were, as Katherine once put it in a letter, 'so beautifully US'; then we were filled with peace and all was well. But for the bud to flower it needed the sunshine of an inner peace; and I had no confidence. I was always needing assurance to know that all was well, and demanding a fuller expression of her feeling. Yet there was nothing, yes nothing, that I would not have done to have made one moment of her life more easy, more free and safe.

In March 1921, while Jack was still at the Villa Isola Bella, I went to London finally to shut up Portland Villas, which Violet the maid had been looking after, and to pack, sort, and sell or store all their belongings. It all seemed rather sad. Jack did not want to be there alone and Katherine could not live in England; besides it was too expensive. Also Jack had somehow lost Wingly, Katherine's beloved cat and he had to be found.

These letters which I received while I was at Hampstead throw, for me now, a new light on this woman who, living intensely in all the beauty she found around her, fought so bravely against her illness. She seemed to cut through any falseness or furry edges sharply, yet always with an underlying tenderness.

Tuesday.

This is just a note to let you know that *tout va bien à la maison*. It is the late afternoon of an exquisite day. That heavy, evening rain that made waterspouts of Jack's trousers fell like a blessing upon the garden. When I went out today the air smelt like moss, and there was a bee to every wallflower. The peach leaves are like linnet wings; the branches of the fig are touched with green, the bush of may is just not in flower, I had to lift up the daffodils and set them on their legs again and to give a finger to the reclining freezias. But nothing had come to harm. As to that white rose bush over the gate and the gas meter it is sprinkled with thousands of tiny satin-fine clusters. This is a darling little garden when one can get out of one's shell and look at it. But what does it profit a man to look at anything if he is not *free*? Unless one is free to offer oneself up wholly and solely to the pansy – one receives nothing. It's promiscuous love instead of a living relationship – a dead thing. But there it is —— And my gland is a great deal more swollen for some reason. The blood goes on tapping squeezing through like a continual small hammering, and all that side of my head is numb. It's a vile thing.

I hope you had a good journey. Will you please wire me immediately if you want any money and I'll wire it to you. I am now v. serious. Don't go to other people first. I can so easily overdraw for now; I don't care a button. But you must feed properly in London – eat nourishing food – not scones and coffee – and you must take taxis. Don't buy things in bags and eat them. Make Violet cook you porridge, bacon and eggs for breakfast. That climate is the devil. And wear a thick scarf when you go out and change your shoes and stockings when you come in. And burn the anthracite. And get people to come and see you if you want to see them and make Violet cook for them. I feel you will never be sensible enough to keep warm, dry shod and fed. I have no confidence in you.

I wish I were back in that Hampstead house – wafted to the top landing – allowed to linger on the stairs to look out of the windows to see if the lemon verbina is still alive. It should have been a perfect little house: it never came to flower. And the view of the willows – bare now – and the room that was mine – so lovely – the light was always like the light of a pale shell.

Tell me what happens. Take things easy. I beg you to wire me for money without hesitating. Don't work too hard.

Try and be happy; be sure to keep well.
Katherine.

(Confidential)

Sunday.

I really must tell you this or jump out of bed or out of the window. You'll appreciate it so. I paid the surgeon on the nail yesterday. That was all right. I'd expected to (only 100) but Jack came down and paid the cocher. When I said I'd paid the surgeon he replied "The *cocher* : , mine. I agreed on the price 20 franc beforehand." Just now – making out the weeks bills he asked me for 11 francs for the carriage – half – plus a 2 franc tip! I think its awful to have to say it. But fancy not paying for your wife's carriage to and from the surgery! Is that simply extraordinary or am I? I really am staggered. I think it is the meanest thing I ever heard of. It's not the fact which is so queer but the lack of fine feeling. I suppose if one fainted he would make one pay 3d for a 6d glass of salvolatile and 1d on the glass. That really does beat Father.

Things are serene otherwise. My head hurts but not more than is to be expected. Cousin Lou* has been in today. She is infinitely kind and affectionate. In fact she lavishes kindness on me in an old fashioned family way.

The old villain† is being as sweet as sugar. Hangs up my dresses, puts away my hats – brings up supper for 2 into this room without a murmur. I feel like Koteliansky when he says: "Let her be beaten – simply – but to death!" I hope to hear from you tomorrow.

Don't rush things. Keep well and be happy.

ALL IS WELL

Katherine.

. . . Friday (Later)   Menton 10.3.21

I haven't heard from you today. Again I have forgotten your letter for Broomies.‡ Here it is.

Bouchage came today and my neck was again tapped. But it was no go. He was not very satisfactory or helpful, I must say. I think he is tired of the patient for the moment. He has exhausted his not v. rich resources. But he did say most definitely that I can't stay here later than May. Positively not. This means, therefor, finding another place for four months at least. I should like tot ry Switzerland. It's not really fashionable and there are doctors

---

* Connie Beauchamp's sister.
† Marie, the maid at Isola Bella.
‡ A cottage on Chailey Common, Sussex, which JMM had actually bought in March, 1920, though they never lived in it.

there. Peira Cava, *par example* is no good. I couldn't bear hotels for so long and I don't imagine there is any medical man there. I feel Switzerland might be much the best place. Would you go and look at it for me? I mean – when you come back. Would you, as soon as possible – go off there and look for a v. small chalet? I shall write Marie Dahlerup to send me a list of places near Geneva. And perhaps there is a bureau – I am *sure* there is in London where you can get information. Do try and find one. The Swiss Consulate would put you on its tracks, wouldn't it? You see there is no time to be lost. Here's March over. There'll be nothing left if we leave it any longer. I had hoped *in a way, only,* not *really,* to stay off and on here until the end of July but its definitely out of the question. And I shan't come back here until the end of September. I have a vague idea I've seen advertised a *Swiss Information Bureau* but I can't be certain.

What about going to Switzerland from – No, you have a return ticket and besides one can't talk out such important plans from afar.

I think that's all. I'm sorry your little neffy is ill with malaria. How unfair for a child to have fever.

The weather has quite changed this last week. Spring has really 'set in' as they say. The air is different and now at night one hears, not one *moustique,* but a regular tuning up. I wish I could change too. Perhaps Switzerland will do the trick. In spite of what Bouchage says to the contrary I have a perpetual suspicion that this place is a bad place. Lovely, and dear, in a way, but *bad.* And it has caused these glands. For they are now plural – another having been discovered at the apex of the right lung, pressing on the bronchial tube. GOOD. I believe it may be all the fault of this relaxing climate. At any rate the climate is never helpful. You have to do all your own bracing, as it were. It clings round your neck. So help me to get to Switzerland soon – will you? And always we must behave as though J. were a visitor. Not a person to consult, or to expect from or to count on. If he comes along – he comes and that's all. Farewell. Katherine.

Thursday.
I shall try and reply to your two letters. I wish to Heaven you didn't refer some of these silly little points to me. It's really idiotic

to ask me if I wish to take the advice re cleaning of Shoolbred's man. Of course I do. Why not? Am I an idiot? They sound alright and satisfactory. Go ahead.

(a) Yes, sell matress of camp bed. Keep mattress of grey bed.

(b) I'll send a note to Broomies.

(c) Arthur had better have the writing paper for scribbling paper.

(d) Of course give the rabbit or any other small thing to the baby.

(e) Let both the wooden clocks go – especially the beehive one. I mean I do not want them kept.

Do you mean *destroy* by *put away?* Is that a delicate refined way of referring to the *morts des objets cheris.* I don't know? May I put them away? What does it mean? You'd scarcely be silly enough to destroy my old blotter if it were possible to keep it – and the velvet curtain you say has only one small hole. ∴ it's not bad enough to destroy. And does *keep* mean *store?* for I asked you to bring my Chinese skirt and yet I certainly don't want these other things. As to the remains of that rubbishy plaid velvet – I groan with horror at the thought of its perpetuity. It is extremely confusing. I have wired you about Jack's things. Its no good saying if you don't hear by Thursday you'll do so and so. Today is Thursday and your letter is only just come.

The weather is fine here. All is as usual. The house 'goes', and the servants are just the same. Please do not hurry back. That is my one really urgent cry. My health is also – the same.

Katherine.

But, as the result of this letter stop writing to me – *please.*

Sunday

D.I.

Your telegram about Wingly came late last night.* It was very thrilling. I long to know how he was found, and even more, if

* 'I had tramped the streets to search for Wingly and then I found him a few streets away sitting on the top of a wall with a bevy of enemies or admirers round him and looking rather dishevelled. I took him and Athenaeum to a vet nearby where they had to stay for several weeks.' LM

possible, what was the meeting like between Athy and him. I envy you seeing that. I hope you really saw it and tell me what happened. It is a great triumph to have found him. But now the question is – what to do with them? If we were not leaving for Switzerland I wouldn't hesitate. But all these train journeys – arriving at hotels – and so on? Would it be torture for cats? I feel the cat's first need is a settled home; a home that never changeth. And I know that is just what I am not going to have. At the same time the idea that they should be destroyed is *horrible*! . . . You see, just suppose you and I hear, when we are in Switzerland, of another place and decide to try it. Or decide to make a sea voyage. Or . . . so much is possible. We couldn't ever leave the cats with Jack and to take cats where they are not wanted is cruelty. I confess I don't see a way out. If Richard were older I'd suggest asking him to mind them. I'd better leave it like this. If when you have thought it over you decide it would be an unhappy life for them or unpractical for you – have them destroyed.

Elizabeth Bibesco has shown signs of life again. A letter yesterday begging him to resist Katherine. 'You have withstood her so gallantly so far how can you give way now.' And 'you swore nothing on earth should ever come between us'. From the letter I feel they are wonderfully suited and I hope he will go on with the affair. He *wants to*. 'How can I exist without your literary advice,' she asks. That is a very fascinating question. I shall write to the silly little creature and tell her I have no desire to come between them only she must not make love to him while he is living with me, because that is undignified. He'll never break off these affairs, tho', and I don't see why he should. I wish he'd take one *on* really seriously – and leave me. Every day I long more to be alone.

My life is the same. I get up at about 11. Go downstairs until 2. Come up and lie on my bed until five when I get back into it again. So I am infinitely worse than when I left England. There's no comparison. I wish I could consult Sorapure. It's all a great bother. I 'note' what you say about your Thursday letter. I'll destroy it.

I find it possible to speak to you today. I am not in despair about my health. But I must make every effort to get it better *soon*, very *soon*. You see Jack 'accepts' it; it even suits him that I should be so subdued and helpless. And it is deadly to know he

NEVER tries to help. But I was not born an invalid and I want to get well – I long for—— Do you understand? I feel every day must be the last day of such a life – but I have now felt that for years. Ida – let us both try. Will you? Bouchage has failed. Help me to escape!

Later

. . . I have decided to give up this villa for good and to really try Switzerland. I shall try and find that man *Spahlinger* and see if his treatment suits me. Jack goes to England in the first week of May. I have arranged with him not to return abroad, at any rate until the winter. But to spend the summer in the English country, with a bicycle. It would be *impossible* to have him in Switzerland while one was 'looking round' and deciding. I can imagine it too well. He is v. willing not to come. So we'll burn our French boats and go off together. I wish you could get Spahlinger's address or an address where the treatment is followed. But how can you? I don't know . . . I must now make a real effort to make money for this. Somehow, it *must* be done.

Take things easy – and look after yourself. I hope the little boy is better.

Yours,
Katherine.

Dear Ida,

I have not written to you quite lately because I did not know how soon you intended leaving London. All your letters have come.

Will you come here to morrow at about 10.30? Then I shall be free and able to talk to you in the salon. The early morning, here, is as you know rather a distracting time. I am v. anxious to hear your news.

In this month that you have been away I have discovered I am not nearly so in need of assistance as I thought I was. So will you, as far as possible, forget our relationship of the past four years and look on me *not* as a friend who needs looking after, but only as a friend?

I mean that in all its implications.

I hope you are not too tired after your journey.

Yours,
Katherine.

In April 1921 I returned to Isola Bella.

Katherine had hoped to be able to stay on at the villa but Cousin Connie and Miss Fullerton, perhaps influenced by the fact that Katherine had slipped through their religious fingers and was not converted, decided that they wanted the place for another friend. So her thoughts had turned towards Switzerland and the new treatment of which she writes in her letters. It would be high and she would have the clear air of the Alps; Isola Bella, as Dr Bouchage had already warned, was too low-lying and enervating for her lungs during the summer months.

In May, therefore, we left the lovely villa of Isola Bella, Murry returning to England where he had to deliver some lectures at Oxford,* and Katherine and I travelling to Baugy near Montreux.

* On 'The Problem of Style'.

CHAPTER XIV

Baugy – Sierre – Montana:
May 1921 – January 1922

Travelling was now more difficult for Katherine and there was little provision on the railways for a sick woman. I had to arrange everything beforehand: reserve seats, obtain foolproof tickets and visas, pack every little comfort she might need, and fill the picnic basket. One essential item was a small square clock which went with her everywhere; it always stood on the edge of the folding table under the window in the train. She set great store by this, for while we were in Menton I had lost the gold watch given me by my factory friends, and I don't believe Katherine had a wrist watch at any time. We started early because progress down the long platform was slow and Katherine must not be hustled by crowds; then, with every eventuality catered for, we settled down for the long hours of travel.

Baugy proved to be most unsatisfactory, with a hotel that was not very comfortable perched on a steeply sloping hillside, and I think Katherine must have been disappointed over the Spahlinger treatment, since she never heard very much from him.

It was at Baugy that we met Miss Franklin. She was a delightful, sincere woman on holiday from India, where she was working at a mission hospital. She wanted me to go back with her as housemother for the home. It would have been wonderful work, especially for me with my early memories of India and love of the people, and I found it hard to make her realise the impossibility of my leaving Katherine, who also liked Miss Franklin and appreciated her fine character. We corresponded for a long time and Katherine mentions her in one of her letters.

So we tried another place, Clarens, lower down and nearer to the lake of Geneva. While we were waiting there, uncertain what was best to be done, there was a great flower festival, honouring the narcissus which grew wild all over the lower slopes of the mountain – great sheets of the strongly scented little pheasant-eyed blossoms. People came in from all the country around with great bunches, and the roads seemed to be strewn with flowers. It was too much for Katherine to go down among the crowds, so I brought the flowers to her. I was never able to discover the mean- of the ceremony, though. When Katherine was ill or unhappy, I seemed unable to take note of outside things.

Katherine had heard of the little village of Montana-sur-Sierre up the Rhône valley and its wonderful curative powers. She de- cided to try it; and after I had been first on an exploratory visit to book rooms in the village of Sierre below Montana, we made our way up the wide Rhône valley. I think on that journey Kathe- rine regained hope. She enjoyed the valley with its endless suc- cession of little cone-like hills crowned by small castles, the spreading rich countryside so different from the low-lying south, and the view of the little silver streams which fall almost perpen- dicularly down the snow topped mountains.

In Sierre we had to rest awhile and wait for Dr Hudson, the English doctor from Montana who was coming down to see us. I had found rooms in a wide, cool, shadowy, peaceful hotel, Château Belle Vue, an old castle transformed without too much change into a hotel. There was a large entrance yard in front, large enough to have taken the coaches of earlier days, and a fine col- oured heraldic sign, the arms of some past owner, over the front door. Katherine had been given a room on the ground floor look- ing out on to a shady garden. Later, we found at the end of the long passage a wonderful circular room preserved from former times, with painted walls, deep, mullioned, grey stone windows, tapestries, a curtained, much carved four-poster bed and rich polished floor. Katherine would have liked to have had that room, but it was much too expensive.

She rested a day at Sierre before Dr Hudson arrived. He spoke promisingly of the air and virtues of Montana. A small funicular railway ran up the mountain to the village, which lay above the winter snow line and 2000 feet above us. Sierre was already 1,000 feet above sea level; as might have been expected, the greater altitude was to cause trouble to Katherine's heart after her long stay at sea level. It did.

Dr Hudson arranged that she should try a large clinic called the Palace, really a hotel for invalids; but when I went to see Katherine the next morning, I knew this could only be a very temporary arrangement. Luckily Dr Hudson's mother owned a chalet in Montana which she was not using, so we came to a satisfactory agreement: Chalet des Sapins was to be our home until the beginning of the next year.

It promised everything. The house was set among pine trees, overhanging the valley, and behind it the mountain rose up to the glaciers and the great heights of Switzerland. Katherine's occasional drives took her through pine woods, past a lake, and on to the open mountainside with its glorious views across the valley below, to the faraway mountains beyond, all snow covered in the winter. Then the wheels of the carriage could be detached, so that it became a comfortable sleigh.

Katherine's bedroom was at the top of the house with a large square balcony, to which came many birds from the woods to feed on the coconuts that we put out for them. The stairs kept her prisoner sometimes though, when she was not strong enough to climb up and down.

The living-dining room was on the first floor, which was not so bad for Katherine, but the bathroom was at ground level beside the kitchen, and this meant two flights of stairs which often she could not manage. So I would carry up a round tin bath and enormous bath towels and take them to her room, where I poured hot water over her, and wrapped her round to dry, much as her grandmother must have done twenty years earlier.

It was a friendly house and we were happy there; Katherine made it a real home for a while. She was getting stronger and more peaceful in herself, and hoped that her heart would stand the strain of the altitude. The quietness and good air refreshed her and she was able to go for short walks. She would come down if she was not working and take an interest in the little house; for instance, as I struggled to clean a big plate-glass door that had become dim, 'Methylated spirits!' said Katherine. She enjoyed the good vegetables I brought from the shops, and we used the cellar as an enormous refrigerator to keep piles of huge cabbages fresh for the coming winter.

Sometimes Elizabeth, Katherine's cousin, would visit us. She lived at Randogne about 1,000 feet below and would come walking over the snow in her little black gaiters.

In June Murry finished his Oxford lectures, and, as he had left the *Athenaeum* and had no home in England, he decided to join Katherine in Switzerland; he stayed with us in Montana all through that summer and winter until the following January.

As he had come, Katherine found a Swiss woman of 'very high birth' called Ernestine, to come and do the housework. Being of such high birth, when she went to a Festa she wore all the traditional family clothes with their elaborate embroideries, and looked wonderful. She was a kind girl, very solid in appearance, with the strong ankles and feet of a climber and a gentle smile, and she served us well, even if her cooking was strangely erratic. On one unforgettable day Katherine told her to roast a chicken whole instead of cutting it into joints. The English being so strange, she could not tell what they liked; so she cooked it whole, insides and all!

Now that Ernestine was established, I considered taking a job helping a young French woman in a clinic at the end of the village. Moreover, three was proving to be an uncomfortable number in so small a house, and soon we heard of a chalet in the village where I could get a room. But first, in August, I went to London. Katherine needed warmer clothes for the coming winter, and Wingly was to be collected from the vet in London.

I stayed there about a week before I returned with Wingly. He travelled all the way in a collar and lead, like a dog. He was a beautiful, lordly, black-and-white cat and when the train stopped, as it frequently did, he and I walked up and down the platform to the astonishment and admiration of the French countryfolk. But, somehow, I never could persuade him that the tarred platforms were made of grass, with the necessary soil for him to scratch with fine soft paws. I began to despair, till on one very long platform we found a little grassy garden – and all was well.

Eventually we arrived safely at the chalet in Montana, and Wingly settled in, rather as a king might graciously accept a country house as the best his subjects could do. Presently, when the snow set in, he would sit at Katherine's window with his head going up and down like a mandarin watching these strange large white things falling, falling, but never going up again. It was freezing hard and Wingly soon learnt that the heavy curtain over the bathroom window was movable, and he would go out, coming back later with the snow on his coat frozen into tinkling drops of ice. Every evening, at ten o'clock, he would sit and lick his coat till it shone, then his ears and soft white paws. Katherine said that then he picked up his top hat, fixed a buttonhole in his fur and went out for his nightly stroll. It really looked like it!

I had returned to Montana to find Katherine and Jack happy and working hard, writing and talking over what they were doing. They spent weeks discussing Proust and later Keats. Murry wrote good and successful essays on both, I believe, but no one pointed out that Katherine had been giving him all her ideas! I think she had planned to study and write on Keats herself. But they seemed happy and Katherine was certainly in better health. The good air and peace were what she had needed most.

So I started work immediately at the French woman's clinic. Nursing was not difficult, once I had grasped French methods and standards of hygiene, and it was interesting at times. I learnt to 'cup' the patients, an old-fashioned treatment of hot air suction on the lungs. The doctor had ordered it, and when I confessed my complete ignorance he replied, 'It's quite easy: just burn some cotton wool soaked in methylated spirit inside the little glass cup – this will create a vacuum – and then put it on the patient's back.' So I did – producing a shriek of pain from the wretched patient! The doctor had forgotten to warn me that the glass rim quickly became burning hot. However, I was forgiven and learnt how to do the cupping properly.

I had many adventures, some at the clinic and some on my way back to Chalet des Sapins, where I spent my late evenings before going home to the room which I had rented in the village. There was no heating in this room, and I used to put a large metal warming-pan on the electric plate at the chalet to heat, and then carry it across to my bedroom. One night – I must have been talking late or worrying over some problem – I filled the pan and put it on the stove without unscrewing the lid. Then I forgot all about it till I was halfway to my room. I could not go back as they had gone to bed, so I thought I would have to waste the electricity and suffer for my folly by staying cold that night. At about 2 a.m. there was a terrific explosion at the chalet. Jack ran down and found that the metal pan had boiled dry and then burst. The shelf above came down, the electric stove was cracked right across and many things had fallen and broken! They told me the next evening but, bless them, they never said a word of reproach.

While I was at the clinic I had this letter from Katherine sent to me at my rented room:

Montana

7.iX.1921

My dear I,

It's not possible to say all I wish to. I'll write it. Do you feel inclined to take this *job* – really? I mean to manage things for me as if I were a man. It's like this. I have gone to a new agent,* he's got me work which will keep me busy until Christmas at earliest. Then the *Daily N.* has asked me to do some especial articles for them and so has the *Daily Chronicle*. All this is *extra*. I can't devote myself to it if I have to look after the house and my clothes and so on. It's impossible. At the same time I *must* do it without delay. I can pay you between £10–£12 a month. But tho' payment is important – it's not the important thing. Can I rely on you? Can I ask you to do just simply what is necessary – i.e. what I should do if I hadn't a profession. In a word, can I feel, payment apart and *slavery* apart and false pride apart – that you are mine? That you will accept this situation as the outcome of our friendship? Does it satisfy you? May I consider you as permanently part of the scheme and will you consider me in the same light?

The truth is friendship is to me every bit as sacred and eternal as marriage. I want to know from you if you think the same.

yours ever,
KM

As for my *illness* and so on I could explain all that, too, but it takes too long. Try and accept it while it lasts.

My answer was that of course I would – there was no need for her to ask. With all her illness and all the work she wanted to do, Katherine could not always count on Murry and needed to feel certain that she could rely on me.

* Pinker, KM began to deal with this agent in the winter of 1920; up till then JMM had handled her stories.

The difficulty was that when she and Jack were happy together I always felt that I must try and be independent too and make my own plans, though it was bitter pain for me to do this. So that now, as all was well between them at the chalet in Montana I felt free to go to London again for a few weeks at the end of September to see my sister, who had come home to have her second baby; and I arranged to escort an English girl on my way back to Montana. This would cause Katherine to call me a flirt, as she does in the following letter which I received while I was in London – as though by going away I were trying to squeeze out of her an assurance of her friendship.

Chalet des Sapins.
Montana S. Sierre.

Saturday.

Dear

Thank you for your letter. I would have written a card before but the Furies have been busy. I have been – am – ill ever since you left with what Doctor H. calls acute enteritis. High fever, sickness, dysentery and so on. I decided yesterday to go to the Palace but today makes me feel I'll see it through here. Jack is awfully kind in the menial office of nurse and as I can't take anything except a little warm milk E. can't do her worst! It's very unfortunate because it holds up my work so. Just when I am busy. But can't be helped. If I were to tell you how I've missed you even you might be satisfied! At the same time – this is serious – don't hurry back – will you? The worst is over. Don't rush. I shall manage. Don't come before you have arranged– i.e. the 6th. At the *same* time don't just to oblige a Glasspool* – come later.'

I am glad you are safely there. Not a word about your new neffy – or haven't you seen him yet. Oh, I would *hate* to be in England. If only, in the next two years I can make enough money to build something here. But my soul revolts at your pension talk again. I suppose it gives you a trumpery sense of power, to take

* The English girl LM was to escort back to Montana.

on one job and pretend all the time you're perfectly free for any
other that comes along. A pity you can't resist the female in you.
You're the greatest *flirt* I ever have met, a real *flirt* I do wish you
weren't. With all my heart I do. It seems so utterly indecent at
our age to be still all aflutter at every possible glance. But – there –
I still hope one day you will be yourself. I am not going to flirt
back, Miss, and say how I want you as part of my life and can't
really imagine being without you. The ties that bind us! Heavens.
They are so strong that you'd bleed to death if you really cut
away. But *don't* – Oh please don't make me have to protest. Accept! Take your place! Be my friend! Don't pay me out for what
has been. But no more about this. I've no doubt I'll get a card
today saying your idea is to go out to Africa and so on and so on.
I really mean it *is* detestable.

E. is as mad as a sober Swiss can be. I think she puts all the
thick soups into my hot water bottils.

When you send papers get a label the size of the papers!
Otherwise the copy arrives *torn, black torn* and *disgusting*. Didn't
you know that? And I can't keep the illustration. It was so like
Olive to ask who he was – so tactful!

You can, in spite of my rages, read as much love as you like
into this letter. You won't read more than is there.

Katherine.

By the end of September I had seen my sister and was back in
Montana again.

*For KM and JMM, this time at Montana seems to have been peace-
ful, harmonious and productive. To Murry, at least, it was an extension of their great happiness at Bandol; the disease in KM's lung
appeared to be arrested, they were living in a beautiful place, both
working hard and able to discuss their writing together: Murry wished
that this state of stability might continue. Certainly the months July
to November were highly productive for KM. She wrote her second
great spate of stories, in these four months completing* Sixpence
(Sphere, *August 1921*), At the Bay (London Mercury, *January
1922*), The Voyage (*published first with* The Garden-Party,

February 1922), The Garden-Party (Weekly Westminster Gazette, *February 1922*), The Doll's House (The Nation, *February 1922*), Mr and Mrs Dove (Sphere, *August 1921*), An Ideal Family (Sphere, *August 1921*), Her First Ball (Sphere, *November 1921*), *and beginning* Susannah, By Moonlight, Widowed, *and* A Weak Heart – *though these were not completed.* (Marriage à la Mode *was also published in the* Sphere *in December 1921, though it is not certain that it was written at this time.*) *In January 1922 she began* The Doves' Nest, *though this was not finished, and completed* A Cup of Tea (Storyteller, *May 1922*) *and* Taking the Veil (Sketch, *February 1922*).

By the October 1921 she had begun to feel the strain of this great output, though in her Journal *she repeatedly chides herself for idleness. She was again prey to that restless need to be well completely, to recover perfect health, and by October had already written to Koteliansky for suggestions. She saw her health as linked to her state of being, and longed to find the miracle cure which would heal her altogether and at once. In her* Journal *for 20th January 1922 she wrote: 'I have a suspicion like a certainty that the real cause of my illness is not my lungs at all, but something else. And if this were found and cured, all the rest would heal'; and later on 6th February, 'The weakness was not only physical. I must heal my Self before I will be well.' This had now become her one aim.*

Having been at Montana for six or seven months, Katherine began to realise that though she was much stronger in herself, the disease was not fully under control and she once more began to despair of ever being completely well again.

Then in the first days of January she began reading a book which made a very deep impression on her; it was called *Cosmic Anatomy**. She told me about it, but said she did not think I would understand it easily; she would explain it later. It was un-

---

* *Cosmic Anatomy; the Structure of the Ego* by 'M. B. Oxon' (published by Watkins) had been sent to JMM for review by Orage. The author, Dr Wallace, was a theosophist who had been much interested in the Douglas Credit System, (a monetary system which had also interested Orage at one stage). Dr Wallace had written for *The New Age,* and for a period made regular anonymous payments to support it. His book outlined a compact model of the Universe, providing a framework in which to see man, his place in this universe, science and religion in a

fortunate that she never did, because I think that it provided the first step towards what she later found in Ouspensky; though this she did try to explain to me a little.

Earlier that October Kot had recommended to Katherine a man in Paris called Manoukhin, who apparently had a new treatment for TB, making use of X-rays. It is difficult to realise now how very little was known in those days about tuberculosis and its cure. One felt so completely helpless. Manoukhin claimed much and had had some success, so Katherine thought about it, and at the beginning of January 1922 wrote to Paris. He answered that he would see her with a view to giving her treatment if she wished.

She did wish, but she hesitated; the weather was still so wonderful and she was taking drives on the snow, Murry was so happy and well, he had learnt to skate and was thinking of skiing. She said he looked like a great bird swooping about on the lake. But she was warned of the much less pleasant period in the mountains between the seasons when the thaw set in, the mists came and the snow turned into slush, and she decided she must try Paris. Murry would not go; he was working well and enjoying the winter sports.

Katherine sent for me and told me he would not go. What was she to do? She begged me to help: would I go to Paris with her? I thought even then that there was no need to *beg* me to do anything; of course we would go. I told the French woman at the clinic that I would have to give up my work. I then left my rented room (rather gladly!) and went with Katherine.

---

new way. KM seems to have been fascinated by this book, and her journal entries for January and February of 1922, published in *The Scrapbook*, are full of quotations from it.

CHAPTER XV

Paris – Randogne – Sierre:
January 1922 – July 1922

Katherine and I arrived in Paris on 31st January and took a small suite of rooms – two bedrooms and a private bathroom – at the Victoria Palace Hotel, 6 rue Blaise Desgoffe. Katherine went to see Manoukhin that same afternoon. The X-ray treatment sounded strenuous and Manoukhin advised starting straight away, while Katherine was already in Paris, to avoid the hazards of yet another journey. He said she should stay till May, and then return for the second part of the treatment in the autumn. She settled to do this and I began to look for cheaper accommodation for our headquarters.

My journeys took me from second class hotels – which Katherine came to inspect, turning down the unclean sheets and smelling the unswept passages and dusty windows – to a magnificent luxury flat, obviously belonging to some writer or artist now on holiday, with wonderful silk curtains and rich rugs and palm trees.

However my troubles were cut short, before anything suitable was found, by Murry, who, finding that the chalet at Montana under Ernestine's control was not so enchanting as when Katherine was organizing his life, decided that, after all, he would come to Paris. He arrived on 11th February. I was to return to look after the chalet and Wingley, while he and Katherine would share her rooms at the hotel and stay in Paris until the end of May. She would then be better and they would pack their bags and together wander through Europe till they found a home. A splendid plan! But it was Murry's idea, never Katherine's. She was by now a sick woman and the treatment, as I knew, was proving to be more exhausting for her heart with every day. She was too tired after her sessions to do anything, and (as I learnt later by letter) Murry filled every part of their room at the hotel with his newspapers spread all over the floor and on the furniture.

That February in Paris Katherine completed The Fly (The Nation, *March 1922*) *and worked intermittently from about May till August on a 'long serial' called* The Doves' Nest, *though this was never completed. She also prepared another list of stories for her next book of the same title* (*printed posthumously in June 1923*). *Several of these stories she listed and had started, were never finished and only fragments now remain, published in the* Journal.

On 23rd February her book The Garden-Party *was published by Constable and was extremely well received, getting more than twice the number of reviews that had welcomed* Bliss *the previous year.*

Glad for Katherine to be in Paris, I returned to Switzerland in mid-February expressly to deal with the chalet, for there were five months left of our tenure. The one thing which filled my mind was how to help by minimising the financial strain on Katherine's limited resources. To me everything seemed to turn on this. My first thought was to find another tenant and then return to England; another possibility was to stay and take in paying guests; but everything was surrounded by thorns made fierce by my poor knowledge of French. How could I find out about the cheapest way of sending Katherine her belongings? How to sort out the distracting Swiss and French laws and customs? What to do when faced with the law that one could not take in paying guests? How to get goods to the station, the post? It was all a nightmare!

Meanwhile in Paris Katherine equally distracted by my silence, waited and wondered. When her exasperated letters came, they only made things worse; and instead of laughing and telling the truth – explaining how difficult it was for me to manage and making a joke of it – I felt I could not burden her with my stupidities, and retreated hastily into my shell of silence and worked all the harder. Poor Katherine! Poor indeed, bravely going on with her painful treatment while parcels flew about and keys were lost or arrived without immediate acknowledgement. Parts of these letters I received then will show a little of this confusion.

Paris

14.11.22

Dear Ida,

I am writing to you so that you shall have a letter and because I want one from you. We have heard nothing from Mrs Maxwell* about sub-letting. I think you'd better not even make inquiries until we do hear with Doctor H. on the spot to report to her. It is annoying. We shall look v. silly if she says 'no'. . . .

What has E. done with the newspapers? She has not sent on *one*, and Jack asked her to. I suppose she has just thrown them away. Make her look after you properly. Please write and tell me how you found things and so on and what was the *feeling* of the place. I am longing to hear about everything. You mustn't be so silly as to imagine because I am such a horrible creature I don't love you. I am a kind of person under a curse, and as I don't and can't let others know of my curse you get it all. But if you knew how tenderly I feel about you after one of my outbreaks. You do know. I can't say 'nice' things to you. In fact I behave like a fiend. But ignore all that. Remember that through it all I love you and *understand*. That is always true.

Take care of yourself, ma chère

Katherine.

Saturday.

Dear Ida,

Can you tell me (1) what my boxes would cost to send by rail and (2) how long they will take. I have been thinking it over. It seems from your card today there is a chance the Chalet may not be let as soon as we had thought. In that case I can't do without my clothes. In fact I feel the need of them very much, so perhaps they

* Dr Hudson's mother, the owner of the Chalet des Sapins.

had better come along as soon as you have the keys. Yes, that's best. They had better be sent at once.

If the Chalet is not let I have been thinking what had better be done. These last few days have made me feel I don't want any flat before May. I prefer to stay here (in the Victoria Palace Hotel). It's simpler and it would be cheaper in the end – of that I am *certain*. Here we can tell what all costs to a halfpenny. *La-bas* there is food, servant, concierge and all the unforseen expenses. . . . It is not very gay here but it's clean and one is independent. One soon gets into a routine and is free to work. It's a good hotel and the people are decent. But if the Chalet remains unlet it will mean a loss of about £50, and that is horrible. In fact I can't easily meet it. Also we shall have to keep it open and warmed and cared for. Here is a suggestion. What about you staying there until May, keeping Ernestine, and taking in a married couple as pensionaires? At not less than 32 francs a day the pair. Does the idea revolt you? As far as I can make out one would then pay for the heating, lighting, E's wages, your keep, and you make a profit of £10 a month (that is allowing £1 a day for all expenses, i.e. food, heat, light, laundry). I'd put them in the top double bedroom of course and *ask* 35 francs. Tell me what you think of this idea. It would be a terrific help if it could be done *easily*. No help at all in fact a horror if you don't care about the idea or if it sounds difficult. It is indeed only a suggestion – an in case – to be answered as such – to be taken 'lightly'.

As I write I am conscious I exaggerate a bit and that is not fair to you. If I have to drop that money on the Chalet – well I must drop it, that's all. But I want to tell you it's a little bit hard to do so. The first fortnight here I spent in all £50. And I must earn to keep up with it. This plan would save your fares down and up again. There is that to consider. It would also give you your £8 a month clear and perhaps a little over. I want you to believe I am not just making use of you. I am treating you as my friend, asking you to share my present *minuses* in the hope I can ask you to share my future *pluses*.

Talk it over with me – will you?

> Yours ever
> Katherine

Friday.

Dear Ida,

Your Tuesday and Thursday letters have come. From them it
seems you are waiting to hear from me *still* about the boxes. But
your wire said you were sending them by G.V.* unless you heard.
I naturally kept quiet which meant SEND. Do please get them
off at once! Any way Grande – Petite – as long as they are here. . . .
Later.

I have broken open this letter to say after two mornings spent
at the Post Office we have managed get the second parcel and found
it contained 1 belt and 1 pr stockings. If it wasn't comic it would
be too much of a good thing. It's a sight to make the Wings
themselves look down. There was a letter from you, too. I don't
believe in your shivering and shaking because of my barks. That's
fantastic. If you don't yet know the dog I keep you never will.

Glad to know – very glad about the birds. Why should it be
extravagance. Buy another coconut if you like. I shall look at the
bills and reply in the next letter. I am 'off' bills for today. My
boxes – mythical, tantalising boxes, I 'note' are packed to perfection. But Oh – why don't they come. You torment me – shew
them to me – and whip them away again. I freeze I burn for my
kimono my Anne† coat. Tell Wingly to *wriggle and stamp*‡ until
you take them to the post.

I don't want your old money if you do keep a pension. The
whole point is – it should pay for the house and E. and then pay
you.

That's enough of letter writing. My hand shakes because I
have been writing very fast. It's not paralysis or the family washing.

The Lord be with you.

KM

* *Grande Voiture.*
† A coat given to KM by Anne Estelle Rice.
‡ A quotation from Walter De la Mare's story *The Three Mullar-
Mulgars,* about a tribe of monkeys burning down their own house to be
warm and rejoicing in the great fire quite forgetting that in fact they would
be much colder.

2.III.22

My dear Ida,

Your Saturday–Sunday letter gives me the impression that
you are unhappy and restless. Is that so? Tell me! What do you
do now. I suppose I hope and trust the 'settling' of the Chalet is
over. All is in order? And Ernestine capable of doing all there is
to be done. Do you see your girls? Do you find people to talk to?
How do you spend your days. I should be very interested to know.
Don't *focus* on Wingly, though he is a nice cat. You have books
in plenty and wool. But books and wool don't make life. I don't
want you to feel stranded up there – cast away.

. . . The longer I live the more I realize that any life but a life
remote, self-sufficient, simple, . . . eager, and joyful, is not worth
living. Cities are ashes. And people know it. They want the other
thing; they feel their own 'poverty' in their several ways. It is
sad. However the only way to help others is to live a good life
oneself. It's a round about way but I see no other.

. . . I hope your May* doesn't go in for town life and trying to be
a social success in Bulawayo. I hope Roger gets a real chance.
You'll have to gallop off there one day and look after him if you
love him. Don't you feel that?

This is just a little chat with you. Now I must work. I have mas-
ses to do. Keep well!

Yours ever
KM

3.III.22

Friday.

Dear Ida,

Your Ash Wednesday letter is rather ashy. I confess it makes
me feel impatient. Will you reply to this speak out. Say exactly
what you want. I can't tell. I must know.

(1) We can afford £2–10 to £3 a week quite well. I would great-

* LM's sister.

ly prefer the Chalet *not* to be left. If it costs a little more it would
be far better than leaving the keys with anyone.

(2) No. While you are there please keep Ernestine. That is
final. So for Heaven's sake don't go on about it. Rubbish! I must
say it all sounds dreadfully ineffectual and vague and foolish. If a
pensionnaire did 'turn up' as you say what about your servant?
You must have one. In any case there is no need for E. to go and
no earthly need to work miracles at keeping down the *chauffage*.
Ugh! I think its extremely ungracious about the cheque.* However, if you feel like that you must act like that. It's not good or
right or splendid. If you had said: 'How nice to get the cheque.
I shall have a small spree on the spot!' I should have been delighted and warmed! As it is I don't feel at *all* warmed! Please
take things a little more lightly. There is no need to go on 'worrying'. This is what happens when you burrow underground and
suggest and think and so on. Why? It's so unworthy! Please just
say out what you mean. You know what I think now and it's final.
I can't write every day about it.

And I am sorry I can't send the reviews. I must keep them at
present in case I need them for America. I shall not throw them
away however and later on if you care to see them I will send them
to you then. If I get duplicates you shall have them.

But *cheer up*.

Yours ever
KM

The truth was that I was determined to do something on my
own with the chalet to make it pay for itself and so save Katherine
the rent, but I did not want to trouble her. I wanted it to be so
settled that she would not have to think about it any more, and
I could give it to her as a present and say: 'There darling, it's all
quite all right; I'm doing a job, I can manage, you don't need to
worry.'

I always tried to imagine what would be best for Katherine,
and sometimes it would be quite outside my own character. I
was ill at ease, unaccustomed to making business arrangements,
managing things and never quite sure what would be acceptable.

* KM has sent LM a cheque for £2 0 0 as a present.

But I had made friends with a young Swiss girl, Susie de Perrot, a daughter of the Suchard chocolate makers, who was at Montana looking after a younger sister who had tuberculosis. She was a tower of strength and with her position and money was in touch with all the small, sturdy, nice looking Swiss officials. She worked wonders, and found that as a 'group of friends', and not '*pensionaires*', she and her sister and two other Irish friends could all come and live with me in the chalet and share expenses. I was very frank about these expenses, and told them they would have to pay them all, including keeping me to manage the house for them, so that Katherine would have no more fresh bills or other expenses to pay. I wrote to Katherine again, and told her of our plans and what we hoped to do; she sent this letter in return.

7.III.22

My dear Ida,

That's the kind of letter for me! Now keep that in mind as your ideal, 'focus' on it and I'll never be cross again. I cannot tell you how relieved I am to know what you are doing and that you are happy doing it. Thats the important thing. At four o'clock this morning I had decided to write to you again and really tell you what I thought of you for keeping me for so long without any detailed news. Nothing but chauffage and money! When I wanted to know what you were doing, thinking, feeling. However, this is a noble effort and so I say no more Betsy.

Alas! for the distressed gentlewomen. How can I get this vast parcil across? I shall have to write to the English clergyman in Paris if I can find his address somehow. But there is so much that they (the poor) would call fancy dress – little jackets and so on. As to woven combinations (the very height of fancy dress) I seem to have collected the things or they have bred. They are my horror and my box was stuffed with them like peas in a pod. Away they *must* go. All my things looked rather as though they had been washed through the customs – they are very much exhausted. But even a change is such a relief that I fully expect a low hiss of admiration when I go to lunch today in different shoes.

I suppose your Miss Yates would not know of a worthy charity in Paris that would call for a bundle? Is it worth asking?

Yes, large towns are the absolute devil! Oh, how glad I shall be to get away – the difficulty to work is really appalling – one gets no distraction. By distraction I mean the sky and the grass and trees and little birds. I absolutely *pine* for the country – (not English). I could kiss the grass. It's true there is a jampot and a jug in my room full of small daffodils. But exquisite though they are they keep on making me wonder where they grew. It's wickedness to live among stones and chimneys. I keep on thinking of lying under a tree in some well hidden place (alive not dead). But this is not a complaint. It may have the ghost of a moral in it – a 'don't settle in a town whatever you do'. But I don't think you will. Do let me see Olive's letter.

. . . I wish you could stay up there for a bit if you like it. It seems to me *right* for the moment – you felt the place suited you spiritually when you first got to know it and that was the right feeling I believe. I wonder if the Palace would be tolerable? Another small barbed thrust 'I saw you in the Palace (illegible) . . . I don't care – I do think it might be very interesting. Hudson is an extraordinarily decent man – really he is. I have had quite remarkably simple nice letters from him here. He may be stupid but all doctors are that. And I always rather took to that matron. However – its a long way off. Wingly I presume could be a kind of Red Cross *scout*. Which reminds me. After I had unpacked the box I had all the symptoms of terrific bites. They have gone off this morning. But I was certain, last night, that Wing had carefully put in a few for a surprise for me. Have you ever found one of the biters? Are they fleas or what?

Yes, I was glad to hear from Pa. I began of course to plan a visit to N.Z. with Jack – to start this autumn, late, to return at the end of March. I wish I could work it. I should like it more than anything in the world. It would be the compensation prize of prizes. I dream of driving out to Karori in an open cart and showing Jack the Karori school. But I'm afraid it will stay a dream. Father will be over here in June. My 'success' makes a difference to him naturally.

I feel you don't want to jump to Rhodesia just now. Well, there's no hurry is there? You can wait and be godmother to Roger's first. But try to keep in touch with him whatever you do. May is – all she is – I don't know – but you can give him a great deal that she has no idea of and never will.

I have had letters from Elizabeth,* Chaddie Waterlow†
about the book‡ which are a great joy. Letters from strangers,
too, and 'my' undergraduate,§ (*pages* from him) and Clement
Shorter the Sphere man who asked for a portrait for publication
and has ordered 12 stories to be ready in July. This is no less than
staggering. I enclose the *Times* review. Please return it. Jack, who
read my card to you, said off his own bat he'd order you a copy
to be sent direct from London. He also said off his own bat, 'of
course she won't believe it was I who did it'. Well, it was.

Thank you for the grey satin top with all its little blanket
stitches. They made me smile. My writing case looks excessively
sumptuous here. It reminds me of the Ida I love. Not because of
what it cost. *No*. But the 'impulse' – the gesture – what you call
the 'perfect thing'! It carries me back to Isola Bella. Oh, memory!
And back I go to the Casetta and the olive tree before and the
cotton tree along the twisted fence and the red roses and big
starry-eyed daises. Menton seems to hold years of life. How hard
it is to escape from places. However carefully one goes they hold
you – you leave little bits of yourself fluttering on the fences –
little rags and shreds of your very life. But a queer thing is – this
is personal – however painful a thing has been when I look back
it is no longer painful – or no more painful than music is. In fact
it is just that. *Now* when I hear the sea at the Casetta it's unbear-
ably beautiful.

I must begin working. I'll never be a Wealthy Woman. I write
like this because I write at such a pace. I can't manage it otherwise.
Here is some money. Be well! Be happy! Eat! Sleep!

Yours ever,

KM

All went splendidly with the new plan and we had already turned
the chalet into a community home, When I received Katherine's
next letter which made me feel so sick in my heart. For she said
that when she was better, I must leave her and start a new existence, as she must keep her independence and go about the
world: she and Jack were going to travel.

* Countess Russell.
† An aunt of KM's.
‡ *The Garden-Party* (published in February).
§ William Gerhardi.

15.III.22

Tuesday.

Dear Ida,

I have just received your Sunday letter. Don't apologise for writing what you feel. Why should you? It only means I have to cry 'de rien de rien' each time and thats silly. Heavens! what a journey it is to take one anywhere! I prove that to myself every day. I am always more or less marking out the distance, examining the map, and then failing to carry out my plans. It's rather nice to think of oneself as a sailor bending over the map of one's *mind* and deciding where to go and how to go. The great thing to remember is we can do whatever we wish to do provided our wish is strong enough. But the tremendous effort needed – one doesn't always want to make it – does one? And all that cutting down the jungle and bush clearing even after one has landed anywhere – it's tiring. Yes I agree. But what else can be done? What's the alternative? What do you want *most* to do? That's what I have to keep asking myself, in face of difficulties.

But you are saying 'What has this to do with our relationship?' This. We cannot live together in any sense until we – *I*, are – am stronger. It seems to me it is my job, my fault, and not yours. I am simply unworthy of friendship, as I am. I take advantage of you – demand perfection of you – crush you – And the devil of it is that even though that is true as I write it I want to laugh. A deeper self looks at you and a deeper self in you looks back and we laugh and say 'what nonsense'. It's very queer, Jones, isn't it? Can you believe it – that looking back upon our time in Italy and Garavan* – even the afternoon when you were raking the garden and I was proving our purely evil effect on each other I keep on remembering that it was a lovely day or that the button daisies were ducks. How nice – how very nice it would be to bowl along in one of those open cabs with the wind ruffling off the sea and a smell of roasting coffee and fresh lemons from the land. Oh dear! Oh dear! And do you remember standing at your window in your kimono one morning at five o'clock while I sat up in bed behind the mosquito curtains and talked of decomposition? No, we can't simply

* The village next to Menton.

live apart for all our lives from now on. We shall have to visit at least. How can we live? What is the best plan? The future is so wrapt in mystery. Until I am well it's foolishness for us to be together. That we both know. If this treatment succeeds I shall go to Germany for the summer, then to Elizabeth at Randogne and then come back here in September or October. If all goes well I shall then go back to Germany for the winter – or Austria – or Italy. Then – I have not the remotest idea . . . Jack wants to take a little house in the English country in Sussex and put all our furniture in it and so on and have a married couple in charge. I feel it is my duty to spend 6 months of every year there with him. The other six October to March I shall spend in either the South of France or Italy and I hope and imagine that if he has his house, Arthur, his books, his married couple, a little car and friends coming down Jack will not want to come with me. They will be my free months. That's all I can see. Now my *idea* is that we should spend the foreign months together, you and I. You know by that I mean they will be my working months but apart from work – walks – tea in a forest, cold chicken on a rock by the sea and so on we could 'share'. Likewise concerts in public gardens, sea bathing in Corsica and any other pritty little kick-shaws we have a mind to. But here is a brick. Money. If I can manage to pay for those months can you get a job for the others? That's the point. And of course the 'arrangement' is only in case you care to, are not in Rhodesia, are not married, or living with some man. Tell me what you think. If you say 'What the dickens could I do for six months?' I reply 'Why not the Universal aunts? Why not try them? See what kind of jobs they have . . .' But don't fly off and cry 'This is very kind of you to arrange for and dispense my life like this *Merci pour la langouste.*' I'm not doing it. I'm only talking in the dark – trying to keep you – yes, I will own to that, and trying to make things easy, happy, good, delightful. For we *must* be happy. No failures. No makeshifts. Blissful happiness. Anything else is somehow disgusting. I must make those six months with Jack as perfect as I can make them and the other six ought to be fearfully nice. But I know any form of life for Jack you and me is impossible and wrong. (There is all [ILLEGIBLE]; if this treatment does not succeed but I pass it by.)

Now the immediate future for you . . . It seems you are not going to get P.G.s. Can you stay there until it's time for the Chalet to be shut? Do you want to? and then – what do you want to do? Will you go to the Palace this winter? But this is all far away and uncertain. And I must stop writing and begin to work. The great point is – if you can – think of happiness, work for happiness, look for it. I should like to ask you, every day between sleeping and waking, i.e. before you go to sleep and before you get up to practise this. Breathe *in* saying I am and *out* saying happy. Your subconscious, Miss will then take note of that fact and act according-ing. However miserable you will be that has a quite definite coun-ter-action. I suggest you teach Wing on the same principal to say "I like – stopping at home. . ."

Goodbye for now. You say don't write letters and you lead me a terrific dance writing them. Thus it will always be.

Yours ever,
KM

At first glance it is perhaps hard to understand why LM was made so sick at heart. Her reaction throws significant light on her feelings and on the delicacy of the balance in the relationship between herself and KM and Murry. For LM the implication was crystal clear: Kather-ine had decided that 'another way should be tried'. The ambience of her life was again her work and Murry, after a lengthy period since 1919 in which she and LM had been abroad together in search of health, and JMM had been present only as a visitor. In subsequent letters she talks gaily of 'going to Bandol when her time is up in Paris' and of 'getting a maid before she leaves. . . . ' In consequence LM felt again, as she had done before the previous autumn at Montana, that she must be independent and that she must find other work to occupy her.

Katherine's next letter is more explicit.

22.III.22

Tuesday.

I have been waiting for an answer to my last letter, I think, before I wrote to you. It happened on the night I sent it I had a perfectly odious and typical dream about '*us*', and though that did not change my feelings, au fond, it made me feel that perhaps I had been premature in speaking so definitely about the future. You felt that too? Rather you were wiser than I and simply did not look so far. I think that is right. I think it's best to leave the earth alone for a bit – i.e. plant nothing and try to stop cultivating anything. Let it rest as it is and let what is there either grow or die down or be scattered or flourish. By the earth I mean the basis the foundation of our relationship. The stable thing. Let it rest! Depend on me though, even when I don't write. Don't get fancies, will you? I am just the same whatever is happening.

In the host of indefinite things there is one that is definite. There is nothing to be done for me at present. And whenever we do meet again let it be in freedom – don't do things for me! I have a horror of personal lack of freedom. I am a secretive creature to my last bones. Whether that is compatible with asking you to make me some *pantalons* in April I don't quite know. Brett asked what I'd like for April – Easter, and I said some fine linen. But if you feel it is not part of our compact for you to sew for me from afar I must go about with a paper ham frill on each leg instead.

. . . By the way *tell me* if you'd like to go to Rhodesia any time. I could get the money if you tell me early enough. What would a 2nd class fare cost? And you'd want £20 for clothes before you went.

I hope your pensionnaires turn out well. It seems devilish little to pay. Less than the Valpini even. They are in clover in one of the best Chalets in Montana for 13.50. And I suppose you will give up every moment of the day and ½ the night to caring for them. I don't see how you can do it at the price – but you know best.

I must get up. These last days have been very busy. So many letters to write and so much business to attend to. I've sold the Scandinavian rights of the book and the continental and North African of this new one – and it all means agreements and so on – accursed business! However according to plan this is my last really bad week. After this next Friday I begin to go up the hill again. This has been that second bump on the switch back.

I feel more at home in this hotel than I ever did in Switzerland. One blessed thing about Jack is he does ignore one completely – in a *good* way, in the way that is necessary if one is a writer. He is there and not there. Give me warning of the Aylesburys* won't

* The two Irish girls sharing the Chalet with LM, who planned to come through Paris and on the way collect KM's old clothes.

you? Their parcel grows and grows. I mentally put on another brand for the burning each day. I shall be left stripped to my last leaves.

Oh how I'm longing to be in the green country though – with a block and a pen! Oh, for that German village in its nest of green and the hay meadows and the lilac bushes. I shall leave here the first moment I can!

Goodbye for now. Forgive an odd letter. I'm in bed still and rather vague.

Love from Katherine.   K.M.

This letter is colder than I mean it to be. I have read all your letter. I understand what you mean. Look upon it – our time apart, as something that never is permanent. It's just like a long interval between the acts. It had to be. The irony is I should never get well with you who wish me well more than any other being could. But you were always ready to help and the consequence was I didn't have to make those efforts which tire me and at the same time drag one back into the *normal* world. I don't know . . . it's difficult and mysterious. But having tried the one way and found it a failure one must try the other way. We gave the one way a good run nearly four years – over four years in fact.

The truth was that leaving Katherine – and I do not mean only visiting England, France or Switzerland for her, but leaving her entirely for an indefinite period – was always a most bitter anguish for me, physically as well as in my heart. But some stronger feeling helped me not to shew it; I would not let her suffer for *my* pain. If this was to be the plan, so be it; and I turned to find some other occupation to fill my days.

This is where I now acted misguidedly. I forewarned myself that our parting might be for a very long time, but half unconsciously I knew I must not disappear, whether to my sister in Rhodesia, to some other friend or 'to the end of the world'. Thus it was that I let my friend Susie Suchard talk me into starting a tea room with her in England, since she needed someone of English nationality to make her venture possible. I undertook to help her without ever setting any time limit or telling her where my real allegiance lay. The unconscious feeling that I must always be 'on call' for Katherine was to deep that I never thought of mentioning it to Susie, and I agreed therefore, to go to England in May, when Katherine and Murry were returning from Paris, to try to find a suitable tea room for her.

I had letters from Katherine telling me that her course of treatment which was coming to an end had been entirely satisfactory, and that Paris though busy and exciting was too full of social activities. She longed for the peace and air of the mountains to rest for a while. She also advised me on the tea room.

Sunday.

My dear Ida,

Your full house may be amusing but where are you sleeping? I hope the de Perrot girls do not stay. Five is too many for comfort. I cannot see where they all are. Besides feeding five and so on must be a bore in that little house. Don't forget stuffed *nouilles* and *plats* like that; they go farther and are easy to make.

. . . My book is in a 3rd large edition which is more important and the reviews still roll in – still the same – *and* letters. Do you remember Mrs Belloc Loundes? Wrote me at Baugy? She's coming over in May for 'ten days talk'. So are Chaddie and Jeanne, so is Brett, Anne Drey, Richard. The Schiffs are *here*. But I wrote saying I couldn't see them. I shan't see the others either if I can escape in time. I have a horror of people at present. As it *is* one never has enough time to oneself.

If you can manage without the money – good! For my teeth are beginning to give me gyp. I shall have to start with Heppwell in May. And if I don't get my hair washed next week I shall commit suicide. There is a good shop in the rue de Reune that specialises in Henna. I shall go there and come out shinning like a chestnut, I hope .

I am very insincere in my horror of people for the Russians here, writers like Bunin,* Kuporin, Neryskovi and his wife and so on I am longing to meet. Manoukhin has asked me to his flat to

* Besides being a Russian writer the main attraction for KM was that he had known Chekhov in Russia.

see them. It will be really thrilling. But it's the English and French 'crowd', always the same, so ashy, so gossipy, so tiring that I don't want to see. Horrible ingratitude I know!

Forgive a dull letter. I ought to be working. But I wanted you to know I was thinking of you. All goes very well here. Have you really time to sew? And have you patterns of my knickers and nightgowns? In case Brett sends the stuff?

Yours ever,
KM
Love to little Wing – the sweet boy!

Saturday.

Dear Ida,

You have missed my point. Where do you sleep? When do you go to bed? These two important questions you hedge away from. If you omit to put the time why the devil should that put my mind at rest. It doesn't in the least. I still hear midnight strike through the pages. You are a perfectly maddening character to have to do with.

. . . What about *giving* Wingly for always to the de Perrots. If they would take him would it not be a good plan? As regards Jack and me we shall not be settled anywhere for over a year. I hate to think of the cat being pulled about – from pillar to post. He'd be much happier with kind friends – the dear.

When you wrote Thursday with icicles, it was warm, really hot here and sunny. I had a most extraordinary afternoon. Got ready to go to Cox's and lost my cheque book – spent an hour with Jack turning the whole room into a hay stack. No sign. Went off to Cox's – to stop all cheques. I had to wait to explain, to see my entire account, to go to the intelligence department where my name 'Mansfield' was cried like a vegetable and finally escaping prison by a hair we went off to the Bon Marché to buy a very simple light hat. Have you been there? It's one of the wonders of the world. Having fought to the lift we got out on to an open gallery with about 5,000 hats on it 10,000 dressing gowns, and so on. But the gallery looked over the entire ground floor and the whole of the ground floor was taken up with untrimmed 'shapes' and literally hundreds and hundreds of women – nearly all in black wandered from table to table turning and turning over these shapes. They were like some terrible insect swarm – not ants more like blow flies. Free baloons were given away that day and fat elderly women with little eyes and savage faces carried them. It was exactly like being in hell. The hats were loathesome. Jack as usual on such occasions would not speak to me and became furious. If I said 'Do you like that?' he replied 'No. Horribly vulgar!' If I timidly stretched out a hand he hissed 'Good God!' in my ear. We got out of the place at last. Then while waiting for a taxi a woman tried to commit suicide by flinging herself at his umbrella with which he was prodding the pavement. *She* was violently angry. I ran away to where a man was selling easter chickens that cheeped when you blew a whistle. The taxi came and Jack had by this time lost me. Finally both of us raging we got in, drove to the hotel, got out, got in again, and drove to another hat shop. 'Get this damned thing over!' was Jack's excuse. There was a quiet shop we both knew. We found only about 25 people and hats flying through the air. One woman put on another woman's old dead hat with the pins in it and walked off to pay the cashier. The owner dashed after her, with a face of fury and snatched it off her astonished head. My one stipulation was I didn't mind what kind of hat I bought but it must have no feathers. And I finally decided on a little fir cone with 2 whole birds on it!

So now you know what city life is like.

. . . Re Chocolate Shop and tea room. I believe there's an awful lot to be made out of a *good* tea room at the seaside, with morning buns after bathing and so on. But I'd make it really very original – *very* simple – with a real style of its own. The great point is to be 'noted' for certain specialities, and to make them as good as possible. If you go in for chocolates – have the very latest thing in chocolates – and so on. As you realise I could write a book on such a scheme. But when you are in the mood tell me your plans.

. . . Excuse writing. I'm in the devil of a hurry as usual, with a story to send off today. But I thought you'd better have a chat with me or you'd be beginning to make me feel guilty.

KM

11–V–22

Confidential.

Dear Ida,

   As far as I can tell this treatment has been (I hesitate to use this
big word) completely successful. I hardly ever cough. I have
gained 8 pounds. I have no rheumatism whatever. My lungs have
not been re-examined yet nor has the sputum. I'll let you know
about these things. But so far – it seems I am getting quite well.
My voice has changed back. I take no medicines. The only thing
that remains is that my heart is tired and weak. That means I get
breathless and cannot walk yet except at a snail's pace with many
halts. But I have no palpitation or anything like that. And of
course now that I don't cough or have fever my heart will gradually recover. Manoukhin says I ought to be able to walk for an
hour in June, even. I put confidential to this letter because I
don't feel it's fair to tell anyone who may ask you until I have the
facts like Xray and analysis. Should anyone ask – just say I am
infinitely better and that I've gained 8 lbs. I mean Hudson or
Woodifield.*
   Jack told you – didn't he – that we are going to the Angleterre.†
If you have time would you run down and *see* a couple of rooms?
It would be very nice if you could as you are so near. I look forward beyond words to the early summer there for working. Any
other plans would take up so much time. We can settle in there
in a day and start off. Both of us are behindhand. And it's harder
and harder to work here. The weather is really devine. I spent
yesterday in the Bois at a marvellous place with the Schiffs. I
think I should begin to dance if I stayed here long. You can't
imagine how beautifully these women dance in the open under
flowering chestnut trees to a delicious band. All the very height
of luxury. I do like luxury – just for a dip in and out of. Especially
in Paris because its made into such an Art. Murry buys such really
delightful things. And then all is arranged so perfectly. One has
tea out of doors but it's so exquisite. One's cup and saucer gleams

* A patient at the Palace in Montana.
† The hotel in Randogne, the little village below Montana at which
KM and JMM planned to stay when they returned to Switzerland.

and the lemon is a new born lemon and nobody *fusses*. That's the chief point of money. One can buy that complete freedom from *fuss*. But what nonsense I am writing. I must get up and go have my wool washed. The shutters are ½ shut and through them gleams a red azalea that Jack bought at Poitiers. It looked a poor thing then but it has turned into a superb creature in this blessed Oh how blessed heat and light!

Ida – can you take a parcel for me? If not you and I will tie up one here and you'll nip out to the post with it. I must get rid of these old skins. Short of digging a hole in the carpet I can't with Jack about. Jack has accepted more or less a lecture tour in England this autumn. I go to Bandol when my time is up here – to the Beau Rivage. I hope to get a maid before I leave here. But I haven't done anything about it yet. Some one I must have. But really as long as the sun shines nothing is urgent. It is as hot as San Remo. I have slashed the sleeves off my blue charmeuse. Sleeves are intolerable. At 10.30 last night I paddled in the bath. But they still feed one on puree de lentilles and soissons. I had strawberry tartlets with the Schiffs yesterday. Can you make *them*? Forgive a very silly letter.

Ever

KM̄

my deep sympathies for Wingli.* Ether too! I think you'd better call your T room *The Black Cat*. Why don't you send the bills?

I went down to the Hotel d'Angleterre at Randogne, the village just below Montana, not far from Elizabeth's house, to take rooms for Katherine and Murry. I did my best but it was a poor place, unaccustomed to out-of-season visitors, with bare rooms and very little staff left. I felt I was once more leaving Katherine to her fate – and Murry.

I prepared for the journey to England, and at the end of May I closed the chalet, put on Wingly's collar, and called in to see Katherine in Paris on my way home. I found her bravely ignoring the heat and the untidiness of the room. I stayed only a short time,

* Who had been operated on for an infected scratch.

while Wingly, who had been panting and prone on the railway seat, recovered enough to examine everything, even the windows of the neighbouring rooms. I left Katherine with an aching heart and great apprehension, which I think she shared a little. Back in England. I had the following letter from her.

29.V.22

Saturday.

My dear Ida,

I was so infinitely relieved to get your wire and to know you had arrived safely. It was kind of you to send it. My heart was wrung at the last moment of parting from you – as you must have known. I could not believe it. It seemed solemn and wrong. But don't lets call it or consider it a *parting*. We shall make some arrangement sometime that will make it possible for us to be together. Aren't you certain of that? I am. Don't let S. de P. tire you. Don't send me back any money. Spend your money! If you knew what that little account book made me feel. I could have howled for misery like a dog. And then they snatched £5 from you and left you hard up! It is too bad.

I don't seem to have said anything to you at all. But the heat was overpowering and my tooth added to it. Perhaps it doesn't matter so very much. But Oh! how I hate to see you travelling. I feel your fatigue and I know you will hurry and not eat enough and your hat will hurt and so on for ever. When I am rich, my dear Ida, I shall buy you a house and ask you to keep a wing, and a chicken wing and a wingly for me in it. In the meantime I wish you could stay with Mrs Scriven and eat Easter custards or play with Dolly's babies.

It is nice to know the poor little cat is out of its basket. Awful to love that cat as one does. I suppose you imagine I don't care a bean for him because I keep on talking of having him destroyed. I say that and see his little paws dodging in and out of the wool basket, and see him sitting in the scales or returning from his walk with paw uplifted stopping now and then. . . . In fact I shall one day write a cat story which will be *heart breaking*! In the meantime I do hope he will not die and that you will give him an occasional sardine tail. . . .

Its less fearfully hot here. There is a breeze. It has been terrifically hot until tonight (Saturday.) I went to the Louvre this afternoon and looked at Greek sculpture – wonderfully beautiful. The difference between the Greek and the Roman stuff is extraordinary; the Greek lives, breathes, floats; it is like life imprisoned, except that imprisonment sounds like unhappiness and there is a kind of radiant peace in the best of it. – Scraps of the Parthenon frieze – figures greeting, and holding fruits and flowers and so on are simply devine. I never realised what drapery was until today. I had a good stare at the Venus de Milo with all the other starers, and she is lovely as ever – the balance is most marvellous. It's intensely fascinating to see the developement of that perfection – to trace it from heads that are flat as flat irons with just one dab for a nose – then to the period of tree worship when all the bodies are very round and solid like the trunks of trees, then through the Egyptian influence when they begin to have stiff and terrible wings, and at last that perfect flowering flower. It makes one in love with the human body to wander about there – all the lovely creases in the belly and the roundness of knees and the beauty of thighs. The Louvre is a superb place; one could spend months there.

We hope to leave here next Friday evening. Next week will be a rush. We have so many engagements, lunches, dinners and I must go to that dentist every day. I feel we are only just leaving Paris in time; we would be swept away. And these little social affairs take up such an amount of the day – preparing for them, seeing to one's gloves and brushing one's coat and skirt and so on and cleaning shoes. It takes one hours to get ready. But I shall speed up later. Already we are putting off engagements till the autumn. . . . I sound rather smug and as though I like it all – don't I? No, its not that. As one is here it's the only thing to do. Serious work is out of the question in a city. One simply *can't* feel free enough. So one accepts distractions; that's all.

It's half past eleven. Jack is still 'dining out'; I suppose he's gone to a café. As usual, as I lie here I have got *very hungry*. Oh for a cup of tea and something to eat! It's just the hour for it. And there's a jug of old fashioned moss rosebuds on my table smelling of years and years ago. I bought them from a little street boy last night.

Well, this is the awful kind of letter you get from me. I can only make the pen move; it won't really run – or show off its action. Not that I am in the least tired. Only my hand is. How is everybody? Tell me! I had better end this letter quickly for the old feeling is coming back – an ache, a longing – a feeling that I can't be satisfied unless I know you are *near*. Not on my account; not because I need you – but because in my horrid odious, intolerable way I love you and am yours ever

KM

In England I went to my aunt Mrs Scriven's house at Lewes, and there found a permanent, loving home for our dear, brave little cat Wingly. Then I began to look for the tea shop.

For six weeks I tried hard to find a suitable place on the south coast. I had no idea how to set about it, and did not realise there were such things as house agents. I spent all the time bicycling along the south coast road, looking for empty shops. Of course I could find nothing.

Meanwhile on 4th June Katherine and Murry were setting off for Randogne. That fateful journey! Katherine was so weak by now that when she travelled every detail had to be very carefully arranged beforehand, to save her any unnecessary fatigue. It was all she could do to stand the journey. Tickets, reserved seats, luggage, passports, even picnic baskets had all to be in hand, probably under her surveillance; but someone else must do all the work, even to remembering her little clock!

But Murry knew nothing of this. I don't think he had travelled alone with her since she had been ill. And everything went awry: tickets were lost or had not been bought, timing was wrong so that she had to struggle through crowds, and there were difficulties over baggage and refreshments. When the suitcases were hurriedly unloaded, the little clock, the great standby of every journey, was left on the train. Only a short break was possible for them at Sierre before they had to go up to Randogne, by the little mountain railway. When they got to Randogne it was pouring with rain. Katherine did not possess a raincoat, and they were met by an open cart to take them and their luggage to the hotel. When they eventually arrived at the hotel, it was spartan in its lack of comfort. Katherine soon went down with a bad cold and pleurisy, and then Murry sprained his ankle. I have always thought this dreadful journey from Paris to Switzerland may have accelerated her illness and blamed Jack, perhaps unjustly, for being so inadequate and apparently careless of her. Her letter to me describes all the horrors.

Hotel d'Angleterre Randonge
5–VI–22

Sunday.

My dear Ida,

I am at last on the balcony overlooking the same mountains. It's hot with a small wind: grasshoppers are playing their small tambourines and the church bells of Old Montana are ringing. How we got here I shall never know! Every single thing went wrong. The laundry did not come back in time. We were off late. Brett was laden with large parcels which we could not pack and which she promised to store for us – until when? And only when we got to the Garde de Lyon we remembered that it was Whitsun. *No* porters. People wheeling their own luggage. Swarms and thousands of people. Fifteen thousand young Gymnastes de Provence arriving and pouring through one. Poor Jack who had my money gave away a 500 note instead of a 50. And at last arrived at the Couchettes we found an ordinary 1st class carriage with 3 persons a side. No washing arrangements – nothing. It was the cursed *Fete de Narcisse* at Montreux yesterday so conducted parties crammed the train. What a night! And the grime! At Lausanne we both looked like Negroes. Then came a further rush for the Sierre train (registered luggage tickets lost) and finally two hours late we arrived at the Belle Vue, starving, as we had no food with us and there was no food on the train. But that enchanted hotel was more exquisite than ever. The people so kind and gentle, the waving branches outside the windows, a smell of roses and lime blossom.

After a very powerful wash and an immaculate lunch – how do the glasses and spoons shine so? – I lay down and went to sleep and Jack went out. The next thing was: *La voiture est là Madame.* Heavens! Nothing was packed. Jack had not come back. The bill was not paid and so on. I am quite out of the habit of these rushes. Finally we found Jack at the Post Office and just got to the station in time. Then at Randogne there was no room for our luggage in the cart. So we went off without it. (Last bulletin de bagage lost, Jack simply *prostrate*) and, we'd scarcely left the station when it began to pour with rain. Sheets, spouts of cold mountain rain. My mole coat and skirt was like a mole skin. We got soaked and the road which hasn't been remade yet after the winter was exactly like the bed of a river. But the comble was to get here and to see these small poky little rooms waiting us. We took the ground floors three as you said they were so *big* and so *nice*. Good God! whatever made you tell such bangers. They are small single rooms and really they look quite dreadful. Also the woman told us she had *no* servants. She and her sister were alone, to do everything. I thought at first we'd have to drive off again. But that was impossible. So I decided to accept it as a kind of picnic: 'the kind of place R. L. Stevenson might have stayed at' – or 'some little hotel in Russia'. Jack looked much happier then. But there wasn't even an armchair or a glass in my room. No wash table in his. I made the old woman get in these things. She is amiable and kind and poor soul – very frightened. And before supper the luggage arrived and we unpacked and my room looked much better. We were just settling down when I found Jack had left the dear little square clock in the train. I was devoted to that clock – and he found he had lost his only fountain pen!

However, wild horses won't drag me away from here for the next two months. I think we shall be able to get decent food. At any rate they have excellent eggs and good butter milk and their own vegetables. I felt inclined to cry when I saw how hard they had tried to impress us last night at supper with their cooking – even to a poor little boiled custard that floated airy fairy with little white threads in it.

But at last it *is* peaceful. This balcony is perfect. And the air – after Paris – the peace – the outlook instead of that grimy wall – Cities are too detestable. I should never write anything if I lived in them. I feel base and distracted. And all those dreadful parties –

Oh how odious they are. How I hate the word '*chic*'. C'est plus chic, moins chic, pas chic, très chic French women haven't another note to sing on. And the heat! It was frightful. And the stale food. I had to give up my dentist at last until a more propitious moment. I couldn't stand it.

Well, that's enough of Paris. I shan't mention it again. Write to me when you get this. All my underclothes are in rags. Shall I never have time to mend them. All the tops of my knickers are frayed and the seams of my 'tops' are burst and my nightgowns are unsewn. What a fate! But it really doesn't matter when one looks up at the sky and the grass shaking in the light.

What are you doing? What are your plans? How is Wing? How is 'everybody'?

Yours ever,
KM

Murry had in his mind that he and Katherine would wander off happily hand in hand, a pair of near invalids seeking health, until they found another 'Villa Pauline'. But, when it came to it, Katherine soon realised that this new way was impossible for her; she just could not manage. She wanted to call to me for help but felt that she could not write or telegraph: 'Please come after all, Jack cannot manage.' It was not possible for her to let him down like that. So, instead, she wrote this letter to me:

before 9.VI.22
Hotel d'Angleterre

This is shorthand and the result of *weeks* of thinking.

Ida,

If you are not finallyfixed up for the summer – listen to me. It's no go. I am almost as ill as ever I was, in every way. I want you if you can come to me. But *like this*. We should have to deceive Jack. J. can *never* realize what I have to do. He helps me all he can but he can't help me really and the result is I spend all my energy – every bit – in keeping going. I have none left for work. All my work is behind hand and I *can't do it* I simply stare at the sky. I am too tired even to think. What makes me tired? Getting up, seeing about everything, arranging everything, sparing him, and so on. That journey nearly killed me literally. He had no *idea* I suffered at all, and could not understand why I looked 'so awful' and why everybody seemed to think I was terribly ill. Jack can *never* understand. That is obvious. Therefore if I can possibly, possibly ask you to help me we should have to do it like this. It would have to come entirely from you. I'll draft a letter and send it on chance. If you agree, write it to me. It's not wrong to do this. It is right. I have been wanting to for a long time. I feel I cannot live without you. But of course we will have to try and live differently. Dear Ida, I can't promise – or rather I can only promise. If you cannot 'honourably' accept what I say – let it be. I must make the suggestion; I must make a try for it.

Yours ever,
KM

Forgive me for saying all these things *bang out*. There is no other way. I shall understand of course if it's out of the question and if you think my letter – my 'draft' horrid – throw it away. The truth is I can't really work unless I know you are *there*. I haven't got the strength. But I'll manage some sort of compromise if we can't arrange this. This is a black moment because I've got pleurisy badly and it always affects my spirits.

When Katherine's letter came I sent back the letter she needed immediately:

Dear Katherine,

I've been thinking over what you said to me about a maid, and I'd like to suggest something. So far I have not found anything that *just* suits me. Would you be inclined to take me on in a really professional capacity this time – let's call it companion-secretary. I do feel I could help you more than anyone else if we manage to keep things on a proper footing. For instance would you pay me £6 a month – I don't think I could do with less, and keep me? You see I am being quite frank. I want to leave sentiment quite out of it. This is what you would call a proper practical proposition, and I only suggest it until you have finally settled down – whenever you do settle down. Afterwards we could see. Surely we could each have a life apart and yet be of use to each other. Can't we ignore what was so unsatisfactory in the past and start afresh. Pretend you haven't known me and try me as a companion-secretary. Give me a six months trial even. You can always say you don't think it works and there will be no harm done. Let me know as soon as you can – will you? I have thought this over for a long time.

Yours ever,

Ida.

Murry was so uncertain of himself, so vulnerable, that he deeply needed the reassurance of making a success of something. He could now persuade himself that if it was because of his ankle and his cold that Lesley had better come for a while. I wrote to tell Susie that I could no longer wait; I had been unable to find a suitable tea shop and I was going back to Switzerland. I am afraid that she was very angry with me, and justifiably so; but I too felt justified in paying heed to my inner warning voice. I had this letter from Katherine before I arrived.

Hotel d'Angleterre
14.VI.22

Dear Ida,

Your 'letter' came and had precisely the effect it was intended to have. Thank you. I believed in it myself as I read it. It sounded so real. I have had your telegrams. I understand about Susie. Do as you think best. Don't tire yourself by rushing. I don't think the little lady needs too much consideration, though, after the very casual way she treated you. Miss Franklin is the person I like and your Mrs Scriven. They both sound delightful women.

About plans. . . . Do you want any money? I will send you a cheque for £7 to buy yourself any odd clothes you may need. I mean stockings and so on. England is the only place for them, and to pay for your journey. I don't know what it costs. About the *cat*. Where can you leave him? Do you know of anywhere? Would Mrs S. have him if he was doctored? That would mean he'd be a quiet cat and not a fighter. It's impossible to have him here. For my plans are so vague. At the moment, too, I can't write letters. I haven't the time. I'm late now for the *Sphere* and it's a difficult job to keep all these things going. I write to nobody. Please forgive this. Understand it and don't get anxious and don't telegraph unless you have to! I have such a horror of telegrams that ask me how I am! I always want to reply *Dead*. It's the only reply. What, in Heaven's name, can one answer?

. . . And listen to the old Adam in me for a moment will you, my dear? *Don't* take advantage of me because I have begged you to come and say I can't do without you. I haven't turned into a grateful angel. I'm at heart a distraught creature with *no time* for anything for the moment. When this work is done I'll be better. But try and believe and keep on believing without signs from me that I do love you and want you for my wife. And come as soon as you *reasonably* can. Let me know when you arrive and I'll send the cart to the station. Elizabeth* has come. I am glad for it frees me from the worry of Jack a little. I am a bit better physically but the labour of getting up, tidying, brushing clothes, carrying cushions and so on is so great that mentally I confess I feel absolutely exhausted! But it must be got through, somehow. There's no help for it and I am bound to deliver the goods by the end of this month.

Yours ever
KM

So I returned to Switzerland in June 1922 and tried to make things easier for them. I lived quite separately in a different part of the large, empty hotel at Randogne and I went to their 'flat' when I could do things for Katherine or massage Jack's ankle.

Katherine improved a little, but she was not able to think of making a home with Murry at the moment; any such plans had to be delayed. She would go out on to the hillside and sit half-hidden under a tree to try and work, while she saw the mountains above and heard the sound of the cow bells as the herds came slowly down the hills. But though it was lovely high summertime, with

* Countess Russell.

upland flowers and faraway snow-covered mountains and great peace, she was not happy; the effects of the pleurisy that Katherine had caught on that fateful journey were too depressing. Probably she had been forced to realise that though she had been made so much better, Manoukhin had not yet cured her completely. He had urged a second course of his treatment and she saw now that this was probably necessary, though it was a great strain to her heart. And Katherine had always feared that, in the end, it would not be the tuberculosis, but her heart, that would cause her death.

We waited a little and then she decided that her heart, strained by the treatment, could not really stand the mountains and she and I went down in July to the beautiful Château Belle Vue hotel at Sierre, while Jack went to Elizabeth in Randogne. All was not well between Katherine and Jack. I think one explanation of the many separations which broke the steady flow of their happiness, was an ever-growing difference in their essential beings.

The guiding necessity of Murry's life at the time seemed to be to find firm ground on which to stand. He needed the absorbed devotion of a patient, loving soul to stand by and help him resolve the tangled problems of his undeveloped personality, which struggled with a far more mature intellectual self. But Katherine was no nurse or doctor, rather a surgeon, cutting through the outer surface, under which most of us hide, to find and expose the truth of each personality. From this she derived an insight that could lead her to compassionate understanding. It is perhaps, the firmest step towards love of one's neighbour.

The Murrys' great love for each other bridged these divergencies, but it could not altogether prevent the intermittent, and at times, essential periods of separation, with their attendant despair. Katherine herself once told me that only love could assuage these ills and perhaps finally cure them.

But now there arose between them a more particular difference. Jack could not follow the new direction in which Katherine's thoughts were turning ever since she had read *Cosmic Anatomy*. She now saw her physical weakness as a result of spiritual impurity, and strove to find a way to amend this; she desired most deeply to be whole and felt that by her own effort she could achieve this. In this, there seemed to be no meeting place between them, and their most fundamental paths began to separate.

CHAPTER XVI

Sierre – Pond Street – Hampstead – Paris: 1922

The magic, quiet and beauty of the old Château Belle Vue Hotel at Sierre refreshed Katherine a little and she was at peace there, and I believe able to work. The shadowy sunshine of her room was the inspiration of her poem *The Wounded Bird*.

In the wide bed
Under the green embroidered quilt
With flowers and leaves always in soft motion
She is like a wounded bird resting on a pool.

The hunter threw his dart
And hit her breast, –
Hit her but did not kill.
"O my wings, lift me – lift me!
I am not dreadfully hurt!"
Down she dropped and was still.

Kind people come to the edge of the pool with baskets.
'Of course what the poor bird wants is plenty of food!'
Their bags and pockets are crammed almost to bursting
With dinner scrapings and scraps from the servants' lunch.
Oh! how pleased they are to be really *giving!*
'In the past, you know you know, you were always so fly-away.
So seldom came to the window-sill, so rarely
Shared the delicious crumbs thrown into the yard.
Here is a delicate fragment and here a tit-bit
As good as new. And here's a morsel of relish
And cake and bread and bread and bread and bread.'

At night, in the wide bed
With the leaves and flowers
Gently weaving in the darkness,
She is like a wounded bird at rest on a pool.

Timidly, timidly she lifts her head from her wing.
In the sky there are two stars
Floating, shining . . .
O waters – do not cover me!
I would look long and long at those beautiful stars!
O my wings – lift me – lift me!
I am not so dreadfully hurt . . .

The whole hotel, with its large spacious rooms, held an atmosphere of graciousness. In the centre of the building there was a little chapel, now sadly faded and rather dusty. It seemed to have no light left in it, as though it was so long since anyone had called on the Great Spirit in that place that the little altar had almost forgotten Him.

The garden too was restful, with many seats scattered amongst the flowering bushes, and the sunshine filtered through the drooping branches of the tall, willow-like trees. One plant in particular took Katherine's mind many miles from Europe, a wonderful aloe in full flower – her first draft of *Prelude* had taken its name from that tree of her homeland.

As August advanced the air grew hotter, the trailing, swaying trees in the garden lost their freshness, and Katherine seemed to lose her vitality. She gave the impression of getting through the days with difficulty, drifting with little of her normal sense of direction.

It was at Sierre that August that she made her will. She asked me to help her with it, because she felt it should be done. I think death was often haunting her now: not death itself, but the thought that she had so much still to write, to tell people, to make clear, yet somehow could not find the time to put it into words. The will was written in her room at the Château Belle Vue. We discussed each item: she had few ornaments or jewels: there was the small gold watch and chain Jack had given her some time before, which she always wore round her neck. I remember it cost £22 and was a most rare treasure; it seemed remarkable that he should have given her such a present, he who seldom thought of gifts (or could afford them, perhaps) and did not spend! Also a necklace of small round corals which she sometimes wore, and a daisy-shaped pearl engagement ring which Jack had bought for her 'when they were young' and was particularly dear to her.

That she gave her watch to me I could accept and understand, it was a token of her continuing love – almost a living symbol. But when she asked if I would like her Bible, I could not face the thought of her dying and said no. 'Very well, I'll give it to Father.' I wonder if anyone reads it now. I wish I had it after all. She particularly asked Murry to destroy as much of her writing as he could, for she did not wish to leave signs of her camping grounds here for all to see.*

I think Katherine must often have felt Murry's characteristic 'holding-on', or lack of generosity, though she only remarked on it once to me when she said, 'If ever Jack offers to give you money, *take* it, don't hesitate.' She knew my inclination would be to say 'No thank you', and partly for my sake, partly for his, she told me that I must not refuse.

After her death, when I had finished helping him with deciphering and typing her more difficult manuscripts, he asked me if I would like to take charge of a small cottage in Ditchling where he could put their furniture and which he could use for week-ends. I agreed; but I had hardly settled in when he announced he was marrying Violet le Fevre and would need the money from the cottage to start a magazine. He offered me £40 'to get a cow or something', and I, remembering K's words, took it.

I met him twice after that. Once was when he came to the house where I was living to ask for lunch, I think, or maybe a bed, for his brother Richard and himself. My hostess, who was of the old school and did not understand such casual ways, was kind and gracious but rather haughty. The second time Murry asked me to meet him at some station he was passing through, and to bring two antique jars he and K. had obtained from a chemist's shop in Paris, which I had been taking care of. I gave him the jars, and as he by then was printing everything of Katherine's that he could

---

* Other personal bequests were made to Anne Estelle Drey (née Rice) (her Spanish shawl), her mother-in-law, Mrs Murry (her fur coat), Richard Murry (her large pearl ring), her cousin Elizabeth Countess Russell (her copy of Shakespeare), one book each to Walter de la Mare, H. M. Tomlinson, Doctor Sorapure, A. R. Orage, Sydney and Violet Schiff, J. D. Fergusson, Gordon Campbell, D. H. Lawrence, her carved walking stick to S. Koteliansky, to her sisters her writing case, her piece of greenstone and her Italian toilet boxes, and to her father her brass pig and her Bible.

get hold of, including all her private, personal papers, I was angry and told him it was very wrong. We did not meet again.

At Sierre I would first do what I could for Katherine in the morning and then take a picnic lunch, to avoid the expensive hotel meal, and go out to the gardens or for long walks up the mountains; Katherine would stay in quiet, private peace to rest or work or sit in the gardens. We only met later in the evening.

At Sierre that July Katherine wrote Father and the Girls, *describing the Château Belle Vue hotel and also* The Canary. (*The* Nation, *April 1923*). *This latter was the last complete story she wrote.*

Occasionally Katherine went out in the afternoon, driving in an open victoria through the gently sloping foothills. I went with her sometimes, and on one such drive we had an odd conversation. She was saying she would certainly die before I did, and when I protested that she should not talk like that, she told me teasingly that she would send me a coffin worm in a matchbox. 'Oh no, not a worm!' I remonstrated. 'No – all-right, I'll send you an earwig in the matchbox.' I agreed that that was better. A few weeks after she died, when I was most heavy-hearted in my sadness, I had to go to the small cottage in Ditchling that Jack had rented. Arriving tired, my first thought was a cup of tea and I picked up a match-box. Alas! empty. But no. Something rattled in it and I opened it to find Katherine's earwig. Her posthumous message did indeed cheer me and I could not help smiling!

Sometimes Katherine went into the little villages around the gardens of the castle, and one night there was a festa of some sort in the village below the castle, with lanterns and the country folk and a brass band. Katherine had the imagination or vision to see through to the inner meaning of the scene and enjoyed it. I could only hear that the band was excruciatingly out of tune! But it was all pretty and happy and gave an impression of the days when the hotel was still the old castle and lord of all the surrounding villages in the wide valley.

Presently Brett, hearing that Katherine was at Sierre, came to pay a visit; I do not remember whether she was already in Switzerland or if she came from London. She painted a great deal of the time and made a fine picture of the aloe in the garden but she talked too, and often stayed in Katherine's room till late at night. This was a great strain on Katherine and she sometimes asked me to come in to break up the conversation and persuade Brett to leave. I always went in when it was late, but the most open hints and more direct requests failed to move the visitor. I learnt afterwards that this was because she thought that I was jealous!

Murry came down to Sierre from Elizabeth's place at Randogne at the end of August, and I hoped the situation between them would improve, but this was not to be, and Katherine resolved to go to England again before coming to any decision about the second part of the Manoukhin treatment.

We all three journeyed to England. It was the first time Katherine had been back since September 1920. She stayed in the flat on the first floor of Brett's little house in Pond Street, Hampstead, which she had put at Katherine's disposal, while Jack stayed next door and I went to my friend Dolly Sutton at Chiswick, coming up from there to Hampstead every day.

I do not know what arrangement Brett made about meals, but she would go continually at odd times to see Katherine and ask how she was getting on, and these unpredictable interruptions and the lack of privacy were too worrying for Katherine; in the mornings I would find a card hanging by her door saying WORKING, or OUT. Katherine said it was the only way she could defend herself, and when she expected me, I had to slip in quietly so as not to break the rule. She seldom wanted to see people that month; it seemed as if she found the effort of contact was both disturbing and burdensome for her. Her outside life seemed remote, though in reality much was changing.

Most probably due to the influence of Orage, with whom she had been corresponding again and to her reading of Cosmic Anatomy, *Katherine came to England in August before returning to Paris for the second part of the Manoukhin treatment.*

On 30th August she saw Orage, who introduced her to the lectures *that P. D. Ouspensky was then giving in London. Ouspensky was a Russian who had worked with Gurdjieff* for seven years: like him, he taught from an intricate and all embracing system of esoteric knowledge whose main premise was that man is a machine who alone among the animal world, has the possibility of waking up to become a conscious being; that by constantly observing and working on this 'machine' he can achieve harmony between what he called the different 'centres' (body, mind and heart), and so become unified and aware. The idea that through his own efforts a man can expend his consciousness, and that he has a will and can act, appealed strongly to Katherine. She recognised in these ideas thoughts of her own, now expressed in the context of a deeper knowledge.*

These six weeks in Hampstead were spent in going to Ouspensky's lectures, absorbing what she heard, and discussing it with others who had been similarly interested (in her letters to JMM she mentions Orage, J. W. N. Sullivan and J. D. Beresford). In September Murry moved out of London to stay with Locke Ellis at Selsfield. He found Katherine's new way of thinking alien to his nature and he could not follow her in it.

I remember the day Katherine went out to meet Orage. She had always been fond of him, and when she got back after her first visit to him she was happier than I had expected. She said it had been wonderful, he had been so affectionate, embracing her and calling her 'darling', as though in a return to earlier, happier days. It was a great comfort to her that he seemed to understand her new problems and searchings. He took her to the discussion groups on psychology which Ouspensky was holding, and so helped to shed a new light on her difficult path. She talked to me

* A Caucasian Greek, he was fascinated by the occult and his travels in search of esoteric knowledge took him and his fellow companions through the many countries and small states between Turkey and Tibet, including as well India, Mongolia, Jerusalem and Egypt. By 1915 he was teaching in Moscow, where Ouspensky met him and worked with him. Leaving Moscow, he set up his Institute for the Harmonious Development of Man in Essentuki, Tiflis and Constantinople successively. During this time Ouspensky gave lectures in these towns. By 1921 the political situation had made it impossible to continue this work in Russia; Ouspensky came to London and Gurdjieff went to Paris and in the autumn of 1922 set up his Institute at Fontainebleau.

of Ouspensky's meetings and tried to explain some of his principles and teachings, but I could not follow it all.

I believe that her friends the Schiffs and Anne Estelle Drey
were hoping to see something of her while she was in London, and
she did see them once or twice, but in the main she seemed to have
withdrawn from people and the life around her, while the new way
of thinking and understanding was filling her being. Later, she
said, it would be different, but now she was deeply exploring
something new and the old patterns did not 'belong'.

She saw Richard, Murry's brother, and Kot called once. I
opened the door to him, we greeted each other without speech,
and Katherine allowed him to go up to her. I think it was the last
time he saw her. She also went to see Dr Sorapure. He said that
her heart was sound and her lung disease arrested, and I think this
gave her some hope of getting stronger with Manoukhin's treatment; she tried to find an English equivalent, though she did not
continue long with it. Of course, her lungs were badly affected,
and nothing was known about collapsing a lung in those days, so
she was always in danger of a haemorrhage if she risked any
strain. There was not one moment when she did not have to be
careful and conscious of this danger.

In fact, she found the X-ray treatment in London without the
personality of Manoukhin to be quite a different matter, and
everything seemed to push her towards Paris again. She and
Murry had been out of tune since they left Paris and went to
Randogne, and Katherine was making her own plans now. She
decided to give Manoukhin another try.

*That same autumn Gurdjieff had established his Institute for the
Harmonious Development of Man at the Priory in Fontainebleau,
with the Russians who had followed him and a few English people who
came through Ouspensky's London group. At Fontainebleau the ideas
which Katherine had been hearing about were put into practice in community. The participants lived together, putting themselves under the
direction of Gurdjieff and working hard in practical ways on the
different aspects of their being. Of particular interest to Katherine
seems to have been the precise knowledge Gurdjieff possessed of the
human psychological structure, its workings at all levels and his
understanding of the relationship between these levels. She saw him as*

the one man who could make her whole, and felt he knew infinitely
more about this than anyone else she had met.

On 2nd October Katherine and I crossed over the Channel
once more. We stayed in the Select Hotel in the Rue de la Sorbonne – the same hotel at which we had stayed in 1918. It was
small and only provided bed and breakfast, but the top floor where
Katherine and I always went was just what she preferred: cheap
and undisturbed, with queerly shaped rooms, probably the attics
of some large old house, looking out on the roofs of the Sorbonne.
She went back to Manoukhin and had several treatments.
These gradually proved more and more exhausting and she would
come back and lie down in a breathless condition, her heart
beating furiously. This continued for two weeks, then she felt
much worse and was really frightened, terrified by the thumping
of her heart; she said she could not risk another session.
The final decision had to be taken. She was caught between the
treatment offered by Manoukhin with its related dangers and the
unknown possibilities of her new way of thinking as it was being
practised at Fontainebleau. She thought Manoukhin had failed,
though I was privately convinced that he had already arrested the
disease; what more he hoped to effect I did not know. But she
could not continue: the strain on her heart was too dangerous. If
she turned to the new way of living it would mean burning all her
boats; there would be no return. Things seemed then, to me, to be
taken rather out of her hands.
Orage had already decided to join Gurdjieff at the Priory and
had sold *The New Age*. He came over to Paris on 14th October, a
Saturday; on the same day, Katherine's birthday, he arranged to
meet her with a Dr Young from the Priory, who was to give her a
medical examination. She was very anxious and, it seemed to me,
nervously apprehensive. But finally she decided she would go
down to Fontainebleau and see if she could embark on this new
way of life.

CHAPTER XVII

Fontainebleau:
October 1922 – January 1923

Going to Fontainebleau was not a sudden turning-point in Katherine's life, but rather the culmination of a gradual process. She had met Ouspensky and been medically 'passed' by Dr Young: then she had an invitation to go down to see the community for a couple of days.

We took no luggage, only a few necessities for our short stay. I was to be there with her.

Dr Young met us at Fontainebleau. Katherine was given a room in the visitors' quarters on the first floor. We did not meet Gurdjieff till lunch time, when we went down to a pleasant informal meal, though I cannot remember anything of the conversation. I was, of course, an outsider, a stranger, and indeed it was difficult to find me a bed when evening came, but then a mattress was put down for me in Katherine's room. I remember this well for the draught coming under the door affected my neck most painfully.

The following afternoon Gurdjieff invited Katherine to stay for a two-week trial period, and made the necessary arrangements. Then she was moved to a spacious, beautiful room overlooking the garden.

During my few days there I was shown a large garden, where members of the community were working, and then taken over a good sized house in the garden, where the children lived and were cared for. I cannot do better at this stage than quote from a diary I began to keep at that time.

OCTOBER 17TH, TUESDAY

Went down to Fontainebleau. Met by Dr Young. A drive in the sharp air through an avenue of immense trees, arriving at an old château, long and low, with a fountain playing into a round basin in a large courtyard, the flower beds full of crimson flowers and golden autumn leaves.

OCTOBER 18TH, WEDNESDAY

Last evening spent in the salon before an enormous fire of great logs. 'Fire is condensed sunlight.' Music and tambourines – atmosphere intensely alive. Came to Paris for letters, etc. for Katherine. Back for dinner. Dreadfully depressed and self-conscious. Spent evening upstairs alone. K came up radiant, her eyes shining. She is staying for a fortnight under observation.

OCTOBER 19TH, THURSDAY

I left Thursday morning, 'emotional centres entirely out of control'. Packed and took up Katherine's boxes. Spent night at Hotel de la Foret, Fontainebleau. Locked the door in case I was in a disreputable house – too immature to judge by atmosphere.

OCTOBER 20TH, FRIDAY

Came away for last time absolutely dazed. Decided in train to go on the land or to Russia. I ought to bless and sing praises to life. I do in my reason, my heart refuses to join in.

OCTOBER 21ST, SATURDAY

Posted two parcels registered, yellow coat, etc., etc. I feel as if I had come from the funeral of someone who has meant the world and life to me. Indeed I have said goodbye to Katherine. That centre-point of relationship or affinity is what I connect with the state after death; the rest ought to have been killed long ago – it would have been easier to recover from . . . there is so small a part that is left me.

OCTOBER 25TH, WEDNESDAY

Letter from K. She is staying indefinitely.

OCTOBER 28TH, SATURDAY

So anxious about K. Woke in the night hearing K call, so distinctly that I answered aloud. Such a cold wind.

OCTOBER 29TH, SUNDAY

Received a letter from K with great relief, also P.C. answering my letter. Shouldn't have sent that letter, it was a weakness. If only I could keep the personality of independence going on I could write to her. Wrote today. Be sure not to criticize. Should not be difficult for me.

These letters and postcards I received from Katherine in the first few days.

> Le Preiuré
> Fontainebleau. Avon.
> Seine et Marne.

Dear Ida,

This is the address. I have had no post so far. Perhaps its all got lost. Thank you for the things. The warm petticoats vest and scarf are a joy. It is cold here when one stops working.
Cold – but lovely.
I am glad your toothache* is better.
Thank you. *I am happy.*

KM

Whatever clothes the 1000 francs will buy *please send*. Especially a warm jacket for the evening of a bit soft scarf.

POSTCARD   24 Oct. 22

D.I., All the parcels arrived safely. Please send the cloth one. No, I don't want another petticoat or knickers. Don't send the book. Why should you? I don't want any books at present. I'd like another sleeping jacket – a very warm one – and a *Tuteur* for teaching the 'Cello and a book of quite elementary exercises – for teaching. This is urgent.
I am staying here indefinitely. I feel better. But as a precaution I shall send my will to the Bank in case of accidents. I hope your toothache is quite cured. Write to me from time to time won't you? Jack seems to have toothache too. If you go back to England I hope you'll see him.

Ever
KM

* 'Toothache': an emotional trouble, not physical. LM

28.X.22

D.I.

Everything has come. I am so grateful for the red scarf. It is just what I wanted. Here is the pattern. And can I have a pair of galoshes and a pair of garters. I love being here. I am perfectly looked after and I feel one of these people. My only fear is that I may have to go away for a few weeks later on* I don't want to miss a day. The weather so far is perfect. But terribly cold. All the fountain basins were frozen this morning and we have not a flower left. The leaves fall all day and the grass smells good. We are making a Turkish Bath which will be very comforting.

I don't do any 'work' just now except – well, its hard to explain.

I hope you are happy. Haven't you used that 1000 francs? Shall I send you another? Please ask me. And remember you can always get a job at Selsfield, doing chickens for Locke Ellis.

Excuse my writing. It's on the corner of the table under rather awkward condition.

Ever
KM

Alas! I gave my plaid skirt away. But I have the plain panne velvet.

*This is a little ambiguous. Of course Mr Gurdjieff would send me and so on . . .

POSTCARD

Dear Ida,

Send the green skirt. But please don't write to me any more about clothes. I do not want any and I do not want to talk or think about them *at all*. I can't tell you about the other things either. Let me give you Mr Ouspensky's address. It is *38 Warwick Gardens*. If you are in London why do you not write and ask if you may attend his lectures? I shall not write again just now. I do not want to hear about Miss Beach.†
KM

† Sylvia Beach who ran the bookshop, Shakespeare and Co., in Paris.

When I arrived back at the Rue de la Sorbonne from Fontaine-bleau, I gave up Katherine's room and sat down in a completely empty world. I felt utterly alone. My days were EMPTY. My absorption in Katherine's life, caused by her illness, had perhaps been wrong; it was now over. Katherine was walking along a new road, a road of which I knew nothing. That she was happy at last freed me, in some way, from the strain of trying to help her to be happy. But I now realised fully the emptiness of my days, and my very soul ached; Katherine called this 'toothache'. It was hard to accept, but it could have been possible, had I not had a subconscious vision of things to come and known that in fact, our earthly relationship was already at an end: that I should not see Katherine again.

In the meantime, I received her letters and tried to supply her requests, even going to London for that purpose in the middle of November for two weeks. There were still some material matters to be attended to. Katherine wanted me to see Murry. She had a vague wish that we should join in a project to start a farm of some kind, but, when I asked her about it, she could not explain. I was myself exploring the possibilities of staying and working in France. There were several and I looked into them all: the most likely seemed to be at Lisieux near Deauville, where I could work on a farm.

10.XI.22

Dear Ida,

I do not think that Lisieux is a good idea. It is too isolated. You need people and interchange of relationships to take you out of yourself. You will only get depressed and *dull* at the farm, I should think. That is my opinion. Would not the Palace at Montana be better? Or that V.A.D. place at Menton? Why not write to Jinnie F? She might have an idea. I think it would be worse than folly to live a lonely life. Surely you know your need of people! Any kind of isolation is only possible for very great strong people.

Katherine did not realise that it would be impossible for me to return to the south of France or Switzerland; there were too many memories. Nor did she realise how much I would like the farm, and that essentially I was happy with animals and simple people lower down the scale of intelligence. She perhaps never understood the strain for me of constantly trying to live up to people of higher intellectual capacity. For this reason too, it would have been impossible for me to care for JMM on a farm. The letter continues,

Why are you so tragic? It does not help. It only hinders you. If you suffer, learn to understand your suffering but don't give way to it. The part of you that lived through me has to die – then *you* will be born. Get the dying over! But remember you will teach yourself nothing alone on a farm. You are not the type.

No, it makes no difference to me if you are in Paris or not . . . How I am? I am learning to live. But I have not 'disappeared'. Later I may go to Paris or London or Berlin or anywhere and we could meet and have a talk. I am far less disappeared than ever I was.

I meant the cheque to be 500. *Please cash* it and use it.

As for the clothes – later – I shall order them myself.

But you do see that our relationship was absolutely wrong now? You were identified with me. I prevented you from living at all. Now you have to learn and its terribly hard.

Keep my keys, please. Write to me whenever you wish to.

Yours KM

If you loved as you imagine you do how could you make such a moan because I was no longer helpless. Try and look at it like that.

She was so like a child with her new learning, her mind full of the psychology that she was absorbing but had not yet fully understood; like so much fresh paint washed over everything.

about 11.XI.22

My dear Ida,

I am hoping this may reach you before you leave Paris. A major-minor misfortune has happened to me. I have had stolen 3 weeks' laundry including as you must know nearly all my underclothes.

Pyjamas, *crêpe de chine* nightgown, *tricot de nuit*, 3 *pantalons*, 3 'tops' (my best, of course) 3 stockings, woolly petticoat, knickers 18 handkerchiefs and so on. If you are in Paris will you please go to the Galleries or anywhere you think and fit me out again? I'll make a list of what I want. As regards the woollen petty and knickers they are best bought at the Magazin Jones Avenue Victor Hugo *or* Rue de Villefirst [sic] where you buy cream woolen chemise and knickers at 20 francs the set. Quite plain-little closed shape knickers bound in cream silk. The other things I want are

3 tops (can you make them? Quite plain *crêpe* or anything – bound with silk – *cream* I think, or the colour of the tops.

3 knickers (Buy them. You can't make them. Quite plain again as I shall have to wash and iron them *plus tard*.

1 *tricot de nuit* (cream if possible)

3 pairs of woolen stockings (one grey and not thick. There is no difference between thick and thin wool).

1½ dozen handkerchiefs, quite simple.

1 *crêpe* nightgown. The others I have are too thin. The pyjamas I must let go. The nightgown I would prefer to be just a hole cut in the middle the sides sewn up and a ribbon from the sides to tie at the waist at the back – like I did my tops. You know that red shawl you made me. Can you make me a cream one embroidered in cream?

That's all. It's quite enough. Everything else has come. Send me the whole amount please and I will send a cheque by return. If you can't do these things, tell me and I will attack the shops. It's an awful curse to have had this loss but there you are and I am not alone in it. I shall never send another shred out of any kind.

I hope you are feeling better – the weather here is very good.

Yours ever KM

13.XI.22

Dear Ida,

I hasten to answer your letter. Please buy me *no* dress of any kind and *no* shoes. This is final! I can't risk the wrong things again and I prefer to go without. Please understand I am absolutely fixed in my mind about this. No dress – no shoes – no material for dress!

As from this week I have no more money so I can't buy any more clothes. I don't want them either. The coats were in the Paris box, I am sure. Please pack that small silky blanket of mine as well, if possible, with the eiderdown.

Excuse a hasty note. I am busy and my pen is not good. I hope you like seeing Jack and that all goes well with you. Thank you for your letter with the snapshot of the cat.

When I say I have no money I do not mean I have not always money for you when you need it. I have. You only have to ask – so ask *please*.

Yours ever KM

What a pity you and Jack could not start a small farm together. Why don't you suggest it if you like him enough.

When I had finished tormenting Katherine with the wrong and right kind of warm clothing I returned to Paris from London. And then set out for the farm at Lisieux which was on the estate of Madame von Shlumberger, a feminist.

I was driven there from the station in an old-fashioned cart, over the most abominable roads, to join the family who managed the farm.

Monsieur Dubois was a tall, thin, busy man of whom I do not remember much. But Madame Dubois was wonderful. She had been, first, the nurse of the family of von Shlumberger, then her mistress's lady's maid and firm friend and now, apparently, she ruled the whole farm and held all the keys. Her family consisted of two married daughters and their husbands, one unmarried daughter, herself and her husband; in addition to them she had me and about eight or ten farm workers to feed. She made 90 lbs of butter twice a week in an enormous electrically turned churn. She taught me to make butter as well, and when I prided myself that I was getting quicker at it, she dashed me with: 'Not quick, just nervous.' She teased me over my incorrect French: 'Merci oui, ou merci non?' She had travelled a great deal with her mistress and spoke excellent English. I taught her to make English Christmas cake and fudge for the Christmas feasts.

My work was with the cows, helping the young daughter of the family and her husband. They seemed, from their long association with the beautiful animals, to have become a little bovine in their ways of expressing themselves, and they would butt each other with affection. The cows were excellently housed and scrupulously clean in the true old-fashioned manner; we almost danced down the long brick paved corridors between the stalls, sweeping out with our brooms, right, left, right, left, and singing to the rhythm.

One day we looked up across the field to see the cows come slipping and rolling down the road; they had got drunk in a field of cider apples. I know that Katherine would have enjoyed that scene.

One night a calf was born. I was not allowed to be at the birth, but soon afterwards saw the tiny thing being fed by hand in a comfortable hay 'cradle' near its mother. The calves were taken away at birth, which saved the mother greater distress at a later date. That night the moon had seven rings round it, like a huge bubbled rainbow.

If only I could have written all this to Katherine: it would, in fact, have delighted her, but I felt she would not be interested and so I wrote only of the things I could or could not get.

Another night, very near Christmas time, a thousand owls started screeching; the woods seemed to be full of them. And now I am always frightened by this sound of the owls.

I loved the farm. I felt at home in it and I could have been very happy working there looking after the animals, had it not been for the immense hidden weight of sorrow.

I could not keep my despair out of my letters, and so wrote less, and perhaps superficially; Katherine, who could not possibly guess at the trouble, was perhaps concerned, and in one letter suggested that I wanted her to disappear for a little. Alas! At Lisieux near Christmas, the time of the owls' hooting, I had woken early in the morning from a dream of the knowledge of death. I know not whose, but the tears were streaming down my face. And I was not a dreamer. Thus when her last letters came to me, gentle, relaxed, happy and loving, they seemed to come from another world, like precious dreams.

12.XII.22

My dear Ida,

Many thanks for your two letters. The postman has told me this morning that my six *colis* are awaiting me at the post office. I'll send you a line when I have 'examined' them. I am sure they will be very nice. I will also send you a cheque for 300 francs for the coat and skirt in the course of a day or two. If that suits you. I hope you like your farm. Jean S.* is a very good youngish writer, I believe. You ought to try and get hold of his books in your library. Thank you for telling me about Jack. He sounds happy. I don't think I can talk 'fully' about my suggestion that you should join him in a farm. It seemed to me for many reasons a very good idea and I suppose I had deep reasons. But such explanations are futile. He wrote as though he liked the idea but you were not very keen. And remember the fact that beautiful hand weaving is done at Ditchling which might interest you to learn. I think it would be very worth while for you to know Dunning.† I an sure Dunning knows how to *live*. However, it's as you please. And you may find Lisieux absorbing. I would be very glad if you would tell me your *financial position*. Will you? Quite frankly?

It is intensely cold here and very damp. Very rarely the house is heated. I have a fire in my little room though. I live now in the workers' quarters and have the kind of bedroom Gertie Small‡ might have. Bare boards – a scrubbed table for the jug and basin etc. At about 10.30 p.m. we start work in the salon and go to bed at about 1–2 a.m. The windows are like whistling side streets to pass down – icy-cold. My hands are ruined for the present with scraping carrots and peeling onions. I do quite a lot of that kind of kitchen work. But I shall be very glad to exchange a very grubby washing up cloth for an apron or an overall. This life proves how

* The son of Madame von Shulumberger, actually called Paul Shlumberger.

† Dunning, whom JMM saw a great deal of at this time, practised yoga and with his family lived at Ditchling, the same village in which Eric Gill had settled and formed his guild of Catholic craftsmen. People of similar interests were attracted to the village; Ethel Mairet, the wife of Philip Mairet taught the weaving. In the autumn JMM moved to Ditchling with J. W. N. Sullivan to be near Dunning.

‡ The maid at Portland Villas.

terribly wrong and stupid all doctors are. I would have been dead 50 times in the opinion of all the medical men whom I have known. And when I remember last year and that bed in the corner week after week and those *trays*. Here there is no more fine food. You eat what you get and that's the end of it. At the same time I have wonderful what shall I call them? friends. When you leave Lisieux come to Fontainebleau for a few days. I will arrange to meet you there. Not before the late spring though.

I'll write to you again at Xmas – a long letter instead of a 'present'. For I haven't one for you. And tell me all you care to about your new life. I am sure I know a great deal more about cows than you do. I spend hours every single day with them. Goodbye for now dear Ida

Yours ever
KM

15.XII.22

That, the ultimate remark in this letter was what I was driving at when I suggested you should join Jack. I felt then I'd be sure of you.

Dear Ida,

Forgive this paper. The parcels have arrived and are extremely satisfactory, thanks very much. Why are you still so awfully tragic? I feel you must be very ill physically. Tell me your *Physical health*. I am not dead though you persist in pretending I am. And of course I shall not be here all my life. 'Connected' with this work and these ideas, yes, but that is different. As soon as I am cured I shall leave here and set up a little place in the South and grow something. You can come and talk over the fence if you like and are not too mournful. Come and stay with me if you promise to smile now and again. *Dear* Ida! Thank you for the tops and for everything. As I have said I'll write again at Christmas and provided you are a happy nature I shall beg you to join forces with me when I leave here, if you care to, of course, in some kind of farm. So learn all you can for goodness sake.

With love, yours ever
KM

22.XII.22
Le Prieuré

Dear Ida,

This is to wish you a Happy Xmas. I meant to have something for you. For the moment I have nothing and can't get anything. I can't give people commissions nor get to Fontainebleau myself. So take whatever you please that I happen to have and that you think you would like. What about the green cardigan *par example?* Especially as you probably paid for it yourself. In the course of a week or two I shall send you the sleeping vests you bought me. I can't wear them. That kind of wool next to my skin brings me out in a rash. . . . I presume of course, it doesn't you.

We are going to *Fêter le Noel* in tremendous style here. Every sort of lavish generous hospitable thing has been done by Mr Gurdjieff. He wants a real old-fashioned *English* Xmas – an extraordinary idea here! And we shall sit down to table 60 persons to turkeys, geese, a whole sheep, a pig, puddings, heavens knows what in the way of dessert and wines by the barrel. There's to be a tree, too and Father Xmas. I'm doing all I can for the little children so that they will be roped in for once. I've just sent them over coloured paper and asked them to help to make flowers. It's pathetic the interest they are taking.

Our pudding was made in a baby's bath, stirred by everybody and Mr Gurdjieff put in a coin. Who gets the coin gets our darling new born calf for a present. The calf – 1 day old – was led into the Salon to the beating of tambourines and a special melody composed for it. It took it very quietly. But two minute baby pigs which were also brought in and allowed to play squealed and shrieked terribly. I have been v. interested in the calf. The cow didn't seem to mind the affair. She only lowed faintly and when a leg appeared Madam Ostrovsky and Nina put a rope round it and pulled and presently a tall weak feeble creature emerged. The cow's eyes as big as saucers reminded me of Charles.* I wish we gave our cows apples. Some of the names are Equivoqueveckwa, Baldaofim, Mitasha, Bridget. Our mule is Drabfeet.

My existence here is not meagre or miserable. Nothing is done by accident. I understand v. well why my room was changed and

* The cat at Portland Villas, mother of Wingly and Athenaeum.

so on. And to live among so many people, knowing something of them, sharing something th⌐t is for me very great change and *ca donne beaucoup.*

I shall be glad though when the spring comes. Winter is a difficult time.

You know you must not worry about me or say you do or don't. It's exactly as though you took a piece of my flesh and gnawed it. It helps neither you nor me. *Worry is waste of energy;* it is therefore sin. And to see you waste energy destroys energy in me, so you sin in two ways. That's surely easy to see.

As to steering gear, why don't you begin taking photographs of yourself – take them all day. And look at them. Then begin to decide which are 'good' and which are 'bad' ones. Then try and sort the workbag in your mind before you begin to learn to think and direct your thought. Open your mind and really look into it. Perhaps you won't mind what you see. I mind.

I must end this letter. If you'd like me for a friend as from this Xmas I'd like to be your friend. But not too awfully serious, *ma chère.* The whole difficulty in life is to find the *way* between extremes – to preserve one's poise in fact to get a hold of the pendulum.

Jack said he would be delighted to have you whenever you felt like it. He sounds different in his letters, much simpler.

Yours ever
KM

Katherine did not post the following letter. It was found inside her blotter.

Le Prieuré.
Fontainebleau-Avon.
Seine et Marne.

My dear Ida,

I have purposely not written to you before because I felt you wanted me to disappear . . . for a little. I was right, wasn't I? But you have been in my mind today. How are you? How are your cows? As you see I am sending you 100 francs. Play with it. I don't want it. Until your financial position improves, it's no good minding taking any small sums I can send you. And as I have lost my money complex you can take them quite freely.

Very much is happening here. We are in the throes of theatre building which ought to be ready by the New Year (Russian style) on January 13th. It's going to be a most marvellous place. Mr Gurdjieff has bought 63 carpets for it and the same number of fur rugs. The carpets which were displayed one by one in the Salon last night are like living things – worlds of beauty. And what a joy to begin to learn which is a garden, which a cafe, which a prayer mat, which '*l'histoire de ses troupeaux*' and so on. My thoughts are full of carpets and Persia and Samarkhand and the little rugs of Beluchistan.

Do you kill pigs where you are? It goes on here. Two were stuck yesterday and their horrid corpses were dissected in the kitchen. They are frightful things to watch *and* to smell. The worst of it is until their heads are cut off they are still so piglike. But we kill them outright. That is one comfort.

I am looking for signs of Spring already. Under the espalier pear trees there were wonderful Xmas roses, which I saw for the first time this year. They reminded me of Switzerland; and somebody found four primroses the other day. I have moods when I simply pine for the S. of France or somewhere like Majorka. *When* this time is over I shall make for the South or the East and never go North again.

My blue dress is in large holes. Those cashmere cardigans look as if rats have gnawed them. As to my fur coat – it's like a wet London cat. The last time I was in the stable I caught one of the goats nibbling it. How are you off for clothes? Would you like brown corduroys? That big woman Miss Marston* whom you took such a fancy to, wears them. She got them from Barkers – out size – 35/-. They are breeks and a smock and long plain coat. Very practical.

Write and tell me how you are will you? Dear Ida?

Our calf is still allowed to be with its mother. I can't understand it. It's a huge creature now. We had great trouble with the mother who had to be massaged daily. Do you massage cows? Will you tell me how your stable is kept. What is the condition

* One of the community, who was put to gardening. LM.

of the floor? I'll tell you about ours in my next letter. It worries
me.

With love from
KM

Then, on 10th January, a telegram came from Jack, who had
gone to see Katherine at the Priory, saying she was dead.

CHAPTER XVIII

Afterwards

On the evening of 9th January 1923 Katherine was taken from us, and on the 10th I got the telegram from Jack. The people from the farm at Lisieux drove me in their cart the long distance to the station. I caught the afternoon train.

At the Priory, Jack and I were given a meal in the little room which had once been Katherine's. It had been made over to him when she died.

A friend of hers, Olga Ivanovna, who had spent much time with Katherine, was told to talk to me a little. She was very beautiful, and had loved Katherine. She tried to explain to me that love is like a great cloud around and above us all, and on Katherine's last evening she was so full of the spirit of love that she was transformed. Her face was shining with inexpressible beauty, and when she left the party in the great hall she was so full of joy that she must have forgotten her physical weakness and she ran, or tried to run, up the stairs. But the extra effort made her cough and so started the fatal haemorrhage.

They had taken Katherine to a small chapel, and the next morning I went there. Several people were walking about, and I stood beside her, as she lay in the light wooden coffin, and thought how cold and bare it looked. She would have hated that. So I fetched her brilliantly embroidered black silk Spanish shawl and covered her with it. That she would appreciate, I knew; it was somehow right.

She had been given back her original fine guest room when Murry came, and this now became mine. I spent my day there, sorting and packing all her things. Her watch and chain on the mantelpiece I took at once. It was a symbol or pledge, which she had left me to assure me that she was still going forward and on.

When the packing was done I went into the garden to look at the Christmas roses she had spoken of, and then someone took me to see the balcony in the stable, really a little hay loft, but spread with rich carpets and cushions. We also went to the house of the children, for whom she had grieved to find them left out of the great Christmas festivities.

That evening there was a gathering of young literary men who had come from London for her funeral; some were friends I think, but others came out of curiosity or perhaps as a sign of respect. Koteliansky had been unable to get permission to travel, to his great distress. They were given a dinner at the Chalet de la Foret, and for some reason I was there too.

I remember walking up and down the garden outside the hotel with Orage, up and down, up and down. I felt that I wanted to stay with him, because of what he had been to Katherine, though I do not think he understood the need.

At the dinner we all sat at a long table. The meal started quietly, but presently, when the young men were warmed and at ease, they began discussing Katherine and making criticisms. Why had she come here? What had led to Ouspensky? How? When? I stood it as long as I could, then something made me stand up – an extraordinary thing for me to do – and tell them I did not think they should be speaking in this manner when Katherine was not there to defend or explain herself.

That broke up the party.

The next day was the 12th. In the afternoon a long procession of cars followed Katherine at crawling pace to the cemetery. I began in the car, then could not bear it and got out and walked, miles and miles very slowly. As a mark of respect it had been decided to take the longest possible way to our destination.

In the cemetery I stood beside Jack at the side of the grave, and after the coffin had been lowered, there was some delay and uncertainty. The chief mourner, it appeared, should be sprinkling something down on to the coffin. It seemed that they were waiting for Jack. He did not move. I touched his arm and he jerked away from me.

A man suggested that the Spanish shawl should be thrown down. No! I knew this must not be. Katherine had told me I was to give this to Anne Estelle Rice. Some further hesitation.

I had brought a bunch of marigolds, a flower she loved, and there were not many other flowers there for her. So I stepped forward, looked down, and dropped them in.

The service was then over.

That evening we all sat round in a kind of amphitheatre, which they had built in rising circles, and an immense number of dishes were carried round to everyone. The centre stage was for the dancers, with music and many lights. When this was over, we gathered in a big room – I think in the Priory itself – and there was much talking and wine was served to everyone. I felt completely numb, as though I had been shattered, like some brittle thing, into tiny fragments all scattered and no more LM left at all.

On the other side of the room I saw Jack talking far too much and laughing hysterically, and one of the men, possibly Orage, came to me and said it would be best if I could get him away and make him go to bed. This I did.

The next day we left, and I helped him to go back to his own country. Katherine would have wanted me to look after him as much as I could.

Epilogue

To suggest Katherine in words is like trying to catch a glint of light on a butterfly's wing or describing the shading of a rose. One can only make a kind of diagram. There was a bell-like quality in her rich low voice and her singing was a high, pure soprano; she was neither tall nor short but so well-proportioned that one did not notice; she had a sensitive, finely curved mouth and deep, dark, steady eyes that really *looked*: but above all she was herself, clear-cut and individual. In gaiety and joy or in despair, whether in life or in her stories, she was always Katherine.

She was a born actress and mimic, and even in her ordinary everyday life took colour from the company she was in. I think this was what puzzled people. She would give apparently all of herself to a situation or a person as they demanded, and then, if anything came too close, particularly when she had become ill and frail, she would withdraw into her remoteness, only to change colour again to meet some fresh contingency. She was like a lantern with many sides; not octagonal but centagonal. That was why so many thought they were not just her friend, but her *only* friend.

Fastidious in her personal possessions, Katherine had a great love of order, and by striving for just the right material or colour or arrangement she could impart a little of her own personality to the simplest and most modest surroundings. Even a temporary resting-place would take on an atmosphere of 'home'.

Brave and adventurous through her many adversities, it was only in the early years that Katherine ran away from the quicksands of her own inexperience; and then not through fear but to escape to firm ground where, safe from the stress and entanglement of life, she could sit quietly and write the record of it. Paper and pencil were to be her sword and shield: she was upheld continuously by the guiding thought of her work.

To be a fine writer, she said, one must learn to *live* finely. One must have a passionate love of life and all that lives and breathes – not only the sunny, beautiful things, but the grim side too: all that makes up Truth. At the Priory, near the end, she felt that at last she understood what she was to write. All she had done so far she cast, metaphorically, into the fire.

I want to explain some misconceptions. I have read parts of the *Journal* and find a picture that faintly nauseates me, because it is negative. This was Katherine's old habit of elaborating on a feeling, in order to make it up into a picture.

It is true that I have always fallen in with other people's superficial arrangements – they are generally unimportant, and if I love the people I am glad to let them have their way. But the ME that matters cannot be ordered, and if what I have to do is important or necessary, then I MYSELF take charge. The strength of which I am conscious in myself, even now that I am hemmed in by the disabilities of age, is not of myself: it is a power from without.

In our friendship there was complete honouring of individual independence. Her life was vivid, aware and strong; she was always the instigator, consciously choosing and directing her life, down to the smallest detail. I never questioned her right to make her own decisions and to withold anything she did not see fit to communicate. As for myself, except in the fundamentals which we both agreed upon and shared, I had no grand dreams of what life 'ought' to be in the future. I was concerned with the present: I accepted each situation as it arose, and then did what had to be done within that context. I had accepted Katherine as my friend, so naturally I walked her way, beside her.

My faith was and always has been that Christianity means love and service; and just as Katherine expressed herself in writing, so I expressed myself in service. And then for us both there was love, compassion towards humanity. When you have a friend, you admire much, understand all you can, and accept the whole with love. It is a tragedy of life that there is so much judging and by so many different standards.

Our relationship was not man-made. Once Katherine wrote to a friend, in our early days, that she could bind me to her with chains but could not decide whether it was right to do so. She could not have done so. We *were* bound, apart from our wills.

The relationship was simply an integral part of our lives. There was no domination in it. Katherine loved her brother, and she loved Murry. I, too, have ties of love. But our relationship ran beneath or through these, untouched. Katherine, of course, knew this.

There is one thing that I cannot stress too strongly, as it runs all through Katherine's life and in many ways explains her relationships with people. She always gave fully and generously of herself to all who were lucky enough to make contact; the relationship, as long as it existed, was intensely alive. But she herself stood apart.

Our relationship was rather different. Once, at Bishop's flat in Chelsea, we tried to put it into words. We suggested that I was like a very high green pillar, rooted, always there above the trees. Katherine likened herself to a bird – a white bird – who rested on the pillar, then flew away experimenting, adventuring, seeking, living, but always returning to rest on the pillar. In later years she used another metaphor: sailing on the River of Life. She wanted me to have a boat of my own, so that we could sail together, always at hand but independently. If only I could have been myself, had a boat of my own and been happy in it, I could have done so much for her.

Katherine kept her relationships separate, and this will explain those occasions when I was not included in her social life, to meet and be a part of her friends and acquaintances. If two relationships were similar, then the individuals mixed, as once when Walter de la Mare brought his children to tea at 'The Elephant' and I had tea with them. If he had come to see Katherine personally, I should have been ill at ease had she asked me to join them, and this was completely understood between us. We both knew how uncomfortable I should have been if caught up in the wrong situations. I cared and lived not just for the Katherine I loved, but for the work which she lived for and in which she believed. I came and went, joined in or stood aside as that *faith* dictated. There were no small personal strings attached that I can remember. I did not think about this or understand it at the time. It just *was* so.

One other thing needs explanation, if only because people have so often angered me by saying, 'She must have been a very difficult person to live with'. Most of the belittling remarks Katherine made about me, generally in illness, and mostly from her letters to Murry which he published, were just a freeing of herself from some momentary vexation. As expressed in Katherine's words, however, they sounded worse – and I surely must have vexed her often. Katherine's so-called rages and cruel speeches were all what might be called clean rages, due to frustration – the breaking point of her tolerance under stress of constant pain.

But at other times Katherine's complaints were deliberately made, and I knew it, to give Murry just the kind of self-support that his character needed, an assurance that he was the first, the all-important, the master in the sometimes difficult intimacies of three.

Speaking of Jack, I feel I must explain that my frequent remarks of how he failed, or hurt, Katherine are not meant as criticism: they are just the side of the picture as I knew it. I have no right to give a picture of Murry, because for one thing I can say little to describe the joy and happiness of their private relationship. I can only write of their times of separation or unhappiness.

Jack's charm was very strong and appealing, and his very need of support called on a woman's sympathy. Several times he shook me out of the impersonalness, which I had unconsciously adopted, by some act of kindness or sweet thoughtfulness. On one such occasion I came down from Katherine's room in the evening, exhausted and bitterly unhappy over her frail health and my inability to help; I was reduced to tears on the dark staircase. Jack, waiting in the sitting room, heard my distress. Coming out and drawing me into the room, he put his arm on my shoulder, kissed me and tried to comfort me.

I think that Katherine was right when she said in a letter to me, after she had learnt to see and think in the new way at the Priory, that I had identified myself with her life. Partly because she needed so much care, I had for some time been growing to her more and more, day and night. Her small needs and larger distresses took my entire mind and heart. I suffered, too, from the continual realisation of my inadequacy. In the periods when I was not actually caring for her I was almost vacant, resting rather than living. At the Priory I left her to a new future, in which I could have no part.

I was to see her once again, and that was some months later, after she had died: she passed through the room where I was working with Jack, and seemed to smile. For me, this was the summation of our friendship.

Index

HARRIET MARTINEAU'S AUTOBIOGRAPHY
Volume I

Harriet Martineau (1802-76) was renowned in her time as a controversial journalist, highly respected political economist and government adviser, abolitionist and lifelong feminist. She was also a dutiful daughter and invalid, a woman caught in the constraints and contradictions of Victorian life, yet refusing their stranglehold. Born in Norwich into a Unitarian family, the sixth of eight children, she considered herself ugly and unloved, a child 'with cold feet and a longing mind . . . looking on while other children were at play'. Given a sound classical education, unusual for a girl at that time, she buried herself in books. Later, in conflict with her mother, at odds with her role as a woman, she struggled to become a writer, working in the early mornings and late at night while her daylight hours were devoted to 'proper' womanly pursuits. At thirty, her popularising 'tales', *Illustrations of Political Economy*, began to appear. Overnight she achieved national fame—and a degree of independence.

In 1855, thinking that she was about to die, she produced her autobiography at break-neck speed. In this, the first volume, she covers what she called her 'winter and stormy spring', writing with intensity and passion of her childhood and middle years and offering an honesty and insight quite unique in Victorian biography.

'Provides a fascinating insight into the constraints and contradictions of [a] Victorian upbringing'—*History Today*

HARRIET MARTINEAU'S AUTOBIOGRAPHY
Volume II

In this, the second volume of her autobiography, Harriet Martineau recounts those years that she saw as 'the summer' of her life: at thirty-two, through her *Illustrations of Political Economy*, she had become a national figure. The *Illustrations*, presented in the highly original form of fictional 'tales' to explain the principles of political economy, were an astounding success: appearing monthly for two years, they sold 10,000 copies of each issue. Lionised by London Society, Harriet Martineau met Darwin, Harriet Taylor and John Stuart Mill, Coleridge and George Eliot; Florence Nightingale and Charlotte Brontë later became friends. And through those years she wrote authoritatively and widely, producing articles, pamphlets and books on political reform, history, education, hypnotism, accounts of her travels in America and Palestine, and several novels. She used her pen and her influence on behalf of the enfranchisement of women, the abolition of slavery, the repeal of the Contagious Diseases Acts, and the establishment of a national system of education, writing sometimes six leaders a week for the *Daily News*.

In 1855, when it was thought she was dying, all England was found to be 'in a life stir about Harriet's opinion'. In that year she wrote her extraordinary biography. Published posthumously in 1877, and now appearing in paperback for the first time, the two volumes provide a fascinating and perceptive portrait of mid-Victorian life and a moving account of the profound changes taking place in women's lives at that time.

'A vivid view of political and literary life ... This autobiography is a great classic. It has power and drive which insist on being noticed'— *The Times*

APPEAL of One Half of the Human Race, WOMEN, Against the Pretensions of the Other Half, MEN, to Retain them in Political, and Hence in Civil and Domestic, Slavery

William Thompson

With a new Introduction by Richard Pankhurst

This passionate summons to 'Women . . . wherever ye breathe degraded—awake!' was written in 1825. William Thompson described the *Appeal* as 'the joint property' of himself and Anna Wheeler, and parts of it as the exclusive product of her 'mind and pen' for, as he wrote, although he had thought much about 'the inequalities of the sexual laws', it was she who suffered from them.

The *Appeal* was provoked by James Mill's cryptic dismissal of political representation for women. Thompson, in responding, decried woman's reduction to 'involuntary breeding machine and household slave', and called upon men to throw off the 'tattered cloak' of male despotism. Today, more than a century and a half after its original publication the *Appeal* remains a landmark in the history of both the women's movement and of socialist thought.

'Key nineteenth-century text . . . at last made available in a popular edition, expressing the roots of English feminism'—*City Limits*